Media, Persuasion and Prop

Media Topics

www.euppublishing.com/series/MTOP

Media, Persuasion and Propaganda

Marshall Soules

EDINBURGH
University Press

Edinburgh University Press Ltd
The Tun – Holyrood Road
12 (2f) Jackson's Entry
Edinburgh EH8 8PJ
www.euppublishing.com

Typeset in 10/12 Janson Text by
Servis Filmsetting Ltd, Stockport, Cheshire,
and printed and bound in Great Britain by
CPI Group (UK) Ltd, Croydon, CR0 4YY

A CIP record for this book is available from the British Library

ISBN 978 0 7486 4416 2 (hardback)
ISBN 978 0 7486 4415 5 (paperback)
ISBN 978 0 7486 4417 9 (webready PDF)
ISBN 978 0 7486 9643 7 (epub)

Contents

Figures

Acknowledgements

Important intellectual influences at Rutgers University include Maurice Charney, Richard Poirier and Paul Fussell – they set the direction. And later, Edmund Carpenter, Harald Prins, Gary McCarron, B. W. Powe, Ray Ellenwood, Jennifer Wise, Velcrow Ripper and Pete Steffens shaped my worldview with their passions. Thanks to Babatunde Olatunji for the chance to improvise in music and life, and Ajay Heble for encouraging me to write about it. Many colleagues at Vancouver Island University helped turn the dream of a Media Studies programme into reality, too many to mention here, but particularly Ross Fraser, John Lepage, Steve Lane, Marni Stanley, Doug Stetar, Naava Smolash, Debra Pentecost, Marian van der Zon and Robin Davies. Thanks to Ray Siemens and Geoffrey Rockwell for taking me deeper into computing code.

Valerie Alia, series editor at Edinburgh University Press, is extraordinary. Her confidence in the project, her experience, guidance and patience has been exceptional. I cannot thank her enough. Also, Gillian Leslie and Richard Strachan at EUP and copy-editor Elizabeth Welsh were keenly supportive and professional.

Through their own talents and expertise, Jon Soules, Jane Webster and Nancy Hood gave more than they know. Finally, without the loving support of my daughter Tonya and amazing partner Donna Soules, this work would never have been completed. I dedicate this to them, with humility and thanks.

Preface
Tricksters at Play

Eshu's cap

This is a book about persuasion, deception and trust and begins with a trickster's journey. We take our lead from Robert Farris Thompson, who eloquently traces the spread of West African culture throughout the diaspora of the New World. He begins by acknowledging the central importance of *orisha* (gods) in carrying African expressive genius – the 'flash of the spirit' – across the Atlantic. When calling on the *orisha* for guidance, West Africans begin with Eshu-Elegbara, a powerful Yoruba and Fon deity endowed with *àshe*, the 'force to make all things happen and multiply' (1983: 18). As with other tricksters, Eshu is sexual, of ambiguous gender and a messenger to the gods about human affairs. Eshu represents chance and uncertainty; where the trickster rules, anything can happen. Eshu creates disorder to test the status quo and keep culture moving along. And Eshu is associated with the crossroads, both as a physical place to offer tribute and symbolically, as a place to speak in riddles and paradoxes, where the mind might go in many different directions searching for answers. At the crossroads, we make decisions about which way to go. We take a risk and learn to trust.

In a West African folktale about Eshu, two men swear vows of eternal friendship without first paying tribute to the god of chance. Eshu decides to test them and fashions a cloth cap with black on one side and white on the other. Wearing this two-coloured cap, Eshu passes along the road between the friends, who are working in neighbouring fields. One of the men insists he sees Eshu wearing a white cap, while the other is certain the god is wearing a black one. The ensuing argument is heated and attracts the attention of their neighbours.

Eshu soon returns, appearing cool and pretending not to know what is happening. When the men explain their disagreement, Eshu declares they are both right:

As you can see, one side is white and the other is black. You each saw one side and, therefore, are right about what you saw . . . When you vowed to be friends always, to be faithful and true to each other, did you reckon with Eshu? Do you know that he who does not put Eshu first in all his doings has himself to blame if things misfire? (Ogundipe, in Gates [1988] 1989: 35)

Cultural critic Louis Henry Gates finds deep insight into the 'indeterminacy of interpretation' (35) in this myth. For Gates, both friends are right, and both are also wrong. The hat is both black and white, but the 'folly depicted here is to insist . . . on one determinate meaning, itself determined by vantage point' (35).

The story of Eshu's cap illustrates the paradox that deception can reveal truth – an important insight into persuasion and propaganda. Eshu teaches us that context shapes meaning; point of view determines belief; and truth is contingent. Do we know for certain that we perceive the same events as those around us? Eshu reminds the two friends to make allowances for difference, ambiguity, uncertainty and possibility. Eshu's trick reminds us to question our certainty when interpreting symbolic communication.

Gates takes Eshu's playful deceptions as a model to define the cultural critic's role. The critic 'improvises' on the given materials, repeating and revising previous works, translating meanings, making connections, circulating new texts. Gates calls this work 'signifyin(g)' to suggest its dual association with semiotics (signifying) and African-American word play (signifyin'). The signifyin(g) cultural critic searches for connections to express cultural values and beliefs, always with intent to invigorate, renew and foster understanding. Interpretation is always 'indeterminate' – unfinished and provisional – because we have different points of view, and these differences can make communication difficult and messy. In this text, we will perform as signifyin(g) critics by looking at various cultural practices regarding persuasion and influence, trying to remain open to differences of interpretation and opinion. In difference lies truth.

In her exploration of Winnebago Native American culture, anthropologist Barbara Babcock-Abrahams (1975) uses the phrase 'a tolerated margin of mess' to describe the trickster's role in creating productive disorder. Out of the trickster's mess come new perspectives and insights. The Greek god Hermes, North American Coyote, Norse Loki, Yoruba Eshu, Sufi Nasruddin and Hindu Krishna all may be 'foolish' and disruptive, but they bring gifts as well, including the gift of communication and the arts of persuasion and deception.

Their tricks are teaching stories. Krishna steals butter as a child and then denies it, asking his mother: 'Doesn't everything in the house belong to us?' 'All tricksters do this', comments Lewis Hyde, '[t]hey lie in a way that upsets our very sense of what is true and what is false, and therefore help us reimagine this world'. Aristotle attributes the birth of Western literature to Homer's creative lies: the Greek oral poet 'taught us the art of framing lies the right way . . . [c]lever at deceit, tricksters are clever at seeing through deceit, and therefore at revealing things hidden beneath the surface' (Hyde 2011: n.p.). Hyde emphasises the paradox of the trickster's performances: 'the origins, liveliness, and durability of cultures require that there be space for figures whose function is to uncover and disrupt the very things that cultures are based on' (1998: 9). Cultures need creative disruption to evolve and survive, as long as that disruption occurs within a tolerated margin of mess.

Anthropologist Victor Turner identifies tricksters with play, crossing boundaries and renewing culture. Noting the trickster's presence throughout diverse cultures, Turner associates the archetype with the brain's limbic system – a neural crossroads where physical sensations are translated into emotion, decision-making and action on the fly. Turner describes play and ritual as evolving into performance and theatre: 'Like many Trickster figures in myths . . . play can deceive, betray, beguile, delude' ([1987] 1988: 169). Play, the essence of improvisation, takes what we have at hand – what is – and recombines it to create something new – what could be. A stick becomes a magic wand. We make paper airplanes. The improvising jazz musician takes a popular melody as the inspiration for creative revisions. For Gates, Turner, Hyde and others, the trickster's creative play is cognitively complex and a gift to culture. We find the trickster's beguiling deceptions in advertising, entertainment, publicity, propaganda and culture jamming – all aiming to influence culture at the crossroads of change.

In what follows, we approach persuasion and propaganda as rhetorical performances involving playful, creative and even devious communication filled with suspect reasoning, colourful language and possible trickery. We will work across disciplines as signifyin(g) cultural critics to reveal the strategies and tactics of the persuasive arts. This theoretical and practical work is filled with paradox and contradiction and requires a doubleness of vision to see both sides of the story, the black *and* white of Eshu's cap. While advertising, marketing, public relations, political lobbying, rhetoric, persuasion and propaganda are sometimes described as curses of contemporary civilisation, they all depend for their success on creativity, invention, improvisation and lively performance – the 'flash of the spirit'. These activities may be disruptive, messy and in bad taste; as with Eshu's tricks, however, they push culture in new directions, both invigorating and destructive.

Exercise questions

1. In your own words, tell a trickster tale to your study group and discuss what it means.
2. Describe two examples of persuasive performance, one that successfully persuades you and one that does not. What accounts for the difference? Distinguish between the language, the argument and the beliefs or values expressed. Where do your beliefs influence your evaluation?
3. Illustrate how a cultural critic develops new insights by repeating and revising the work of others on one of the themes introduced in the Preface.
4. How do we know what is true or false?

Figure 1   'Compose'. Photo: M. Soules, San Francisco, 1991.
Improvisation and performance are important in creative communication.

Introduction
The Spectrum of Persuasion

Media maelstrom

> Ours is the first age in which many thousands of the best-trained individual minds have made a full-time business to get inside the collective public mind. To get inside in order to manipulate, exploit, control is the object now. And to generate heat not light is the intention. (McLuhan [1951] 1967: v)

The Mechanical Bride was Marshall McLuhan's early attempt to warn readers that the media, saturated with advertising and persuasive messages, were pulling the public into a whirlpool of narcissism, distraction and confusion. McLuhan announced his intent by asking: 'Why not assist the public to observe consciously the drama which is intended to operate upon it unconsciously?' ([1951] 1967: v) McLuhan was troubled by what he saw. Advertisers had successfully turned the automobile into an object of erotic desire – the 'mechanical bride' of McLuhan's title – and the Catholic media critic did not condone adultery. Original at the time, McLuhan's early 'probes' became the clichés of our time.

In 1957, Vance Packard revealed that motivational psychology had been adopted by advertisers and other compliance professionals. While today we might find Packard's warning mundane, at the time of publication *The Hidden Persuaders* was alarming:

> Large-scale efforts are being made, often with impressive success, to channel our unthinking habits, our purchasing decisions, and our thought processes by the use of insights gleaned from psychiatry and social sciences. Typically these efforts take place beneath our level of awareness . . . (Packard [1957] 2007: 31)

Smokers learned – as the TV series *Mad Men* reminds us – that they were not buying cigarettes for their taste, but for the brand's image. In blindfolded taste tests, they could not distinguish between brands.

Packard was equally disturbed to see Eisenhower and Nixon packaged and sold to voters like products, with PR firms acting as election strategists. While Packard's claims were widely disputed at the time, new research in message processing affirms his assertions and more. Scientists now know that cognitive overload depletes self-control, leaving us more vulnerable to suggestion (DeSteno 2014: 220; Vohs and Faber 2007). McLuhan retells Poe's horror story 'Descent into the Maelstrom' to convey the increasing sense of disorientation created by the deluge of persuasive messages in 1950s media, especially from television and illustrated magazines. In Poe's short story, a sailor narrowly escapes death when he and his ship are pulled into a giant maelstrom or whirlpool. The sailor saves himself by overcoming his panic and remaining observant, 'studying the action of the whirlpool and by co-operating with it' ([1951] 1967: v). For the remainder of his career, McLuhan followed his own advice by immersing himself in the media maelstrom to investigate the strategies of observation, analysis and action needed to survive in the electronic 'global village'.

In the 1960s, McLuhan became famous for observing that electronic media extend the central nervous system into the equivalent of a global network. (This network was like a village, because electronic media such as television, radio and satellites reassert orality and community against the dominance of print technology, which McLuhan considered isolating and individualistic.) Opportunities for learning and cooperation through the new technologies were potentially transformative, but he worried that the deluge of messages would result in 'Narcissus narcosis' – a condition of numbness and self-absorption caused by fascination with reflected images, reverberating echoes and sensory overload. Narcissus' delusion was not falling in love with himself, says McLuhan; rather, it was mistaking his own reflection for someone else. Narcissus lacks discernment and deceives himself with a reflected image. McLuhan concludes that humans 'become fascinated by any extension of themselves in any material other than themselves' ([1964] 1994: 41). McLuhan pioneered the 'Media Ecology' approach to communication (media-ecology.org/) that explores the ways media shape cultures and discipline audiences.

Sixty years after the publication of *The Mechanical Bride*, O'Reilly and Tennant ([2009] 2010) echo McLuhan's concerns by concluding that 'we live in an age of persuasion, where people's wants, wishes, whims, pleas, brands, offers, enticements, truths, petitions, and propaganda swirl in a ceaseless, growing multimedia firestorm of sales messages' (xiii). For the authors, this is not a conspiracy, but something we bring upon ourselves: 'We are – all of us – its creators and its practitioners' (xxvi). O'Reilly and Tennant do not want to take themselves or their subject too seriously, since 'our culture has bigger worries than fallout from a daily profusion of advertising' (xxvi). As O'Reilly proves in his popular CBC radio broadcasts (*The Age of Persuasion, Under the Influence*), advertising can be creative and entertaining, as well as misleading and hazardous to human health.

The spectrum of persuasion from rhetoric to propaganda

Persuasion and propaganda are built on the foundation of rhetoric – a topic explored more fully in Chapter 1. From the Greek *rhetor* for public speaker, rhetoric is the art of communicating effectively and persuasively in a particular context. Aristotle defines rhetoric as 'the faculty of observing in any given case the available means of persuasion' (350 BCE: *Rhetoric* 1.2.1). For Aristotle, rhetoric leverages *logos* (logic and reason), *pathos* (appeals to emotion) and *ethos* (character, ethics) to persuade audiences. Rhetoric has a history of abuse, and in our time 'rhetoric' often refers dismissively to language filled with empty phrases and false sentiments. Ideally, rhetoric gives language additional interest and impact and is judged by its effectiveness. Leith suggests the potential of rhetoric to command attention in his title *Words Like Loaded Pistols: Rhetoric from Aristotle to Obama* (2012).

Persuasion seeks to change attitudes, values, beliefs and behaviours, with mutual needs being met. Trust affects persuasion directly. For O'Reilly and Tennant ([2009] 2010), persuasion always involves an implied contract – some benefit is promised. The contract is broken and trust undermined if the promise is not delivered (29). (In Aristotle's scheme, an undelivered promise would be a failure of *ethos*, of the communicator's character.) When a persuasive message is designed to benefit only the sender, it moves toward propaganda or coercion. Propaganda involves 'systematic and deliberate attempts to sway mass public opinion in favour of the objectives of the institutions (usually state or corporate) sending the propaganda message' (Snow [1998] 2010: 66).

Persuasion requires an 'anchor' – an existing belief or attitude – to be successful. Anchors provide focus, motivation and salience (prominence or significance) for target audiences. Peer pressure and social norms exert powerful influences and act as anchors of belief. Persuasive communicators build trust and rapport by acknowledging values and attitudes to anchor their argument. Since the existing anchor has already been internalised, the persuasive message is perceived as arising naturally from the self, often appearing as common sense rather than persuasion. Schwartz (1974) describes persuasion as 'striking a 'responsive chord' when the message does not tell the audience what to think or feel, but instead triggers a thought, feeling or memory associated with the pitch. Ellul ([1965] 1973) says that propaganda attempts to 'take hold of the entire person', with an 'organised myth' acting as an anchoring belief. 'Through the myth it creates, propaganda imposes a complete range of intuitive knowledge, susceptible of only one interpretation' (11). Appeals to national values, social dreams or religious justifications serve as anchors to define – and limit – the persuasive argument. The assertion '[f]or all freedom-loving people, this is the only sensible approach' uses the anchor 'freedom-loving' to define a community of belief and then argues that this community has only one 'sensible' option.

As noted above, persuasion moves toward propaganda when it is consciously misleading or exploits beliefs, values and attitudes for the propagandist's benefit. An audience will tolerate a deceptive message to serve its own needs – as with climate change denial or the war on terror – but the 'propagandist cannot reveal the true intent of the message' (Jowett and O'Donnell 2006: 38). Audiences feel betrayed when they learn they have been manipulated, a common sensation for soldiers returning from conflict and seeing the effects of propaganda on the home front (Davis 2011; Fussell 1989).

Critics generally distinguish propaganda from persuasive campaigns based on considerations of intention, scope, consequences and sponsors. Paul Rutherford (2000) says that 'propaganda is both the language and the instrument of power' (8) and acknowledges the difficulty of distinguishing it from marketing, public relations and advertising. In his broad definition, public service announcements (PSAs) and advocacy campaigns are examples of 'endless propaganda'; a battle for 'that most valuable (because most scarce) of commodities, public attention' (7). Snow (1998) and Aufderheide (2007) define propaganda by its powerful sponsors: governments, large organisations or corporations.

To distinguish between persuasion and propaganda, it helps to go back to first principles, since propaganda has become widely associated with totalitarian regimes in the twentieth century, as popularised by Orwell's *Nineteen Eighty-Four* and *Animal Farm*, as well as Huxley's *Brave New World*. In 1622, Pope Gregory XV founded the Sacred Congregation for the Propagation of the Faith (*Sacra Congregatio de Propaganda Fide*) as a department within the Catholic Church. Significantly influenced by Jesuits, this agency was charged with missionary work in newly discovered territories and in European countries where Protestantism threatened the Vatican's dominance. In this sense, propaganda propagates the faith through education and conversion. (The original congregation is now known as the Congregation for the Evangelisation of Peoples.) In its original meaning, propaganda promotes belief and ideology leading toward conversion and action. While education ideally stimulates the mind to reflection and discovery, propaganda presents an 'organised myth' (Ellul [1965] 1973: 11) that limits options for discovering truth. From the beginning, propaganda had mixed results, some of them life-destroying. As Joseph Boyden relates in his powerful historical novel *The Orenda* (2013), Jesuits spreading Catholic teachings in North America's wilderness in the seventeenth century may have been well-intended, even when they were struggling with their own faith, but their propaganda campaign was disastrous for the First Nations.

In their three-volume analysis of propaganda as the 'symbolic instrument', Lasswell and his colleagues attempt to disprove the misconception that propaganda is chiefly a product of the twentieth century, the 'spontaneous' creation of authoritarian regimes under Stalin, Hitler and Mussolini (1979: xii). They argue instead that propaganda supplemented military force and diplomacy to build civilisations throughout recorded history, though its reach and scale accelerated in the late nineteenth and early twentieth centuries. Propaganda campaigns waged during the Great War (1914–18) and the Russian Revolution (1917) emerged from a complex matrix of influences: new communication technologies, including telegraph, newspapers, photography, radio and film; the ascendant power of large corporations seeking new markets; the rise of reform-minded (muckraking) journalism from 1890 to 1914; and the influence of art movements, psychology, sociology and marketing.

Taylor's *Munitions of the Mind* (1995) is a history of propaganda since the Trojan War mainly concerned with military conflict, but he finds that conflict waged in the collective mind is as consequential as battles fought for physical dominance: 'If war is essentially an organised communication of violence, propaganda and psychological warfare are essentially organised processes of persuasion' (9). Using similar reasoning, Strangelove (2005) argues that capitalism 'operates as a form of empire, one that works not merely through the marketplace and the much maligned military-industrial complex of modern states, but also through the mind itself' (3). The clichés 'battle for mindshare' and 'battle for hearts and minds' reflect these insights.

Jowett and O'Donnell (2006) define propaganda as the 'deliberate, systematic attempt to shape perceptions, manipulate cognitions, and direct behaviour to achieve a response that furthers the desired intent of the propagandist' (7). Their definition reflects the common view of propaganda as self-interested manipulation – an assumption that can be difficult to prove, because propagandists try to conceal their motivation and intent. In 1943, Churchill famously said to Stalin: 'In wartime, truth is so precious that she should always be attended by a bodyguard of lies' (Jablonsky 1991: 172). Was Churchill's propaganda during WWII deceitful, self-interested manipulation or diplomacy in the national interest?

Propaganda differs from advertising and advocacy, because it must be broad in scope and must dominate messaging in mainstream media; the stakes (risks) are high, with considerable consequences; and there must be significant action – or inaction – based on changed attitudes. There is a difference between an advertising campaign to sell home security systems and the massive social mobilisation needed for a war against terror, even though both hinge on questions of security. The 'greenwashing' of the Canadian tar sands is propaganda and not public relations, because tar sands extraction contributes to massive air and water pollution, and the Canadian Government misreported environmental impact statistics to the United Nations (UN) (de Souza 2011). The energy company BP – formerly British Petroleum, but rebranded as Beyond Petroleum in 2000 – engages in public relations spin when it claims to invest heavily in sustainable energy. But this campaign becomes propaganda when BP participates in an industry-wide effort to discourage alternate energy sources. Self-interest and conscious deception hide BP's true motivations (Landman 2010).

Propaganda aims to win the compliance of its mass audience and mobilise it to act, or not act, in the propagandist's interests. To influence mass audiences, it requires the cooperation and agency of major communication channels. Only wealthy and powerful individuals and organisations can conduct propaganda campaigns. While many 'public service' organisations – from Greenpeace and Amnesty International to trade unions – aspire to that degree of influence, unsympathetic coverage of their campaigns in the corporate media undermines their effectiveness. They produce advocacy campaigns struggling for mindshare in the marketplace of ideas.

Categories of propaganda [1]

Ellul (1965) identifies four categories of propaganda, each with its own motivations and strategies. While these categories complicate any attempt to define propaganda simply, they are useful for illustrating the idea that persuasion operates along a spectrum of influence.

- *Political versus sociological propaganda*
  Political propaganda is organised by a centralised body – government, political party, interest group – with specific goals. It is clearly distinguished from advertising and social advocacy by its political agenda. In contrast, sociological propaganda is embedded into the fabric of technological cultures. It has diverse origins and is more loosely organised. Entertainment and news media play an important role by defining fashions, trends, values and ethics and exporting those styles and values abroad as advertisements for national culture. 'Sociological propaganda produces a progressive adaptation to a certain order of things, a certain concept of human relations, which unconsciously moulds individuals and makes them conform to society' (Ellul [1965] 1973: 64).
- *Agitation versus integration propaganda*
  Agitation propaganda stirs up its target audience to participate in revolution, war, increased production or rapid social change. It is highly visible and short-lived, because it is difficult to sustain at a volatile pitch. In contrast, integration propaganda promotes conformity, adjustment, acceptance of authority. Intellectuals and religious leaders contribute to integration by defining what is proper, appropriate and ethical. In revolutionary Russia, Lenin advocated agitation propaganda (agitprop) for the working classes to provoke them to action – mainly through drama, art or music – while propaganda proper was education in communist principles reserved for the more advanced vanguard (Lenin 1902).
- *Vertical versus horizontal propaganda*
  Vertical propaganda is an exercise of authority directed by power elites, religious leaders and governments downward to the masses. It is often planned in secret, but executed with significant resources through mass media. Horizontal propaganda travels through grassroots, community and volunteer organisations. Leaders are guides and animators, rather than authority figures. In 1961, immediately after the success of the Cuban Revolution, the new government sent out an army of travelling students – *maestros ambulantes* – to teach illiterate workers to read and write using primers that communicated revolutionary values (Keeble 1961).
- *Irrational versus rational propaganda*
  Propaganda is widely described as irrational, filled with false logic, arguments to emotion and appeals to beliefs, myths and

symbols. In contrast, rational propaganda presents itself as scientific evidence, sound reasoning, realism and common sense. As we will see, climate change denial or the justification of economic ideologies are buttressed by an apparatus of statistics and other evidence that is selective, distorting and misleading. (Ellul [1965] 1973: 62–87; Marlin 2002: 36–9)

Ellul says that propaganda's chief task is to 'solve problems created by technology, to play on maladjustments, and to integrate the individual into the technological world' ([1965] 1973: xvii). George Grant analyses propaganda designed to promote technology and has observed that leaders promote the 'dynamism of technology', because it promises the 'mastery of chance' (1969: 113). Those who promise to master chance in a technological society are rewarded with power. Postman (1992) coined the term 'technopoly' to describe the 'surrender of culture to technology', impossible without integration propaganda.

Propaganda must create a total environment of persuasion, using all available media and leaving no gaps to be filled with opposing views. Ellul considers propaganda necessary in a democracy simply because the masses participate in political decisions; paradoxically, propaganda 'renders the true exercise of [democracy] almost impossible' ([1965] 1973: xvi). Political propaganda endlessly promotes elite interests at the expense of public sentiment. Effective propaganda 'cannot be individual; it must be collective' (28), because 'in the collective passion created by propaganda, critical judgement disappears altogether' (170). Ellul's idea that collectives – whether crowds, mass audiences or nations – are incapable of 'discernment' (170) remains controversial (Lévy 1994; Surowiecki 2004; Castells 2012).

Performing in the public sphere

Persuasion and propaganda are performances for an audience. Erving Goffman's work on the 'presentation of self' advanced the idea that people inhabit 'multiple social realities', acting out their identities in bounded 'regions' equivalent to 'backstage' (informal, private) and 'front stage' (formal, public) performance spaces (Goffman 1959: 106ff; Alia 2004: 23–4). Goffman's analysis led to the performance studies of the 1980s and 90s. Schechner (1991) uses ethnographic studies of ritual drama by Turner (1982, 1987) and others to demonstrate the continuum of performance from play and ritual to stage drama and performance in everyday life. A bounding frame – a ritual setting, a stage with props – defines the performance space, where anything can happen. Performance involves a 'consciousness of doubleness', where the performer's action is 'placed in mental comparison' with some ideal or potential (Carlson 1996: 5). The everyday self is transformed through performance and given additional communication powers. In 1927, Hans Hoffmann took a remarkable series of photographs of Adolf Hitler rehearsing his future role as Führer in his studio (Hoffmann [1955] 2012; Ewen 1996: 156).

Persuasion and propaganda occur in a bounded performance space defined by Habermas (1962) as the *public sphere*. The public sphere is 'made up of private people gathered together as a public and articulating the needs of society with the state' (176). Individuals inhabit a private *lifeworld*, where they are relatively autonomous and become active members of society when they enter the public sphere – any place they can engage in dialogue about the affairs of state: cafeterias and restaurants, public meetings, churches, schools, online discussion forums, blogs, social networks, call-in radio programmes, demonstrations and marches. Citizens assemble in the public sphere to engage with the *system*: the market economy, state apparatus (government, courts, law enforcement, military) and its agents, such as corporate media and special interest groups. This dialogue legitimates and endorses the authority of the democratic system. In turn, a healthy public sphere requires its media system to circulate trustworthy information and a range of opinions useful for citizen decision-making. Recall that propagandists need sufficient resources and the cooperation of mainstream media to communicate their dominant message.

Habermas believed the ideal public sphere should be accessible to all citizens, who are autonomous, free of coercion and protected by the rule of law. Fruitful debate requires commitment to reason and civility, and the supreme communication skill is persuasive argument based on rhetoric. The right of assembly and freedom of speech are necessary for a productive public sphere, and security at public gatherings is closely observed as a sign of tolerance for dissent. For citizens seeking social change through displays of solidarity, the public sphere is their stage.

This ideal public sphere has never been achieved. In the nineteenth and twentieth centuries, ethnic, gender and class distinctions were reduced, but Habermas argued that the public sphere was deformed by expanding social engineering, culture industries and powerful private interests. Many critics, Ellul included, observe that system propaganda interferes with democratic dialogue by setting its own agenda and framing issues to reflect elite interests. For example, large, profit-making newspaper chains turned the press into an agent of influence, rather than dialogue – 'the gate through which privileged private interests invaded the public sphere' (Habermas [1962] 1991: 185). According to Chomsky (2006), the system maintains the illusion of a functioning public sphere only to sanction the decisions of leaders. Limited public dissent is tolerated, even encouraged, to maintain the illusion of democracy.

Decoding media discourse: ideology, hegemony, power

To understand discourse in the public sphere, we need a suitable communication model to describe message circulation. In Stuart Hall's model of *encoding* and *decoding*, the sender encodes 'raw' data into a message using a code suitable for transmission, such as an alphabet, Morse code, or binary code. The sender transmits the message through a suitable medium and the receiver must decode the message to understand it. The transmission medium influences the message and must be taken into account during encoding. For example, the same story is encoded differently for television and for print publication. Message transmission is degraded by noise and other forms of interference, including distractions. Both encoding and decoding depend on 'technical infrastructure' (a medium), 'relations of production' (ability to encode and decode) and shared 'frameworks of knowledge' (for mutual understanding) (Hall [1980] 2006: 164–5).

Ideology and power relations influence message encoding and decoding. *Ideology*, and its relation to power, is defined as the 'shared ideas or beliefs which serve to justify the interests of dominant groups' (Giddens 1997: 583). Ideology legitimises power relations and is necessary for maintaining those relations. Persuasion and propaganda are necessary in democracies, because the powerful must constantly reaffirm and rationalise their dominance to pacify citizen doubts and complaints, make the social order seem natural and encourage trust in the system. Antonio Gramsci (1971) adds to our understanding of ideology and power with his concept of *hegemony*, where dominant ideologies are so widespread and accepted that they are 'taken for granted' (172) and expressed as common sense. For example, the claim that capitalism represents economic freedom and fits naturally with democracy's political freedom is a common hegemonic construct. Closer inspection reveals that capitalism and democracy as practised offer more freedom for some than others.

While the sender encodes the message to encourage a certain interpretation, there is no guarantee the message will be decoded as intended. In Hall's model, the receiver has an opportunity to co-create the message with the sender or to respond if there is a feedback loop. For communication to persuade, the sender must anticipate the receiver's response – a premise developed in the Theory of Mind: the idea that humans can infer and anticipate what other humans are thinking and feeling. 'The ability to see the world from another person's vantage point is . . . essential for constructing a mental model of another person's complex thoughts and intentions in order to predict and manipulate' (Ramachandran [2011] 2012: 118). Hall identifies three decoding strategies:

- *Dominant-hegemonic decoding*: the receiver accepts the message as reliable and authoritative. For example, universal health care is a common good that should be provided by the government.
- *Negotiated decoding*: the receiver accepts the dominant view with some reservations. We might accept that universal health care is a common good, but oppose a particular plan advanced by the government.
- *Oppositional decoding*: the receiver understands the message and rejects its meaning outright. Universal health care is not a common good and should not be legislated. This opposition may be thoroughly reasoned or ideological, based on beliefs or biases. ([1980] 2006: 172)

When negotiating meaning, people frequently rely on a network of 'texts', such as religious teachings or historical events, to guide their responses. Persuasive communicators thus enter into a dialogue with other texts, perhaps by citing a well-known story or famous quotation. Bakhtin's (1982) idea of *dialogism* – that all cultural texts, in any media, can engage in dialogue with one another – is related to Gates' idea of cultural criticism as 'repetition and revision', as discussed in the Preface. We often refer to other people's words and thoughts to add substance and credibility to our own communications. The result is dialogical discourse – a blending of voices reflecting the give-and-take of dialogue, ideally open-ended and context sensitive. In contrast, monological discourse speaks with one authoritative voice and attempts to restrict possibility. Monologic discourse is typified by the military command or voice of authority seeking no response but obedience, as in G. W. Bush's 2001 pronouncement '[t]hose who harbour terrorists will be brought to justice' or Orwell's 'BIG BROTHER IS WATCHING YOU' (*Nineteen Eighty-Four* [1949] 1989).

Michel Foucault thinks of discourse as having a 'genealogy', in which history is revised to suit the purposes of the present. The 'effects of power' alter history and thus shape the negotiation of meaning

(1984: 55), as they did when Stalin and other Soviet leaders revised the history of the Communist Revolution (Priestland 2009). In his 'people's history' of the US, Zinn (1980) shifted the focus of attention to redefine American perceptions of power and justice. For Foucault, power is not a commodity to be possessed, but a system of rhetorical practices that must constantly be rationalised, (re)asserted and exercised or power will change hands. Especially in a democracy, demonstrations of power are more successful if they are not experienced as uniformly negative (Foucault 1984: 61). Power is not merely a force of repression. It can control and accomplish things, be productive. These practices, often repeated and revised in unacknowledged ways, make the exercise of power a performance.

In persuasive communication, the sender often tries to position the receiver in a hierarchy of power by claiming authority, knowledge or moral superiority. Foucault identifies three ways to turn subjects into objects of power:

- *Dividing practices*: Subjects are divided either within themselves or from others by a process of exclusion that is justified by science or social science. For example, in the eighteenth century, a scientific definition was required before 'insane' people could be incarcerated. Cohen ([1972] 2002) shows that identifying 'folk devils' can precipitate a 'moral panic'. Current dividing practices label people 'terrorists' whether they are killing for revenge, fighting for political determination or demonstrating for environmental protections.
- *Scientific classification*: The subject is defined as a statistic, a type, a representative, a demographic, a psychographic, a unit of production, a member of a discipline or profession. Officials identify, catalogue, institutionalise and discipline anyone considered antisocial or perverse.
- *Subjectification*: Subjects objectify themselves by self-identifying with others: left, right, conservative, progressive, Muslim, atheist. People also repress their true subject positions to avoid being singled out as different. (Rabinow 1984: 7–11)

Case study: Orientalism

As a dispossessed Palestinian, Edward Said embraced Gramsci's idea in the *Prison Notebooks* (1971) that critical intelligence begins with self-knowledge, of knowing oneself 'as a product of the historical process' that leaves behind 'an infinity of traces, without leaving an inventory'

(Said [1978] 2000: 90). *Orientalism* (1978) is Said's personal inventory, written in response to the Arab–Israeli War of June 1967, and remains an influential study of hegemony. Said is centrally concerned with Western scholarly and media portrayals of the Orient – the Middle East, North Africa and Islam – for ideological purposes:

> The Orient is not only adjacent to Europe; it is also the place of Europe's greatest and richest and oldest colonies, the source of its civilisations and languages, its cultural contestant, and one of its deepest and most recurring images of the Other. In addition, the Orient has helped to define Europe (or the West) as its contrasting image, idea, personality, experience. ([1978] 2000: 68)

Orientalism is 'a way of seeing that imagines, emphasises, exaggerates and distorts differences of Arab peoples and cultures as compared to that of Europe and the US. It often involves seeing Arab culture as exotic, backward, uncivilized, and at times dangerous' (Arab American National Museum 2011: n.p.). Orientalism becomes a hegemonic construct through 'supporting institutions, vocabulary, scholarship, imagery, doctrines' (Said [1978] 2000: 68) that circulate and cross-reference these views of the Orient. Western experts on the Orient present their observations as conventional wisdom and common sense, when, in fact, they are expressing a 'Western style for dominating, restructuring, and having authority over the Orient' (69). Objectifying the Orient allows the West to define itself as separate and different, a classic example of Foucault's dividing practices. Long-standing religious differences between Islam, Christianity and Judaism contribute to these dividing practices.

Orientalism is a story divorced from reality. Said uses an example from Flaubert's travels to Egypt in 1849–50 to symbolise Orientalism's strategies and illustrate that Europeans describe their Orient without its consent:

> Flaubert's encounter with an Egyptian courtesan produced a wildly influential model of the Oriental woman; she never spoke of herself, she never represented her emotions, presence, or history. *He* spoke for and represented her. He was foreign, comparatively wealthy, male, and these were historical facts of domination that allowed him not only to possess Kuchuk Hanem physically but to speak for her and tell his readers in what ways she was 'typically Oriental'. ([1978] 2000: 72 [emphasis in original; all instances of italics in quotations are emphases in original])

Flaubert's story illustrates that ideas of dominance and superiority are embedded in ethnography (or history) and that 'these representations rely upon institutions, traditions, conventions, agreed-upon codes of understanding for their effects, not upon a distant and amorphous Orient' (88). Flaubert's narrative gains additional resonance for Said from the obvious sexual nature of the encounter, with its themes of dominance, exploitation and possession.

In *Covering Islam* (1981), Said supplements his analysis of historical Orientalism with an examination of contemporary media coverage of the Middle East. It is an 'unacceptable generalisation', he asserts, to identify many societies and beliefs and over a billion people all as Islam; this approach 'could never be used for any other religious, cultural, or demographic group on earth' ([1981] 1997: xvi). When such generalisations are embedded in cultural discourse and accepted without question, they provide the foundation for propaganda. Huntington (1993) frames global conflict as an epic confrontation between civilisations, though he places greatest emphasis on the clash between Islam and the West, asserting that 'Islam has bloody borders' (35). Said challenged this reduction of both the West and Islam into crude stereotypes similar to the cartoon figures of Popeye and Bluto. According to Said, Huntington, and those following his lead, are 'presuming to speak for a whole religion or civilisation' (Said 2001: n.p.). Hegemony lives through its sweeping generalisations.

Instead of this biased narrative of warring civilisations, Said demands wider frames and fewer stereotypes:

> These are tense times, but it is better to think in terms of powerful and powerless communities, the secular politics of reason and ignorance, and universal principles of justice and injustice, than to wander off in search of vast abstractions. (2001: n.p.)

The clash of civilisations theory is a gimmick, he concludes, 'better for reinforcing defensive self-pride than for critical understanding of the bewildering interdependence of our time'.

Frames and narratives

Orientalism and the clash of civilisations hypothesis act as frames to construct a picture of cultural identity. Frames are cognitive structures that shape the way we perceive, reason and act. They allow us to understand reality in the form of narratives. Goffman (1974) compares a frame to a dramatic script, complete with actors, roles, props and motivations. As a sociologist, he observed that all institutions require frames to define typical activities and their sequence, employee roles and hierarchies and expectations for clients or customers. Political candidates mount the stage to make speeches, while handlers and strategists work the back rooms, corridors and auditoriums. They all perform within expectations, using scripts. Talking points frame a political or public relations message to ensure all the players stay 'on message'. News editors and reporters use frames to define the context and significance of stories and to encourage conclusions. As a narrative device, framing exerts a powerful influence on storytelling and audience interpretation.

Cognitive scientist George Lakoff thinks frames are central to political discourse because '[w]e live our narratives' (Lakoff [2008] 2009: 33). Frames anchor political narratives:

> Language gets its power because it is defined relative to frames, prototypes, metaphors, narratives, images, and emotions . . . If we hear the same language over and over, we will think more and more in terms of the frames and metaphors activated by that language. ([2008] 2009: 15)

Constant repetition reinforces neural circuits, enhances memorability and encourages acceptance of the frame. Political discourse is thus a contest to see who can define the dominant frames. These stories are neurally inscribed into familiar pathways of thinking and feeling and seem to arise spontaneously when sufficiently widespread.

Frames operate mainly in the unconscious and require conscious reflection to bring into awareness. Narrative constructs, such as the British Empire, the Irish Troubles, American exceptionalism, Canadian peacekeeping, Western decadence, Eastern mysticism, the war on terror and the clash of civilisations are so deeply encoded they are hard to reframe. By bringing assumptions, expectations and scenarios into consciousness, frame analysis makes it possible to adjust or contest hegemonic narratives. For example, Tony Blair's speech to the US Congress frames the invasion of Iraq as a question of religious fanaticism:

> That is what this struggle against terrorist groups or states is about. We're not fighting for domination. We're not fighting for an American world, though we want a world in which America is at ease. We're not fighting for Christianity, but against religious fanaticism of all kinds. (Blair 2003: n.p.)

Notice what Blair excludes from the frame and what he places squarely within it. He is silent on a number of important factors: there is no mention of oil or insecurity or global markets, because these concerns fall outside the current ideological frame. Framing determines what is included and excluded from accounts and stories and thus involves ethical issues of transparency and deception.

Ethics of persuasion

> It must be evident to everyone that it is more praiseworthy for a prince always to maintain good faith, and practice integrity rather than craft and deceit. And yet the experience of our own times has shown that those princes have achieved great things who made small account of good faith, and who understood by cunning to circumvent the intelligence of others; and that in the end they got the better of those whose actions were dictated by loyalty and good faith. (Machiavelli [1532] 1997: 67)

Ethics is a central concern in the persuasive performance. While it is common to assume that deception in persuasion is unethical, no matter the motivation, an opposing narrative praises clever deception and pragmatic Machiavellian realism. The extreme of this position is the saying: 'If you're not cheating, you're not trying hard enough'. In a text almost as relevant today as it was in sixteenth century Italy, Machiavelli (1532) plays on this ambivalence when advising his prince on affairs of state. We find this ambivalence in studies of advertising and public relations (O'Reilly and Tennant 2009; Twitchell 1996; Bernays 1947); in television dramas such as *Mad Men*; and in documentaries on Nazi Germany fascinated with the propaganda of Goebbels (*Das Goebbels Experiment* 2005) or Riefenstahl (*The Wonderful, Horrible Life of Leni Riefenstahl* 1993). The Machiavellian *realpolitik* (practical politics) of Henry Kissinger, Secretary of State for Richard Nixon and Gerald Ford in the 1970s, remains controversial. Winner of the Nobel Peace Prize in 1973 for brokering peace in Vietnam, Kissinger is also associated with Operation Condor – a covert effort to displace socialist leaders and organisers in South America (Hitchens 2001). The aphorism 'all's fair in love and war' captures the sense of this ethical dilemma. A popular title among contemporary business readers, Sun Tzu's *The Art of War* ([500 BCE] 1962) advises that 'all warfare is based on deception' (66): 'He who knows the art of the direct and indirect approach will be victorious. Such is the art of manoeuvring' (106).

Plato and Aristotle both recognised that ethics depends on perceptions of truth, and Plato warned of the dangerous use of rhetoric to deceive. The more pragmatic Aristotle catalogued rhetorical techniques and related them to the dramatic arts. Aristotle believed that rhetoric should be more concerned with performing an effective argument than with discovering ideal truth. However, if persuasive communicators are not held accountable for deception and lack of transparency, they are encouraged to take a 'free hand' in the future: 'Without pursuing matters of truth, we open ourselves to accusations of disinterest in wrongdoing and share the responsibility that goes with willful blindness' (Marlin 2002: 200). We share responsibility for safeguarding a climate of truth-telling based on the 'principle of veracity' that honesty is preferable to deception, because it needs no defence (Bok [1978] 1979: 32–3).

Questions of objectivity and bias complicate the study of persuasion and propaganda, as they must, since we are dealing with perceptions, perspectives and beliefs. The story of Eshu's cap reminds us that point of view, or context, determines perceptions of truth. Alia (2004) describes the 'Rashomon Effect' in news reporting: '"truth" is really *truths* and is always based on multiple realities' (23). She refers to Kurosawa's film *Rashomon* (1950), in which a crime is witnessed from four contradictory points of view. While some debates can be resolved by evidence – for example, the existence of global warming, weapons of mass destruction or species evolution – belief and opinion often trump evidence where human loyalties are involved. We return to the question of ethics and persuasion in the final chapter.

Exercise questions

1. Describe a recent discussion you have had in which there was a dispute over the interpretation of facts. How was the dispute resolved (if it was)?
2. Illustrate Ellul's four categories of propaganda with contemporary examples.
3. Describe, in writing, an example of unethical behaviour – and what makes it unethical – and then discuss your example with your study group.
4. In what ways do you experience the system's 'colonisation' of the public sphere?
5. Hall distinguishes between dominant-hegemonic, negotiated and oppositional decoding of messages. Using your own examples, illustrate the differences between these responses.
6. Provide examples of 'dividing practices' in recent media reporting.
7. Describe the framing devices used in a news story or magazine article.
8. Hegemony (Gramsci 1971) is an important concept in the study of

propaganda. What is your understanding of this term and where do you see it operating in your country?

9. Describe a propaganda campaign currently active in your country. In your description, define propaganda and distinguish it from advertising, advocacy, public relations and lobbying. What roles do ideology and hegemony play? Who is responsible? Who provides funding?

Figure 2 'Army of one'. Photo: M. Soules, Las Vegas, 2014. Words compete with weapons for power.

1 Rhetoric and Persuasion

Media Ecology and the bias of communication

Because of its action in extending our central nervous system, electric technology seems to favour the inclusive and participational spoken word over the specialist written word. (McLuhan [1964] 1994: 82)

The Media Ecology approach to communication begins with the observation that communication technologies 'affect human perception, understanding, feeling, and value ... [Media Ecology] tries to find out what roles media force us to play, how media structure what we are seeing, why media make us feel and act as we do' (Media Ecology Association n.d.: n.p.). Media extend the senses just as tools – and weapons (!) – extend the hands and wheels extend the feet. For McLuhan, electronic technologies extend the central nervous system. Through our various screens, we can witness global culture, exposing ourselves to new understandings and possible shocks to our senses.

Media ecologists believe that communication technologies shape both the message and the communicator's consciousness. 'Writing develops codes in a language different from oral codes in the same language' (Ong [1982] 1988: 106). 'Greek literacy changed not only the means of communication, but also the shape of the Greek consciousness' (Havelock 1986: 17). According to this argument, literacy supports abstract analysis and categorisation that orality cannot support. Havelock's conclusion parallels arguments made by McLuhan (1962) and Eisenstein (1980) that the moveable type printing press of the 1450s created typographic (print) consciousness.

Media have a bias because they extend some senses and diminish others. People who talk on cellphones while driving are at greater risk of accidents, because their sensory equilibrium and focus of attention have shifted. Readers in trains and buses focus their vision to enter an alternate reality. In *The Bias of Communication* (1951), Innis develops this theme when he distinguishes between time-biased and space-biased media. Time-biased media communicate over time, because they are durable (stone monuments, earthworks, metal), while space-biased media communicate more effectively over distance (parchment, paper, smoke signals), giving them greater speed and range, but less durability. Innis argues that orality is time-biased – despite its apparent transience – because it depends on personal contact; it fosters social relationships and provides the continuity necessary for community- and nation-building. Oral histories, myths and stories are important cultural artefacts and demonstrate remarkable longevity (Havelock 1986). Bringhurst (1999) writes about Haida oral culture in the Pacific Northwest and describes the difficulty of translating oral stories into print: 'All classical Haida literature is oral. By definition, therefore, it is something printed books cannot contain, in precisely the same sense that jazz, or the classical music of India, is music that a score cannot contain' (14).

N. Katherine Hayles thinks we are becoming increasingly 'posthuman' in our ability to interact with intelligent machines even to the extent that we do not always know if we are communicating with a human or a computer. She cites Turing's 1950s intelligence behaviour test, in which a human communicates by computer terminal with two entities in another room, one human and the other a computer. If the human sending the messages cannot tell whether the responses come from a human or a machine, it proves that machines can think. Cynthia Breazeal's pioneering research at MIT into human–robot interaction comes close to passing Turing's difficult test (Breazeal 2011; DeSteno 2014: 164).

Hayles believes that communication with computers continues the trend that marked the transition from orality to literacy. When communicating with computers, we depend on 'the formal manipulation of symbols' as a sign of intelligence and not on the presence of a human body (Hayles 1999: xi). Compare this with the equally radical discovery following writing's invention that it no longer matters if the sender is in the receiver's physical presence – an essential condition for primary orality. The increasing influence of writing in Greek oral culture called for studies of rhetoric and persuasion appropriate for this new medium. The transition from orality to literacy altered notions of identity and performance for classical Greek philosophers, just as communication through digital avatars will affect our own understanding of identity and performance (Turkle 1995).

In the early 1960s, McLuhan associated electronic technologies with 'inclusive' orality and expressed a bias against the 'specialist written word'. Havelock tells a story to explain a surge of academic interest in orality in the early 1960s. In previous decades, scholars and the general public were impressed by radio's power: 'We had all been listening to the radio, a voice of incessant utterance, orally communicating fact and intention and persuasion, borne on the airwaves to our ears' (1986: 30). Radio played an important role in WWII propaganda. Roosevelt, Hitler, Mussolini, Stalin and Churchill all used radio effectively to mobilise for war. Radio reconfigured orality dramatically by extending broadcast range and audience numbers, making it an international medium of persuasion. Havelock describes students and faculty at the University of Toronto listening to a radio broadcast over loudspeakers in October 1939. At the time, Canada and Britain were at war with Germany:

> [Hitler] was exhorting us to call it quits and leave him in possession of what he had seized. The strident, vehement, staccato sentences clanged out and reverberated and chased each other along, series after series, flooding over us, battering us, half drowning us, and yet kept us rooted there listening to a foreign tongue which we somehow could nevertheless imagine that we understood. This oral spell had been transmitted in a twinkling of an eye, across thousands of miles, had been automatically picked up and amplified and poured over us. (1986: 32)

Havelock remarks that Hitler's oratory – while partially improvised and certainly a performance – was also scripted and distributed in print form. This was not primary orality, but a hybrid form, a 'remarriage' of the written and spoken word (33). Like McLuhan, Havelock appreciated orality's expressive power and was biased in its favour for certain communication tasks.

Rhetoric: room for argument

A great debate about the ethics of rhetoric began soon after the introduction of writing in seventh century BCE Greece. Orality's patterns of thought evolved toward writing's greater abstraction, analysis and categorisation, allowing a systematic study of rhetoric. Plato occupies a pivotal and paradoxical position in Western thought: as a literate person steeped in oral traditions, he was sceptical about writing. In *Phaedrus* (360 BCE), he expresses reservations about the loss of memory resulting from widespread literacy, and writing's inability to engage in real-time dialogue with an audience. On the other hand, he excludes poets from his ideal republic, because their oral discourse does not allow the close analysis and reflection made possible by writing (*The Republic* 360 BCE). In recording the Socratic dialogues in written form, Plato uses Socrates to advance a new conception of consciousness. Socrates clings to oral habits, while using words in 'a brand new manner, no longer as an exercise in poetic memorisation, but as a prosaic instrument for breaking the spell of the poetic tradition' (Havelock 1986: 5). Writing encouraged a different kind of thinking – more conceptual, abstract and reasoned – and was thus able to articulate the city state's ideals.

As orality and literacy were vying for the stage in Athenian democracy, Plato and Aristotle took differing positions on rhetoric's role. Plato was suspicious that rhetoric, with its origins in oratory, was more concerned with persuasion than with truth, especially as practiced by the Sophists, who considered rhetoric an end in itself. Plato describes Socrates as troubled by the possible abuse of rhetoric. When he challenges the rhetorician Gorgias on the matter, Gorgias replies with a classic rhetorical defence:

> Socrates: ... [T]he rhetorician need not know the truth about things; he has only to discover some way of persuading the ignorant that he has more knowledge than those who know?
> Gorgias: Yes, Socrates, and is not this a great comfort? Not to have learned the other arts, but the art of rhetoric only, and yet to be in no way inferior to the professors of them? (Plato *Gorgias* 380 BCE)

For Socrates, rhetoric trades more in appearances and wit than in truth or justice. Rhetoric is like cooking, 'producing a sort of delight and gratification'. It is 'not an art at all, but the habit of a bold and ready wit, which knows how to manage mankind'. Rhetoric is the 'ghost or counterfeit' of politics; it is 'ignoble' because it describes appearances, not essences. We recognise Gorgias' approach to rhetoric in the confident predictions of pundits whose accuracy is questionable (Tetlock 2005).

Aristotle took a different, more pragmatic approach. Rhetoric is both useful and necessary for political discourse – a civic art with the power to shape and sustain communities. Aristotle identifies three modes of persuasion: *logos* – reasoned discourse, including logic and dialectic (argument); *pathos* – appeals to the emotions, sympathies or imagination; and *ethos* – the speaker's moral character, as perceived by the audience (linked to the speaker's alignment with community ideals). Aristotle sees rhetoric as 'the faculty of observing in any given case the available means of persuasion' and makes no distinction between benign persuasion and deception (*Rhetoric*, Ch. 2). Its first and only requirement is that it be effective for a particular audience.

Rhetoric exploits the ambiguity and instability of language. 'Rhetoric is language at play – language plus. It is what persuades and cajoles, inspires and bamboozles, thrills and misdirects' (Leith 2012: 6). Rhetoric is the language of tricksters. Hermes, the Greek god of cunning, deceit and trickery, was also the god of persuasive speech and oratory. Like Eshu, Hermes was a messenger to the gods and interpreter of human affairs. Leith notes that Corax (whose name means crow in Latin) is credited with being the first to define the art of persuasion. Corax refined his approach to rhetoric in the courts, and rhetoric is often adversarial in nature. In the justice system, opponents present their arguments and a decision is made by a judge, jury or the public. Ideally, the successful argument uses credible evidence, emotional conviction and personal character to influence the judgement. Corax 'grasped the essential notion that in rhetoric you are dealing with likelihood rather than certainty: there is room for argument, and it is precisely in that room for argument that the art of persuasion flourishes' (Leith 2012: 20).

Rhetoric from orality to print

Despite their differences, legal advocacy and public relations both inherited elements of orality's agonistic spirit – its tendency to approach rhetoric as a contest, a battle of wits. Walter Ong (1982) finds this tendency when he compares oral, written (chirographic) and print-based (typographic) discourse to argue that the medium influences both rhetorical style and consciousness. Ong used research by Milman Parry and his student Alfred Lord on performance practices of Serbo-Croatian oral poets, which provided insights into the oral formulas in Homer's epic poems (Lord 1960). Okpewho (1979) and Goody (1977) conducted similar research into oral performance. They found that oral performances were often staged as contests, where poets 'stitch things together' (from *rhapsōidein*, stitching) to demonstrate their language skills. Because oral poetry depends on memory, it uses repeated or formulaic phrases, epithets, word forms and clichés, all of which must fit into the metrical pattern of the composition. Poets working in the oral tradition stitch their poems together from component parts, never in exactly the same order. They are improvising, like jazz musicians. When Homer's poems were written down in the seventh century BCE, they became literary texts, fixed in place, with strong residual orality.

Orality has distinctive psychodynamic characteristics. Spoken language is fleeting – it disappears as it is spoken – which profoundly impacts the communications environment for both speaker and listener. Because spoken words are propelled by breath, they are dynamic in ways written words cannot be. Sound, emerging from the body's interior, draws listeners into closer physical presence and binds the listening community together. Oral poets rely on 'memorable thoughts' (Ong [1982] 1988: 34) patterned for retention, ready for recall. They portray 'heavy' characters, who are bigger than life, though psychologically flat by literate standards. 'Colourless personalities cannot survive oral mnemonics' (70). Contemporary comic book superheroes originate in orality's heavy characters. Formulaic phrases, such as 'enemy of the people', 'weapons of mass destruction' or 'capitalist war-monger', demonstrate residual orality. Orality is marked by fluency, redundancy and copiousness; a dense, analytic writing style is only possible with reflection and editing.

Orality preserves traditions when it remembers the past and brings it forward as a form of knowledge, binding communities together over time through shared words and stories. Talk radio hosts and evangelical preachers are equally concerned with community-building around shared language, beliefs and values. Orality frequently 'situates knowledge within a context of struggle' (Ong [1982] 1988: 44). Ong notes the prevalence of reciprocal name-calling ('flyting') in oral cultures, as illustrated by the African-American practice of signifyin', or playing the dozens, both important influences in rap music. Bargaining in oral cultures is a series of manoeuvres, a duel of wits, a performance.

In contrast, text-formed thought shifts sensory equilibrium from the ear to the eye and gives rise to abstract categorisation, formal logic and reasoning, definitions, geometric figures, comprehensive descriptions and self-reflection (Ong [1982] 1988: 55). While orality is dynamic and body-centred, text is static and removed from physicality. 'Writing moves words from the sound world to a world of visual space, but print locks words into position in this space. Control of position is everything in print' (121). With this control comes ownership of words and copyright and 'closure' of the printed text through a process of editing, printing and distribution. The evolution of communication from primary orality to writing to print and back to the secondary orality of radio, film, television and social networking requires a parallel evolution of rhetoric. While Manovich's *The Language of New Media* (2001) remains an important early text, there is still much research to be done on the rhetorics of computer-mediated communication.

Rhetoric in disguise: identification and mystification

Rhetoric in any medium can be disguised. Kenneth Burke observes that 'a rhetorical motive is often present where it is not usually recognised, or thought to belong' ([1950] 1969: xiii). For example, identification is an important persuasive manoeuvre that does not announce itself as rhetoric, but comes disguised as something else. For Burke, persuasion

> . . . ranges from the bluntest quest of advantage, as in sales promotion or propaganda, through courtship, social etiquette, education, and the sermon, to a 'pure' form that delights in the process of appeal for itself alone, without ulterior purpose. And identification ranges from the politician who, addressing an audience of farmers, says 'I was a farm boy myself', through the mysteries of social status, to the mystic's devout identification with the sources of all being. (xiv)

Burke's theory of rhetorical identification is illustrated by Tony Blair's speech to the United States Congress on 17 July 2003. Blair tells an anecdote about his son to frame a rationalisation for the war on terror:

> Actually, you know, my middle son was studying 18th century history and the American War of Independence, and he said to me the other day, 'You know, Lord North, Dad, he was the British prime minister who lost us America. So just think, however many mistakes you'll make, you'll never make one that bad'.
>
> Members of Congress, I feel a most urgent sense of mission about today's world. September 11 was not an isolated event, but a tragic prologue, Iraq another act, and many further struggles will be set upon this stage before it's over. (Blair 2003: n.p.)

Blair identifies with a former British Prime Minister, Lord North, and leverages the reference about losing America to a spirited defence of the US-UK coalition in Iraq. The story about his son casts Blair in the roles of father, friend and protector, and his use of self-deprecating humour implies that he is a humble man of the people. These multiple identifications establish Blair's credentials (*ethos*) and suggest his motivation through a symbolic transformation: he elevates his status from father and friend to responsible statesman. Simultaneously, he elevates the Iraq War to a struggle for liberation and freedom that parallels the United States' struggle for freedom from Great Britain's tyranny more than 200 years earlier. The shifting identifications that establish Blair's credentials disguise his abrupt transition to a direct personal statement: 'I feel a most urgent sense of mission about today's world'. It is an impressive rhetorical performance accomplished in plain language, relying not on evidence or reason to make its point, but on identification and personal belief.

Burke uses a 'dramatistic pentad' model to investigate the performance aspects of rhetoric. His model includes five interrelated components of persuasion: the act (what happens); the scene (context for the act); the agent (actor); the agency (means); and the purpose (motive) (Burke [1941a] 1973). In his speech to Congress, Blair acknowledges its performative context by referring to September 11 as 'a tragic prologue, Iraq another act'. In Blair's drama, the world is threatened by terrorists (the scene: 9/11, Iraq) and needs decisive leaders (actors) working together (the means: UK–US coalition) to safeguard freedom from tyranny (the motive). He cunningly develops an argument from sensory experience (his son's comment), to an image (of a world in peril), to a transcendent myth (of liberty, freedom and security). Burke identified this progression from sensory experience to transcendence as a form of mystification or rhetoric in disguise. His analysis of motive in 'The Rhetoric of Hitler's "Battle"' ([1941b] 2006) illustrates another example of rhetorical mystification and includes a warning to avoid 'similar medicine in America' (149).

Burke describes ascending or descending hierarchies of images as other ways to obscure rhetorical motives. The hierarchical movement can be oriented towards glory, glamour, charisma and celebrity or it can descend from concern and fear to tragedy and annihilation. Beginning with actions and events in a plausible world, the rhetorician builds a ladder of identification from sense impressions, to symbols, to transcendent narratives (myth, magic or mystery) motivated by belief or faith. Blair ascends from the sense impressions of his talk with his son about American history, to the symbolism of September 11, to the transcendent myth of paternal protection from tyranny – his mission. As in dramatic tragedy, pity and fear motivate audiences even more powerfully than visions of order and harmony, subjects more suitable for comedy. Thus, Blair increases the dramatic impact of his speech by warning of a possible descent toward tragedy: 'and many further struggles will be set upon this stage before it's over'. Blair's performance before the US Congress exhibited a masterful use of identification and mystification to disguise the contest between rhetoric and reason – the focus of our next section on logical fallacies.

Logical fallacies: rhetoric trumps reason

Aristotle's study of logic and reasoning (collected by his followers as the *Art of Rhetoric* in the fourth century BCE) systematises reasoning and provides a method to evaluate the validity of statements. Deductive logic makes inferences ('If . . . then' statements) using the syllogism structure to combine premises into a conclusion: if [the average temperature of the planet is rising], and if [the rising temperature is caused by human activity], then [we can do something about it]. Premises are assertions that must be either true or false, and sound logic only confirms the validity – not the truth or falsity – of the conclusion. The conclusion is not a statement of truth, only a statement of possibility should the premises prove to be true.

In contrast, inductive logic – the basis of scientific inquiry – collects evidence through observation and testing to arrive at probable conclusions. Though many discoveries start out as valid deductions awaiting further proof, what science has discovered about the natural world is largely based on induction. Election exit polls predict winners; laboratories administer drugs and observe the results; and corporations plan budgets based on previous economic data. While the outcome is not guaranteed, the prediction's likelihood is thought to increase with sample size. The story of Eshu's cap reminds us that contingency – unexpected possibility or chance – always leaves a residue of uncertainty in predictions. Propagandists exploit this uncertainty to justify a fear, a doubt or a lack of action, even in the face of overwhelming evidence. Taleb (2007) makes a convincing case for the possibility of a 'highly improbable' event – a black swan in a world of white swans – coming as a complete surprise and instantly redefining what is possible. The events of 11 September 2001 offer a dramatic illustration of the black swan effect. Monbiot (2006) and Hoggan (2009) note that 'experts' sponsored by oil companies exploited perceived uncertainties in the science of climate change to delay political action for at least twenty years. The overwhelming scientific evidence was 'an inconvenient truth', according to the Guggenheim and Gore documentary (2006), and roused the climate change deniers to action.

Logical fallacies are errors in deduction and induction. They can be highly persuasive, especially when skilfully framed with rhetorical devices, ambiguous language, figures of speech and compelling emotional appeals. The Nizkor Project website, established to refute the claims of Holocaust deniers, includes a comprehensive section on logical fallacies. Lanham's *A Handlist of Rhetorical Terms* (1991) is a reliable guide to classical rhetoric, and Harris (2013) regularly updates a useful online resource, the *Handbook of Rhetorical Devices*. A few examples of logical fallacies:

- *Equivocation* uses vague and ambiguous language to obscure the truth: 'We will do everything in our power to ensure that those responsible are brought to justice'.
- The *ad populum* fallacy suggests that something is right or acceptable because the public agrees with it. 'The (British) people want us to do the right thing'. Similarly, the *bandwagon* fallacy justifies

a course of action because everyone is doing it. Technology adoption often plays the bandwagon card.

- *Appeals to emotion* bypass careful reasoning and play on biases, short cuts (heuristics) and prejudices (see Kahneman 2011).

- A *red herring* introduces an irrelevant topic to divert attention away from the main issue. Other sources of distraction include *ridicule*, which uses mockery instead of evidence, and *ad hominem attacks*, which attempt to discredit an opponent's character, instead of addressing the issues.

- Shermer ([1997] 2002) lists twenty-five fallacies, including a number that influence scientific discoveries. *Pseudoscience* uses anecdotal evidence, rumour and an insufficient number of samples (48). *Post hoc* (after the fact) reasoning, like superstition, argues that close correlation and coincidence equal causation (53–4).

- *Special pleading* – the relativist fallacy – occurs when people apply standards, principles and rules to others, while exempting themselves from those standards. Liars often use special pleading to exempt themselves from ethical standards (Bok 1978).

- *Misleading vividness* uses a small number of dramatic events to dispute significant evidence. With the *spotlight fallacy* – similar to the *availability bias* (Kahneman 2011) – the most familiar or recent case is perceived to be more significant than it is. Media attention on violent crime creates the false impression that crime rates are increasing.

- The *slippery slope* fallacy argues that consequences must inevitably follow from an action or decision, even when no causal connection can be shown: 'If we intervene in this conflict, we'll be committed to future involvement'.

- *Appeal to authority* uses the testimony of an authority to support a claim, even though the person might not be an expert on the particular issue or might be biased in some way.

- *Ipse dixit*, the *bare assertion fallacy*, translates from the Latin as 'he, himself, said it' and claims a statement is true merely because it is asserted. As transparent as this fallacy appears to be, it is the basis of arguments to authority and expert testimony: 'What he says must be true because he's an expert'. Even more profoundly, *ipse dixit* implies the argument is over: 'That's just the way it is', no further proof necessary.

- *Hasty generalisations* make universal conclusions based on too few examples. In 2014, Canadian Prime Minister Stephen Harper addressed the Israeli Knesset: '[T]his is the face of the new anti-

Semitism. It targets the Jewish people by targeting Israel and attempts to make the old bigotry acceptable to a new generation' (Goodman 2014: n.p.). Criticising Israel is anti-Semitic, according to Harper's argument, and an overgeneralisation. *Stereotypes* are hasty, often unconscious generalisations, as are the *genetic fallacy* and *guilt by association*, both of which make judgements based on where people come from or who they associate with.

- The *false dilemma* states that either X is true or Y is true, but both cannot be true: 'Every nation has to either be with us, or against us. Those who harbour terrorists, or who finance them, are going to pay a price' (US Senator Hillary Clinton, 13 September 2001). This common fallacy attempts to limit options and control how an issue is framed.

Figures of speech

Figures of speech constitute a broad class of linguistic constructions contributing additional emphasis, originality and vividness. While frequently used to clarify or enhance a message, figures of speech can be distracting by introducing ambiguity or further complexity. For example, *irony* plays on multiple meanings of a word or expression to create a message opposite to that which is expected, often for satiric purposes: 'We will use all our military might to ensure peace in the region'. Irony trades on ambiguity and double meanings.

Figures of speech are further classified into *schemes* and *tropes*, the nuts-and-bolts of rhetoric used to enhance persuasive effect, create emphasis or obscure meaning. Schemes reorganise usual word patterns for emphasis or to create new meanings, while tropes extend meaning by substitution, comparison or transformation. Common schemes summarise previous arguments in a forceful manner (*accumulation*), arrange words in order of increasing importance (*climax*) or repeat words or expressions, while adding detail for emphasis (*amplification*). Inverting usual word order (*anastrophe*), juxtaposing opposing or contrasting ideas (*antithesis*) and summarising a preceding argument with a single, wise statement (*sententia*) are only a few of the many schemes categorised in classical rhetoric.

Tropes include *allegory* – the use of a story to illustrate a moral using symbolic characters and events; *allusions* – short references to a familiar person or event; *analogies* – comparing two things to suggest that an unfamiliar concept is similar to a familiar one; and *false analogies* – which are misleading when superficial similarities obscure important differences: for example, equating the Alberta tar sands to 'ethical oil' (Levant 2010).

G. W. Bush used the analogy of a crusade to describe the US response to the 9/11 attacks and was criticised for using inflammatory rhetoric (Bush 2001; Cockburn 2002). Ironically, Osama bin Laden used the same analogy to describe Western interference in Arab affairs (2005).

Euphemism substitutes a less offensive term for another: 'collateral damage' for 'civilian deaths', 'downsizing' for 'termination', 'enhanced interrogation' for 'torture'. *Hyperbole* deliberately exaggerates for effect ('shock and awe'), while *innuendo*, or insinuation, is an indirect reference, usually involving criticism: 'Some people hint at corruption in the highest offices'. *Metaphor* compares two different things by referring to one in terms of the other. Unlike *simile* or analogy, metaphor is a form of identification and asserts that one thing *is* another thing. *Metonymy* substitutes an associated image to stand for something or someone: 10 Downing Street (UK Prime Minister), Fleet Street (British press), Madison Avenue (US advertising), the Pentagon (US military). *Satire* uses irony, sarcasm, ridicule and parody to criticise with humorous effect. In a classic example, Swift's *A Modest Proposal* (1729) satirised British foreign policy by proposing that the Irish should eat their children during a famine caused by that foreign policy. During a White House Correspondents' Dinner in 2006, comedian Stephen Colbert performed a 'blistering' satire in mocking tribute to George W. Bush (Goodman 2006; *Colbert Roasts Bush* 2006). In his speech, Colbert identified himself with Bush, because both made decisions from the gut, not the head. In 2005, Colbert had gained notoriety as a political satirist for coining the word 'truthiness' to describe an assertion made 'from the gut' or because it 'feels right', without recourse to evidence or logic (wikipedia.org/wiki/Truthiness). Ironically, recent scientific findings seem to confirm that Bush's 'from the gut' decision-making process can be highly effective: we need emotion to inform reason.

Descartes' error and the limits of reason

Logic and reasoning are tools used to assess validity, truth and falsehood, but reason is often inadequate to the task when it does not account for the complete body/brain in its social context. Noë ([2009] 2010) contends that consciousness is not like digestion, something happening within the individual body: 'Consciousness requires the joint operation of brain, body, and world. Indeed, consciousness is an achievement of the whole animal in its environmental context' (10). Consciousness is 'more like dancing than it is like digestion' (2009: xii). Standard economic theory assumes that people are consistently and reliably motivated by self-interest; they act rationally; and their tastes are consistent (Kahneman 2011: 269). Humans are considered to be irrational, illogical, uninformed or inattentive when misled by false reasoning and manipulative rhetoric. Recent discoveries in neuroscience, behavioural economics and social psychology are challenging the tradition of dispassionate analytical reasoning espoused in Western culture, beginning with Plato's concept of ideal forms and notably addressed in Descartes' *Discourse on the Method* (1637) and Kant's *Critique of Pure Reason* (1787). Humans are 'predictably irrational' (Ariely [2008] 2010; Kahneman 2011; Silver 2012; Lehrer [2009] 2010), whether playing poker, making economic decisions or assessing the truth of arguments. Reason needs emotion for effective decision-making.

In *Descartes' Error*, neuroscientist Antonio Damasio argues for new conceptions of reason and decision-making to include the interdependence of thinking and feeling, involving not only the brain, but the rest of the body as well. His somatic marker hypothesis positions emotion 'in the loop of reason', where it 'could assist the reasoning process rather than disturb it, as was commonly assumed' (1994: xi). The body makes an early contribution to decision-making through somatic markers, bodily sensations that may be felt as a 'gut feeling' (173). Somatic markers are acquired by experience, quickly pushing us toward certain solutions and narrowing options. Zak's research (2008) into the influence of the hormone oxytocin on feelings of empathy adds substance to Damasio's hypothesis. Without somatic markers to narrow the range of choices, decision-making becomes prolonged and unwieldy. 'Somatic markers probably increase the accuracy and efficiency of the decision process' (1994: 173), concludes Damasio.

In *Thinking, Fast and Slow* (2011), Kahneman qualifies Damasio's conclusions. He identifies two 'systems' of thinking: System 1 (fast, based on biases and heuristics, often unconscious); and System 2 (slow and more effortful, requiring analysis and computation). Emotion – acting through neurotransmitters like epinephrine (adrenaline) and dopamine – is necessary for initiating action quickly, but reason adds deliberation and reflection, so humans can act both quickly and intelligently. Both System 1 and System 2 thinking can lead us astray when applied inappropriately. At times, heuristic short cuts (rules of thumb) lead us in the wrong direction, as when we mistakenly assume an expert is providing objective advice. Sometimes over-analysing a situation confuses us into ignoring our gut instincts. 'At their best, feelings point us in the proper direction, take us to the appropriate place in a decision-making space, where we may put the instruments of logic to good use' (Damasio 1994: xvii). Contemporary conceptions of reasoning and decision-making no longer rely on Descartes' error – 'I think, therefore I am' – to characterise what actually happens in the body-brain-environment.

Cognitive dissonance and backfire

Facts are not always the enemy of deception. Festinger (1957) identified cognitive dissonance as the mental stress people experience when they must simultaneously hold contradictory beliefs, ideas or values. You discover, for example, that the person or nation you love has betrayed your trust. People experiencing cognitive dissonance will actively try to reduce the discomfort or avoid situations likely to increase it. Journalist Joe Keohane reports on research by Nyhan and Reifler (2010), which discovered that 'when misinformed people, particularly political partisans, were exposed to corrected facts in news stories, they rarely changed their minds. In fact, they often became even more strongly set in their beliefs' (Keohane 2010: n.p.). Nyhan calls this phenomenon 'backfire': 'a natural defence mechanism against cognitive dissonance' (qtd in Keohane). People use 'motivated reasoning' or belief to decide which facts to accept and are unwilling to change their beliefs, even when confronted with contradictory evidence.

Communications glut – where gossip, misinformation and rumour have as much currency as verifiable fact – compounds backfire. Denials and accusations are lost in the free market information whirlpool of 'communicative capitalism' (Dean 2008: 102). The more people care about a subject – its salience – the more firmly they retain their beliefs in the face of conflicting evidence. In Nyhan and Reifler's research, people who self-identified as conservatives believed even more strongly that weapons of mass destruction were found in Iraq after their misconceptions were challenged by (lack of) evidence. Keohane connects their research to the findings of Taber and Lodge (2006) that

> politically sophisticated thinkers were even less open to new information than less sophisticated types. These people may be factually right about 90 per cent of things, but their confidence makes it nearly impossible to correct the 10 per cent on which they're totally wrong. (Keohane 2010: n.p.)

Despite common perceptions, conspiracy theories are not generally the result of 'backwardness or ignorance'. Instead, '[c]onspiracy theories originate and are largely circulated among the educated and middle class . . . It has typically been professors, the university students, the managers, the journalists, and the civil servants who have concocted and disseminated the conspiracies' (Aaronovitch [2009] 2010: 338). Ellul observes that educated people are often more susceptible to propaganda, because they are accustomed to being right about the facts and confident they can distinguish truth from lies. Besides, he argues, the 'aim of modern propaganda is no longer . . . to change an opinion, but to arouse an active and mythical belief' ([1965] 1973: 25). A mythical belief is not an idea or opinion susceptible to reason; rather, it is an embodied state expressed as action in the world.

Boyd (2009) says that religious stories 'prove hard to dislodge despite their detachment from fact' (202). The confirmatory bias – where we readily accept confirmation of our beliefs, but reject contradictory evidence – and the conformist bias – which encourages us to think like others – add to this resistance. While religious beliefs contribute to social cohesion, lack of belief may be seen as a 'challenge to group unity and as tantamount to treason' (206). Osama bin Laden accused the political leaders of Saudi Arabia of treachery against the *ummah* (global nation of Islamic peoples) for cooperating and trading with the 'crusader' American empire. As a consequence, he was stripped of citizenship and his assets were frozen by the Saudi Government in 1994 (bin Laden 2005).

The triumph of narrative

Religious beliefs are memes – memorable cultural artefacts that spread like viruses from host to host. As with 'selfish' genes, memes 'act only for themselves; their only interest is their own replication; all they want is to be passed on to the next generation' (Blackmore [1999] 2000: 5). A meme is a self-replicating unit of culture – an idea, song, story, image, viral video or trend – that appears to have taken on a life of its own (though humans are the carriers of memes, just as they are of genes). The test for memes is simple yet decisive: 'successful memes are the ones that get copied and spread, while unsuccessful ones do not' (7). Myths and well-known stories are persistent memes contributing to cultural cohesion, and they are defended vigorously by the tribe.

Storytelling is perhaps humanity's most widespread and persuasive medium for circulating cultural values. Narratives command attention, explain conflict, reveal character, engage emotions and transmit morals, beliefs and memes. Gottschall (2012) observes the importance of conflict in storytelling: 'Fiction . . . is about trouble' (52). Fulford (1999) identifies the origins of narrative in gossip and stories about other people, but we also need to include myths and origin tales as early stories. All cultures have stories about the mysteries of existence, and archaeologists find evidence of early cultural narratives in rock paintings, petroglyphs, monuments and earthworks.

Aristotle (*Poetics* 350 BCE) defines narrative as the imitation of an action, a fabrication involving something familiar. Mimesis, or imitation, acts as an anchor to engage audience interest. To introduce dramatic tension and engage emotions, narrative advances with a series of plot complications moving toward a reversal of fortune. Characters discover the consequences of their actions in a recognition scene – an emotionally powerful moment designed to engage empathy. Characters must be memorable, either more noble or more corrupt than usual. Their tragic flaw is a failure of self-reflection and is more consequential because of their heroic attributes. Larger-than-life ('heavy') characters are typical of myth, religion and oral poetry: '[S]tories with unseen agents who can monitor our behaviour and administer punishment or reward – the stories we call religion – permeate and persist partly because they offer such powerful ways of motivating and apparently monitoring cooperative behaviour' (Boyd 2009: 64).

'Stories', Fulford writes, 'are how we explain, how we teach, how we entertain ourselves, and how we often do all three at once. They are the juncture where facts and feelings meet' (1999: 9). Experts in rhetoric and persuasion must be expert storytellers.

Stories create belief

In her analysis of narrative in cyberspace, Janet Murray reviews the basic components of narrative, beginning with the Romantic poet Coleridge's idea that the work of imagination requires a 'willing suspension of disbelief'. Murray finds this approach too passive, even for oral and print media: 'We do not suspend disbelief so much as we actively *create belief*' (1997: 110). Creating belief is immersive. The imagination works actively to enter into the story's enveloping world:

> [W]e construct alternate narratives as we go along, we cast actors or people we know into the roles of the characters, we perform the voices of the characters in our heads, we adjust the emphasis of the story to suit our interests, and we assemble the story into cognitive schemata that make up our own systems of knowledge and belief. (1997: 110)

Stories are cognitively engaging and immersive, especially when they embed a moral, myth or belief salient to audiences.

If spectacle is added to this active immersion, audiences can be moved to 'another order of perception' (Murray 1997: 112), where they are highly receptive to collective suggestion. From the Greek dramas, Indian Kathakali, medieval morality plays and Elizabethan theatre, to the films, television, computer games, sporting events, religious ceremonies, music concerts and political gatherings of our time, spectacles elevate us with their integration of narrative, sensual stimulation, heightened emotion and sheer scale into a matrix of community and belief. The theatre of Dionysus in Athens strategically positioned the audience to witness the performance, to see others respond and to be seen. Its amphitheatre design creates a 'seeing place' (*theatron*), the prototype of Rome's Coliseum, and sports arenas, stadiums and places of worship of our time. Spectacle of this sort builds community, offers instruction, creates belief.

Collective participation can be contagious and motivating, and a powerful opportunity for orchestrators of spectacle and persuasion. In the next chapter, we explore visual spectacle and its ambiguous, even contradictory, position in communication studies. While societies need spectacle for cultural cohesion and renewal, spectacle's abuse for social engineering and control remains a deeply rooted anxiety. Just as we discovered rhetorical conventions in orality, literacy and narrative, we will find equally powerful conventions in visual imagery and spectacle.

Exercise questions

1. Either in writing or on video, retell a story in your own words that has particular significance in your culture.
2. Describe any preferences or biases in your use of media. For example, do you prefer to send an email or use the telephone, read a newspaper or find your news online? What accounts for these preferences?
3. In *Metaphors We Live By* (1980), Lakoff and Johnson argue that metaphors frequently influence our thinking and behaviour outside our conscious awareness. Identify a metaphor that you live by and describe what purpose it serves in your life.
4. Select ten logical fallacies and illustrate them with examples from recent publications or media broadcasts.
5. Illustrate ten figures of speech (schemes and tropes) from writing or speeches produced since 2012.
6. Describe a widespread belief in your culture that needs to be challenged.
7. Analyse a speech by a public official or celebrity where you focus on the speaker's rhetoric. What rhetorical strategies are used, and how do they influence the speech's substance and credibility?

Figure 3   'Mass media'. Photo: M. Soules, Athens, 1995.

2 Compelling Images

Images to change the world

In 1890, Danish-American police reporter Jacob Riis published *How the Other Half Lives*, an exposé of New York City tenement life. This early example of muckraking journalism relied on photographs, drawings and graphic descriptions to reveal the appalling living conditions among immigrants vulnerable to wealthy tenement owners. New photographic flash technology using magnesium powder allowed Riis to illuminate the dark recesses of slum living conditions, often revealing images of children in squalid surroundings. While his reporting was designed to 'speak directly to people's hearts' (Pascal 2005: 87), he was convinced that disclosing the facts would lead to outrage and subsequent improvements. His photographs were not without artistry, but Riis intended to document the stark black and white reality of how the other half lives.

Fast-forward to 2011: Parisian street artist JR accepts a prestigious TED Prize for his large-scale wide-angle portraits pasted up on buildings, trains and bridges. An early JR project featured portraits of hoodlums displayed in middle-class Parisian neighbourhoods. *Face 2 Face* paired portraits of Palestinians and Israelis in similar lines of work. Many of the large-scale images were pasted onto the separation barrier dividing the two nations. With *Women are Heroes* (2008–9), JR and local collaborators covered walls of Brazilian *favelas* and roofs and trains in Kenya with giant images of women printed on waterproof vinyl. In his presentation to the TED audience, JR explained that his photographic projects attempt to build bridges between people and media. He expressed the hope that art can change the way we see the world and thus, perhaps, change the world (*JR's TED Prize* 2011).

In this chapter, we look at the persuasive power of images: their ability to reveal their version of the truth and their ability to deceive.

Two allegories: the Cave and the Matrix

Picture this: you and everyone you know are prisoners in a large cave, chained hand and foot to chairs, facing forward. From somewhere behind you, a light source casts shadows onto the wall in front of you. You are surrounded by sound and the flickering shadows mesmerise you.

Eventually, you are released from the chains restraining you and allowed to look around. You see that the images on the cavern wall are created by forms paraded before the light source. You are then guided up a set of stairs to an outer world lit by the sun. At first, the light is blinding, but you soon adjust to its brightness and begin to see an unfamiliar natural world. When you return to the dark cavern, you reveal to the other prisoners that they are looking at phantasms, a collective hallucination. These images, you report, are shadows of real forms passing in front of the light. 'Life as we are seeing it', you announce, 'is a spectacle of shadows. Real life is elsewhere'.

This story should sound familiar. Plato has Socrates tell a version of it in Chapter VII of *The Republic*, and it has come down to us as the 'Allegory of the Cave'. The story should also be familiar because it expresses what we hear in contemporary society about the mass media's power to substitute images for reality. We do not see actual conflict in a foreign country; we see selected images of that conflict on our various screens. The popular film *The Matrix* (1999) and its sequels have a similar theme: images can be deceptive, so you should distrust appearances of reality. Neo, the neophyte, with his guides Morpheus and Trinity, must find his way through the illusions of the Matrix into the light of understanding and truth. The Matrix is a façade of simulations constructed to hide the reality that machines are now controlling humans and feeding off their life energies. At one point during Neo's period of disillusionment, Morpheus offers him a choice between taking a red pill or a blue pill. If he chooses the red pill, he begins a heroic journey toward understanding; but if he chooses the blue pill, he remains enslaved to the Matrix.

Both tales suggest we need guides such as Socrates or Morpheus to help discern what is real, what is ideal and what is false in a world of illusions and both reflect a suspicion of the spectacle's power to deceive.

Iconoclasm and image power

Icons (Greek *eikōn*, 'image') were originally small paintings of Christian divine beings. The term 'icon' came to refer more broadly to images or objects that gain power from what they represent. In contemporary culture it describes well-known people and significant objects: a celebrity, symbolic building, influential design or brand. As icons 'borrow' power from the thing represented, they have a controversial history.

When I travelled through Turkey in the mid-1990s, I saw many examples of Christian iconic portraits where the eyes of saints and divinities had been scratched out by followers of Islam. These faithful vandals were expressing their belief that spiritual beings should not be illustrated by human hands, a convention known as aniconism. Prohibitions against images of the divine are found in many religious texts, including the Hebrew Old Testament (Second Commandment, Exodus 20: 4–6) and the Islamic Qur'an (5: 87–92; 21: 51–2). Judeo-Christian doctrine asserts that humans were created in the 'image and likeness' of God, and this jealous God prohibited the worship of graven idols. Similarly, Islamic aniconism prohibits the 'representation of living creatures because humans might create images to be used as idols' (Meggs 1998: 53). Fear of idolatry was partly a reaction to polytheistic fetishes and totems and is ironic when we consider that monotheism replaced one system of idols for another.

Mitchell (1986) cites many examples of iconoclasts defaming the icons and fetishes of an opposing group, only to assert the purity of their own icons. There was a battle over Christian images in eighth- and ninth-century Byzantium between iconoclasts and those iconophiles who believed religious icons, sacred objects and sumptuous decorations should be permitted. Later, Protestants destroyed Catholic icons during the Reformation, as did French and Russian revolutionaries in their time. In British Columbia, the colonial government of the late nineteenth and early twentieth centuries prohibited the First Nations potlatch and confiscated its spiritual regalia. Christian churches with steeples, crosses and altars replaced the potlatch ceremonies, where extravagant gift giving established status and bound tribes together in a network of obligation. Iconoclasm of this sort is ancient, 'grounded in an ideology that supports the inferiority of ethnic minority peoples and has served to justify policies and practices of assimilation, ethnocide and genocide' (Alia and Bull 2005: 3).

More recently, Soviet revisionists destroyed statues of Stalin after 1956 to discredit his leadership. Chinese communists destroyed Tibetan monasteries and artwork during the Cultural Revolution (1966–76) and forced its spiritual leaders into exile (Dhardhowa 2011). Islamic Taliban destroyed monumental Buddhist statues at Bamiyan in Afghanistan in 1991. US soldiers and Iraqi mercenaries toppled Saddam Hussein's statue after the fall of Baghdad in 2003 (Paxman 2010; Maass 2011). In 2005, the Danish newspaper *Jyllands-Posten* published twelve cartoons depicting the Prophet Mohammad to raise issues concerning criticism of Islam and self-censorship in the media. Publication of the images ignited a firestorm of protest in Muslim countries and resulted in many deaths. Yale University Press refused to include the controversial images in Klausen's *The Cartoons That Shook the World* (2009) and defended its decision by claiming that they did not want to incite further protests and possible deaths (Cohen 2009). In January 2015, two armed men broke into the Paris offices of *Charlie Hebdo* magazine and killed twelve people for publishing cartoons satirical of Islam, reigniting volatile international debates about freedom of expression, the limits of satire, and religious tolerance.

The symbolic power of images can be turned, through their destruction, into equally powerful examples of propaganda. The attacks on the World Trade Center and the Pentagon on 11 September 2001 epitomise iconoclasm in the early twenty-first century. In an interview conducted on 21 October 2001, Osama bin Laden identified the iconic significance of the 9/11 targets: 'These young men . . . have shifted the battle to the heart of the United States, and they have destroyed its most outstanding landmarks, its economic and military landmarks, by the grace of God' (bin Laden 2005: 107).

War is waged with weapons and images. On 21 March 2003, the US launched an aerial attack on Baghdad in a campaign the US military and media called 'Shock and Awe'. As reported in the British press, 'the appalling "Shock n' Awe Show" . . . resembled something that might have been conceived by a big-budget Hollywood director' (Whitaker 2003: n.p.). The bombing of Baghdad – a city founded in the eighth century as a centre for Islamic culture – was a propaganda spectacle staged for prime time television. Not even the satirical film *Wag the Dog* (1997) – in which a Hollywood producer and a publicist stage a fake war in the media to save a presidency – anticipated Shock and Awe's cynical iconoclasm.

Images, perspective and control

> The relation between what we see and what we know is never settled. (Berger 1972: 7)

We see before we understand, giving images persuasive power beyond reason's reach. Spectacles like the September 11 attacks or the 'Shock and Awe' campaign send powerful visual messages before audiences understand their significance. Our defence against disturbing images comes after the fact. Western news sources generally do not show the bodies of the dead and wounded without explicit warning, because they are considered too inflammatory. They disturb viewers' emotional equilibrium and undermine motivation for war. Instead, we see soldiers carrying flag-draped coffins to the waiting cargo plane. The 'ramp ceremony' ritual presents an iconic image with an embedded narrative – one of propaganda's most potent instruments, because it merges seen and unseen into an emotional instant.

In cultures where images proliferate, repeat and circulate in the flow of commerce and promotion, it is notable that culturally important images are often censored, hidden away in unseen archives or too costly to be reproduced. Those owing the important images of a culture – including their means of reproduction and circulation – control, to a large extent, how the past is perceived. For example, in late 2013, US judges were still deliberating on the release of images showing the assassination of Osama bin Laden in May 2011 by US Navy SEALs, even though a film of the same event (*Zero Dark Thirty*) had been nominated for an Academy Award (Levs and Cratty 2013). US Government lawyers argued that images of bin Laden, shot in the head and buried at sea, would be used for propaganda and incite violence against America.

Images can move us deeply and beyond our comprehension. Mysterious images take on the power of fetish or talisman, obsessing viewers. Bataille's exploration of eroticism, terror and death in *The Tears of Eros* (1961) includes a series of images showing the public execution of a Chinese criminal, still alive, being cut to pieces. The victim's eyes gaze skyward and convey inexpressible emotion. Bataille owned one of these images and writes: 'This photograph had a decisive role in my life. I have never stopped being obsessed by this image of pain, at once ecstatic (?) and intolerable' ([1961] 1989: 206). Seeing can become voyeuristic and obsessive, especially when images break taboos.

In *Iconology* (1986), Mitchell attempts to rescue images from being measured unfairly against spoken and written language. He wants to challenge an influential discourse by critics such as Benjamin (1936), Sontag (1977) and Barthes (1978) warning about the persuasive power of images. For these critics, images are not merely a 'transparent window on the world', but present the appearance of naturalness masking unseen distortions (Mitchell [1986] 1987: 8). Neuroscience confirms that image perception is not a straightforward recording of what we see, but a translation and re-creation. The brain 'does not recreate the original image', observes Ramachandran, 'but represents the various features and aspects of the image in totally new terms' ([2011] 2012: 47). Visual perception 'involves judgement and interpretation', an 'opinion of the world rather than a passive reaction to sensory input' (49). But Mitchell also wants images to be assessed fairly against language.

Images can be misleading, but they also communicate in ways language cannot. Over the centuries, philosophers and critics constructed hierarchies between images and words: images were thought to be more primitive than language and writing and, thus, inferior; images came to be associated with nature, and language with culture; images depict sensation and experience, while writing reveals unseen worlds and appeals to intellect, instead of emotion. In cultures seeking to dominate and control nature, writing announced the triumph of culture over nature. From this perspective, language 'signifies spiritual, mental things, in contrast to images which can only represent material objects; [language] is capable of articulating complex ideas, stating propositions, telling lies, expressing logical relations, whereas images can only show us something in mute display' (Mitchell [1986] 1987: 78). Seeking equal status for images and words, Mitchell disputes this false dichotomy: 'The mistake is to think we can know the truth about things by knowing the right names, signs, or representations of them' (92).

Images gained credibility in the contest against language when Alberti formulated conventions of visual perspective in 1425. Perspective added scientific information and verisimilitude (lifelikeness) to images and convinced 'an entire civilisation that it possessed an infallible method of representation, a system for the automatic and mechanical production of truths about the material and mental worlds' (Mitchell [1986] 1987: 39). British painter David Hockney (2006) shows that in the early fifteenth century, optics (mirrors and lenses) helped artists structure their compositions more scientifically, with greater precision and detail. Single-point perspective positions the viewer in relation to a vanishing point, where all lines converge on a distant horizon. Perspective thus controls the way we view images and influences what we look at. Through their control of perspective, monumental architecture, urban design and places of worship inspire awe by organising space and positioning viewers in relation to symbols of power.

Perspective is both persuasive and ideological, and the still camera, followed by film and television cameras, inherited perspective's ability to position viewers. Camera technology imposes a particular vantage point determined by perspective and framing. While not strictly forced to adopt these limitations, viewers must make conscious efforts to imagine the physical scene from a different perspective or outside the bounding frame. The controlling frame and point of view also instruct audiences in visual pleasure by showing compelling images. Film critic Laura Mulvey states that film, and especially Hollywood film, manipulates 'visual pleasure' by encoding 'the erotic into the language of the dominant patriarchal order' (1975: 8). The camera frames what is considered erotic – a hegemonic construct – but frequently misses the mark.

The early twentieth century brought new approaches to perspective. Cubism, Dada, Surrealism and Abstract Expressionism abandoned conventional perspective to reflect developments in philosophy, biology, physics and psychology, which collectively displaced individual viewers from their former, fixed position. Collage and montage superimpose multiple perspectives and diverse materials to communicate the 'discontinuous and ruptured' nature of the modern age (Teitelbaum and Freiman 1992: 7). Audiences learned new ways of seeing uncertainty, diversity and difference, as well as their polar opposites: certainty and uniformity.

Aura and the aesthetics of politics

In September 1940, on the border between France and Spain, German cultural critic Walter Benjamin took his life after Spanish authorities cancelled his travel visa. German forces were overtaking Paris, and Benjamin was trying to escape to the United States. As a Jewish intellectual, communist sympathiser and critic of the Nazi regime, he faced certain extradition to Germany (Arendt 1968: 18). Benjamin was associated with the Frankfurt School of cultural criticism, particularly with his friend Max Horkheimer, who had published Benjamin's influential essay 'The Work of Art in the Age of Mechanical Reproduction' in 1936. Benjamin's essay continues to be widely cited for its provocative insights into art, media and politics and particularly for its inquiry into what makes visual images compelling. As he famously concludes in this essay: 'The logical result of Fascism is the introduction of aesthetics into political life' ([1936] 1968: 241).

Benjamin is most concerned with the impact of photography, its evolution into film and their combined role influencing mass audiences during periods of political turmoil, revolution and war. He was especially troubled by the use of reproduced images in the totalitarian spectacles he witnessed in 1930s Germany. While artworks have always been reproducible by copying, Benjamin argues that mechanical reproduction introduces changes of scale, quality and distribution that redefine art's audience and value. For example, the eighteenth century invention of lithography brought illustration into the regime of mechanical reproduction and set the stage for wider image distribution using the rotary and offset press after 1850.

Reproduction creates an independent copy by adding levels of control: lighting, colour management, enlargement, cropping, camera angle, editing and juxtaposition to other images. The image becomes available in places where the original could not be seen: a painting reproduced in a magazine or art book or a photograph reproduced in the popular press. Benjamin claims mechanical reproduction diminishes the original artwork, as 'for instance, for a landscape which passes in review before the spectator in a movie' ([1936] 1968: 221). The original possesses direct material evidence of its creation, which gives it an 'aura' derived from its presence, authenticity (history) and authority. Benjamin's notion of 'aura' is related to the idea that the iconic image borrows from the spirit and power of the thing it represents. Mander (1978) includes this notion of depreciation as one of his arguments for the elimination of television. Manufactured objects display with greater vividness on television, while nature is stripped of its scope and grandeur, diminished by the screen's confining frame.

Benjamin was interested in Jewish mysticism and coined the term 'auratic perception' to describe a culture's renewed appreciation of myth. Regrettably for Benjamin, a profane 'cult of beauty' was replacing sacred myth and ritual in Nazi Germany ([1936] 1968: 224). Politics tried to appropriate the aura and ritual of original art, but instead converted it to kitsch – a vulgar and sentimental reproduction. Fascism turned politics into kitsch and drove Benjamin towards exile and despair.

Branding totalitarianism

Twenty years before Madison Avenue embarked upon 'Motivational Research', Hitler was systematically exploring and exploiting the secret fears and hopes, the cravings, anxieties and frustrations of the German masses. (Huxley [1958] 1965: 43)

Steven Heller (2008) brings his expertise in advertising and graphic design to bear on the visual culture of four twentieth-century totalitarian regimes: Nazi Germany, Fascist Italy, Soviet Russia and Communist China. He begins with a bold claim: 'Starting in the twentieth century, totalitarian states began using the same graphic identity techniques as modern industries and corporations'. Heller asserts that '[d]espots and businessmen alike strove to establish branding narratives . . . used to trigger instantaneous recognition of their ideas and products' (8). Ads are designed 'to infiltrate the subconscious in order to trigger conformist behaviour . . . to capture the loyalty of a targeted, and hopefully malleable, demographic'. For corporate and totalitarian branding alike, Heller concludes: 'If this requires engaging in some ruse or creating a fallacy, then ruse and fallacy it is' (8).

As producers of political aesthetics, the four totalitarian states under review created 'powerful visual narratives' designed for instant recognition using logos: swastika, bundle of fasces (*fascio*), hammer and sickle and the Chinese star. Leaders became the recognisable face of the movement similar to 'trade characters', such as Bibendum (Michelin Man), Mr Clean and Ronald McDonald. Hitler, Mussolini, Stalin and Mao are iconic figures who embody their movements' core narratives. As Heller comments: 'Each totalitarian brand story was designed both to enrage and engage the populace' (9). From monumental architecture to everyday objects stamped with symbols, the regime's presence – and influence – is constantly paraded before the people. Public gatherings, uniforms, statues, images of leaders and party news in the media encourage brand loyalty. As usual, repetition brings recognition and acceptance.

Heller says that '[e]xplaining the visual language and branding strategies of these totalitarian regimes is essential to an understanding of how they developed, communicated, and perpetuated their core ideologies through word, picture, and design' (11). Visual propaganda and branding must appeal to a broad range of tastes, so their visual style is not high or elitist. Stalin thought the Russian Revolution's Constructivist style was too avant-garde for the masses and insisted on Socialist Realism instead. Similarly, the Nazis condemned what they called 'degenerate' art movements, such as Expressionism and Fauvism, and instead enforced their own style of idealised realism (Clark 1997). Above all, the goal of the totalitarian state is to dominate the public display of images, from the mundane to the grandiose. Totalitarian states stage-manage their brand identities carefully, including the circulation of photographs and films documenting their activities. Image control is especially important when totalitarian regimes inflict pain.

'Psychic numbing': regarding the pain of others

[P]hotographs of the victims of war are themselves a species of rhetoric. They reiterate. They simplify. They agitate. They create the illusion of consensus. (Sontag 2003: 6)

Susan Sontag writes that 'a society becomes "modern" when one of its chief activities is producing and consuming images' (1977: 153). She recognises the power of photographs to convey complex messages, but expresses reservations about the ethics of spectatorship and voyeurism. Overexposure to images of pain can lead to 'psychic numbing': withdrawal of attention from traumatic experiences and future threats, equally affecting individuals and whole societies (Lifton

1982). Photojournalist Susan Moeller writes about 'compassion fatigue' resulting from overexposure to traumatic images (1999, 2001), and Stanley Cohen (2001) investigates the 'states of denial' that follow exposure to disturbing images and news reports.

Photographs and films intended to bring awareness to social issues can have the opposite effect by inducing viewers to dissociate from images of suffering (Phan et al. 2003). 'The quality of feeling, including moral outrage, that people can muster in response to photographs of the oppressed, the exploited, the starving, and the massacred also depends on the degree of their familiarity with those images' (Sontag 1977: 19). Images of refugee children lose their impact, she says, because we have seen them too often. 'Photographs shock insofar as they show something novel. Unfortunately, the ante keeps getting raised – partly through the very proliferation of such images of horror' (19).

Case study: Abu Ghraib exposed

> We also have to work, though, sort of the dark side, if you will. We've got to spend time in the shadows in the intelligence world . . . That's the world these folks operate in, and so it's going to be vital for us to use any means at our disposal, basically, to achieve our objective. (Vice-President Cheney talking to NBC's Tim Russert on 16 September 2001; Froomkin 2005)

In early 2004, disturbing images and reports began emerging in the US media. They told a story of torture and degradation of Iraqi prisoners by the American military and CIA operatives in Abu Ghraib prison near Baghdad. The investigation began when Corporal Charles Graner – a main actor in the abuse allegations – circulated a compact disc of photographs taken in the prison (Hersh 2004). The images showed naked prisoners chained to beds and railings, men heaped in piles, dragged by ropes across the floor, forced into compromising sexual positions, threatened by snarling dogs, covered in excrement, hung from the ceiling, wired for electroshock, beaten, bloody, wounded, unconscious and dead. The shocking images provoked immediate international outrage, though the American media was slow to respond to the report written by General Antonio Taguba and released to *The New Yorker*. Taguba concluded that there were 'egregious acts and grave breaches of international law', where 'key senior leaders . . . failed to comply with established regulations, policies, and command directives in preventing detainee abuses' (Taguba 2004: n.p.).

A year later, eleven people had been charged with dereliction of duty, maltreatment and aggravated assault and battery. Two of them were sentenced to prison time. Secretary of Defense Rumsfeld accepted responsibility with the following wording: 'These events occurred on my watch . . . It is my obligation to evaluate what happened, to make sure those who have committed wrongdoing are brought to justice' (Rumsfeld 2004: n.p.). Rumsfeld's phrase 'obligation to evaluate' is equivocal: as Morris (2011) and others note, those ultimately responsible for the order to torture were not 'brought to justice'. *The Economist*, which had supported the Bush administration in the 2000 election, ran a May 2004 cover that blared 'Resign, Rumsfeld' and featured the low-resolution image of a hooded Iraqi prisoner standing on a cardboard box with electric wires attached to his outstretched arms and genitals. By December 2004, the American Civil Liberties Union released evidence that President Bush, by Executive Order, had mandated torture.

Unlike images of the 9/11 attack on the World Trade Center, reproduction and display of the Abu Ghraib images in US mainstream media was subdued and strategic, many sources citing their inflammatory and disturbing nature (Sontag 2004). Editors at Salon.com commented: 'Abu Ghraib in fall 2003 may have been its own particular hell, but the variations of individual abuse perpetrated appear to be exceptional in only one way: They were photographed and filmed' (Abu Ghraib 2006: n.p.). Sontag notes the unusual inclusion of the 'perpetrators' in many of the photographs and compares this with photographs of lynching, 'which show Americans grinning beneath the naked mutilated body of a black man or woman hanging behind them from a tree'. These photographs are 'souvenirs of a collective action whose participants felt perfectly justified in what they had done' (2004: n.p.).

> Warning: Explicit Images
>
> To view images and videos of Abu Ghraib go to:
>
> Abu Ghraib Torture and Prisoner Abuse, *Wikipedia*: en.wikipedia.org/wiki/Abu_Ghraib_torture_and_prisoner_abuse
>
> The Abu Ghraib Files, *Salon*: www.salon.com/topic/the_abu_ghraib_files/

While it is tempting to read these images as evidence of a nation having lost its moral compass, there is another possibility: the thumbs-up gesture recorded in photographs of Sabrina Harman, Lynndie England, Charles Graner and other military personnel signals that the

US is accomplishing what it set out to do after 9/11. These people are following orders, getting the job done and making a record for their superiors.

Linfield thinks the photographs of Abu Ghraib 'not only depict cruelty but celebrate it' (2010: 151). They may be 'the most widely circulated photographs ever made', appearing in newspapers, magazines, websites, on television, on walls around the world and 'on gravestones in Gaza City, where they are accompanied by the promise, "We Will Revenge"' (151–2). As propaganda images, they have been used to recruit terrorists and raise funds for human rights groups. They have 'inspired a global conversation' (152) in a call-and-response of disturbing images of airplanes flying into buildings, public beheadings, torture and imprisonment, suicide bombings, civilian casualties, protests and flag burning – all photographed and filmed to communicate 'mutual loathing and mutual fear' (152–3).

Linfield quotes Sontag's argument that the Abu Ghraib images reveal the 'confluence of torture and pornography' and are thus voyeuristic and deceptive (Sontag 2004; Linfield 2010: 154). Sontag is sceptical that photographs can tell the whole story without accompanying text. The images may be striking and expressive, but they can also be misleading and ambiguous. Writer and filmmaker Errol Morris shares Sontag's concern and made it the central theme of his film *Standard Operating Procedure* (2008, with Mike Gourevitch) and his book *Believing is Seeing* (2011). Morris observes that photographs 'attract false beliefs the way flypaper attracts flies' (2011: 92) and recommends that captions are important for clarifying the subject of controversial images. Linfield challenges this argument:

> The Abu Ghraib images shocked the public, and scared the government, precisely *because* they were photographs; they could not be spun, denied, or explained away, and though they could be interpreted in various ways, they could not be made to mean anything at all . . . The Abu Ghraib images – digital images, taken by amateurs – have strengthened, not undermined the status of photographs as documents of the real. No written account of the tortures could have made such an impact. (2010: 160)

The US administration crafted the narrative that Abu Ghraib was an anomaly perpetrated by improperly briefed 'bad apples'. Subsequent WikiLeaks documents revealed that prisoner abuse was not isolated to Abu Ghraib and continued after the scandal (Baram 2010). While efforts to script the narrative, cast doubt and redirect blame continue, the Abu Ghraib images are now indelible examples of terror's spectacle.

The terrorism spectacle creates fertile ground for propaganda on all sides and elevates security threats to a national priority. In response to prisoner abuse at Abu Ghraib, Al-Qaeda members beheaded American contractor Nicholas Berg in 2004. They captured the killing on videotape and distributed it globally (Zarqawi 2004; Linfield 2010: 155–6). New channels of image distribution allow disturbing images to bypass the usual gatekeepers and circulate more freely. Now, 'any analysis of public space must take into account the effects, speed, rhythms of information and communication, real-time images, differential modes of control, and unprecedented power increasingly deployed by the new media' (Giroux 2006: 40). The consequences are significant, since governments use the threat of terrorism to justify state surveillance, crowd control and rights removal. In his film *The Power of Nightmares* (2004), Adam Curtis argues that politicians on all sides use the spectacle of terrorism to provoke fear and win elections.

A century of spectacle

The idea that contemporary society is notable for its delusional spectacles is now a commonplace of cultural criticism (Baudrillard 1988, 2005; Eco 1986; Giroux 2006; Hedges 2009). Greil Marcus (1989) traces the origins of this notion to an international movement of social revolutionaries organised around a small group of Paris-based intellectuals. Led by Guy Debord and known as the Situationist International, these cultural tricksters emerged in the late 1950s from the Lettrist International – a group of libertarian artists and writers inspired by Surrealism, Dada and Marx. The Situationist agenda was part revolutionary social transformation, part anti-bourgeois art movement, simultaneously serious and playful. Situationist tricks included the *dérive* (unpremeditated drifting through city streets looking for signs of interest) and the *détournement* (appropriation of images and artefacts for other purposes). Graffiti and other forms of street art combine both forms of Situationist play.

Debord's 1967 manifesto *Society of the Spectacle* remains an influential critique of manipulative spectacle in Western societies. Debord argues that the 'accumulation of spectacles' ([1967] 1983: para. 1) in the twentieth century does not merely result from proliferating mass media, but is continuously produced to promote capitalism and its values. The spectacle 'presents itself as an instrument of unification' working though social relations 'mediated by images' (para. 4). It contributes to the 'existing order's uninterrupted discourse about itself, its laudatory monologue' (para. 24) and encourages 'having' over 'being' in its promotion of commodities. The spectacle justifies elite priorities, whether posing as information or propaganda, advertising or entertainment. It colonises the public sphere with its messages and, even more significantly, infiltrates the lifeworld by promoting commodities that engage identity issues and confer status. The system mystifies both commodity and spectacle to maintain power, a trick it learned from ancient religious rituals: 'The spectacle is the material reconstruction of the religious illusion', writes Debord (para. 20).

In this view, religion exploits uncertainties about creation, morality and the afterlife, offering absolute certainty for believers and replacing former idols with new icons of the divine. Similarly, materialist ideologies such as capitalism and socialism address uncertainties about security and happiness with schemes of production, social organisation and means of governance. The contemporary spectacle absorbs and transforms the uncertainties of philosophy, religion and social organisation and converts them into power. 'The oldest social specialisation, the specialisation of power, is at the root of the spectacle . . . Here the most modern is the most archaic' (para. 23). Debord and his colleagues were deeply troubled by the 'archaic' fascist spectacle.

Following Debord's lead, Baudrillard (1988) criticised the increasing power of 'simulations' to create an artificial space for social action he called the 'simulacrum' – a Matrix-like reality defined by simulations. Baudrillard uses the analogy of a map drawn before the territory has been discovered to argue that simulations 'precede' a 'reality' that does not yet exist: the image 'bears no relation to any reality whatever; it is its own pure simulacrum' (1988: 170). Television news broadcasts use state-of-the-art technology – from high definition cameras to Skype and 'amateur' videos – to convey the heightened realism of their visual reporting. Does the television newscast provide a window to the world or does it assemble a simulation of the day's events? Pseudo-events, such as press conferences, leadership debates and photo opportunities, are staged solely to be reported in the media and make every effort to be convincing illusions (Boorstin 1961).

Umberto Eco's related concept of hyperreality announces the triumph of the absolute fake, epitomised by Las Vegas, Disneyland and other fantasies of all-absorbing illusion (1986). The art style called hyperrealism tries to convince viewers that what they are seeing is minutely faithful to reality, even though it is obviously recreated (Bredekamp 2006). Image manipulation programs such as Photoshop put photographic evidence in doubt; visual beauty is now routinely the result of 'Photoshopping'. High-definition (HD) formats in photography, television and film exploit the aesthetics of hyperrealism to create all-absorbing spectacles of illusion.

The public spectacle

The photographic image and mass spectacle can deceive and distract us, but this is a cautionary tale and not the end of the story. Cultural critics have an understandable aversion to totalitarian spectacles, but a blanket condemnation of the mass experience denies the necessity of ancient and sustaining practices of collective renewal. In *Spectacle* (2006), Rockwell and Mau celebrate the other spectacle: not the ideological spectacle of fascism, totalitarianism, socialism or capitalism, but the spectacle of humanity's universal need to gather, celebrate and worship. They approach spectacle not as cultural critics, but as designers and architects of public spaces.

> An empty stadium, an open field or a busy urban thoroughfare – each one a public space – undergoes an alchemical process when transformed by spectacle. A group of strangers fuses into an instant community . . . [Y]ou become part of something greater than yourself. (2006: 15)

Rockwell and Mau present the playful, invigorating face of spectacle, arguing that human spectacles connect, immerse and transform their participants. Spectacles are for everyone, rich and poor, young and old. They happen in real time and, like theatre, involve living bodies. Anything can happen, including surprise and delight beyond expectation.

Contemporary spectacles exhibit a wide diversity of intent and outcome. The Kumbh Mela brings Hindu worshippers together every three years, while the annual Hajj sees millions of faithful Muslims making the journey to Mecca. The celebration of carnival in cities around the world originated as an opportunity for Catholics to prepare for their forty-day period of fasting and reflection during Lent. Crowds gathered on the National Mall in Washington, DC, to hear Martin Luther King; to protest against the Vietnam War; and to bear witness to the first display of the AIDS Memorial Quilt in 1987. In February 2003, up to thirty million people worldwide protested the impending Iraq War, including three million in Rome and over 750,000 in London ('Millions Join' 2003). The Tour de France, FIFA World Cup football, Olympic Games, Burning Man and Glastonbury festivals, demonstrations in Tiananmen Square and North Korea's Mass Games celebrate, inspire and perhaps indoctrinate. Failure to distinguish between the sustaining and indoctrinating potential of these events is to overlook one of propaganda's fundamental strategies: appealing deception. Rockwell, the designer of public spectacles, concludes: 'I think the power of live experience runs the gamut from sublime to horrific; it certainly has been a tool to corrupt. But that is the exception, not the rule' (2006: 20).

The 2012 London Olympics opened with a spectacle promoting international athletes, corporate sponsors and glorious Great Britain.

> As the London 2012 Summer Olympics approached, the tide of scepticism seemed almost irreversible. There was the heavy-handed sponsorship, the draconian security, the ticketing problems, the ballooning budget, and the lurking fear that the Opening Ceremony might be, in director Danny Boyle's pungent description, 'shite'. It took less than four hours on the night of Friday, 27 July to turn the whole country around. Not only was the ceremony demonstrably not shite, it was the most surprising, moving, spectacular cultural event this country had ever seen … It left viewers giddy with delight, feeling that this really was modern Britain, in all its berserk, multi-faceted glory. (Lynskey 2013: 82)

This spectacular event took the form of an iceberg: 10 per cent visible above the water and 90 per cent submerged below the surface as audience delight, nationalism and expectation.

Propaganda exploits the ambiguous potential of spectacle to celebrate or indoctrinate, and we should question what spectacles want us to believe and do. Some spectacles herald the transfer of power to new elites. Gatherings of the faithful, of sports fans and music lovers, are opportunities for celebration, healing and renewal. If we condemn all mass gatherings or ritual displays, we risk abandoning community, collective action and celebration. If people avoid demonstrating for environmental protection, human rights or political freedom because they are mere spectacles, they lose an opportunity to communicate, both to themselves and their leaders. Democracy itself is a spectacle happening within a 'tolerated margin of mess'.

Exercise questions

1. How does your culture attempt to control images and their circulation? What images are forbidden or censored?
2. Describe the symbols, regalia and other visual signifiers used to identify a contemporary ideology, group or movement.
3. Describe an image that made a memorable impact on you and changed the way you see the world. What accounts for the power of this image?

4. Photograph examples of simulations (Baudrillard) and hyperreality (Eco).
5. Debate the reliability of photographic evidence, either orally in class, in a written paper or in an online discussion.
6. Describe a recent spectacle that you feel is propagandistic. What was the intended purpose? How was the audience organised to witness the spectacle? What did the spectacle look like?
7. Make a short video that captures the spirit and meaning of a mass celebration and upload it to the internet for public viewing.

Figure 4   'Ocracy: the unseen elites'. Photo: M. Soules, San Francisco, 1991.

3 Public Opinion and Manufacturing Consent

Interrupting the spin cycle

In March 1914, a women's suffragist named Mary Richardson smuggled a small axe into the National Gallery in London. She found Diego Velázquez's *The Rokeby Venus* (c. 1650) and managed to break the glass and slash the canvas, before being restrained and arrested. At her trial, Richardson said she wanted to draw attention to Emmeline Pankhurst's hunger strike in London's Holloway Prison (Clark 1997: 28). Her action was not isolated. British suffragists had used disruptive means before, but Richardson's vandalism still resonates for contemporary audiences familiar with the agitprop theatrics of the Guerrilla Girls, Femen and Pussy Riot. While her attack 'targeted the point of intersection between institutional power and the representation of femininity' (28), she testified that she admired the painting and associated Venus with Pankhurst: 'I have tried to destroy the picture of the most beautiful woman in mythological history as a protest against the government destroying Mrs. Pankhurst, who is the most beautiful character in modern history' (28). Richardson's performance used myth, symbolism and iconoclastic spectacle to interrupt the spin cycle against women's voting rights, investing the issues with additional gravity and greater news value.

Progressive public relations

In step with the Industrial Revolution and spread of capitalism, the nineteenth century saw the rapid growth of newspapers, magazines, journals and books. In the 1860s, the electric telegraph brought the reading public more information and opinion, more quickly. The speed and range of dissemination increased during the Progressive Era (1880–1920), when reform-minded journalists like Jacob Riis, Lincoln Steffens, Ida Tarbell, Ray Stannard Baker and Upton Sinclair used expanding publishing opportunities to expose corruption in corporations, governments, law enforcement and courts. President Theodore

Roosevelt used the term 'muck-rake' to describe the work of US journalists shining a spotlight on corruption. While Roosevelt acknowledged the need for honest reporting, when his own administration attracted increased scrutiny, he warned that obsessive negativity might undermine public trust:

> Now, it is very necessary that we should not flinch from seeing what is vile and debasing. There is filth on the floor, and it must be scraped up with the muck-rake . . . But the man who never does anything else, who never thinks or speaks or writes, save of his feats with the muck-rake, speedily becomes, not a help to society, not an incitement to good, but one of the most potent forces for evil. (Roosevelt 1906: n.p.)

In fact, the muckraking of Riis, Steffens, Sinclair and others led to important reforms in living conditions, the financial sector and food safety. Two years earlier, in 1904, Ida Tarbell exposed the sins of the oil industry in her *History of the Standard Oil Company* and inspired further muckraking journalism (Basen 2007). Ivy Lee, one of the first public relations practitioners in the early years of the twentieth century, gained a controversial reputation trying to restore the tarnished image of the Rockefellers and Standard Oil (Filler 1939; Harrison and Stein 1974; Brasch 1990). In England, the Fabian Society (founded in 1884) was a broader political movement promoting socialist programs, international cooperation and corporate reforms, while various movements in the United States, Canada and Australia sought similar remedies for industrial ills, labour exploitation and government corruption.

Accounts of early public relations in the Progressive Era feature such men as Ivy Lee, George Creel, Walter Lippmann and Edward Bernays (Ewen 1996; Basen 2007), but women reformers had an equally profound impact (Straughan 2007). Using public relations techniques to promote social reform, they helped secure the vote for women; transform the stigma of birth control to an issue of health care and sound economic policy; raise the age of consent, making sexual exploitation of children a crime; and alter perceptions of lynching to make it a racist crime. From the mid-1800s to the 1920s, the women's suffrage movement conducted an extended public relations campaign involving widespread public education, debate and protest. It provided an international forum for testing foundational public relations strategies, including rallies, marches and parades; advocacy groups; pamphlets and public speaking; newspaper and magazine stories, photos and analysis; alliances with sympathetic politicians and opinion leaders; and community outreach groups. For example, the US journalist, newspaper editor, suffragist and sociologist Ida Wells-Barnett (1862–1931) exposed lynching using eyewitness accounts and careful documentation, then took her case to Britain to gain international support.

The First World War helped public relations evolve into a 'science' of persuasion, but the pioneering efforts of suffragists and early civil rights leaders provided a grassroots laboratory for testing the effectiveness of organising, demonstrating, narrating and showing. In contrast, Ivy Lee was unable to redeem the image of John D. Rockefeller and Standard Oil after the 1914 Ludlow Massacre, in which fourteen miners and their wives and children were killed by agents of a Standard Oil subsidiary. Lee produced a series of circulars titled 'Facts Concerning the Strike in Colorado for Industrial Freedom' (Ewen 1996: 78). Using 'calculated inaccuracies', the circulars claimed the disaster was caused by union 'agitators' and not by 'mine operators and their armies' (78). This approach to public relations established a persistent theme that 'truth happens to an idea'. A claim is true because it is said to be true – an example of *ipse dixit*, the bare assertion fallacy. 'Repeated and dispersed along the grooves of borrowed thought, something asserted might become a fact, regardless of its connection to actual events' (79).

From crowds to the public

> The more fiercely people press together, the more certain they feel that they do not fear each other. This reversal of the fear of being touched belongs to the nature of crowds. The feeling of relief is most striking where the density of the crowd is greatest. (Canetti [1960] 1973: 16)

The Progressive Era's reforming spirit was fuelled by inequities and corruption that allowed male politicians to deny the vote to women, racists to deny equal rights to people of colour and industrialists to form monopolies, exploit common resources and corrupt governments for profit. However, as Lincoln Steffens (1931) observes, genuine reform is not always what people want. They prefer political corruption if it is good for business. Steffens distinguishes between 'principals' and 'heelers' – those who think for themselves and those who consult with the principals before making decisions. 'To get anything done, one must find and win over the free principals, and it is an utter waste of time to talk to or work with the heelers' ([1931] 2005: 627). Social reform is not always polarised along class lines, and a narrative of the rich exploiting the poor will not catch the complexity of social change. One thing remains constant, however: leaders must move the crowd to influence public opinion.

In Britain and North America, the success of progressive movements stimulated a nascent public relations industry to serve powerful clients. As women gained the vote, and refugees from Europe joined the ranks of the unemployed, leaders needed new strategies to communicate with this restless public. Behind the search for new means of social control lurked the fear of what Thomas Hobbes (1651) called the 'Leviathan' – a mythological sea creature that symbolised the powerful, undisciplined mob. Written during the English Civil War, *Leviathan* warned that without strong sovereign power and a social contract within which citizens exchange the right to self-government for protection and peace, there would be social chaos and 'the war of all against all'.

Gustave Le Bon also warned about the power of the masses in *The Crowd* (1896), an instruction manual for ruling in democratic times. 'The destinies of nations are elaborated at present in the heart of the masses, and no longer in the council of princes', Le Bon declared ([1896] 2006: xii). He was chiefly concerned with the threat of socialism and government capitulation to public opinion. Prevailing beliefs in faith, nationality, science and industry were challenged by growing agitation for better working conditions, wealth redistribution and progressive reform. Le Bon, like Canetti after him, argued that individuals were transformed by participating in a crowd. Unlike the more educated and rational middle classes, working class crowds could not be reasoned with. They were ruled by passions, sentiments, beliefs and simple images. In a crowd, individuals feel invincible, while being subject to 'contagious' sentiments and 'collective hallucinations' (8–9). They possess 'the spontaneity, the violence, the ferocity, and also the enthusiasm and heroism of primitive beings'. While crowds could be criminal, they could also be heroic and productive. Crowds, not individuals, can be persuaded 'to run the risk of death to secure the triumph of a creed or an idea' (11).

To persuade a crowd to action, argued Le Bon, one must replace reason with aggressive affirmations and exaggeration, repeat simple images, and appeal to glory, honour and patriotism. Coherent argument is unnecessary, because crowds are moved by theatrical presentations of 'marvellous' and 'legendary' images that terrify or attract (39). 'Whoever can supply them with illusions is easily their master; whoever attempts to destroy their illusions is always their victim' (76). The most persuasive words and images are often the hardest to define and are therefore prone to deceptive abstraction and mystification: democracy, socialism, equality, liberty, nation, honour, self-sacrifice, faith, patriotism, glory. Above all, crowds are susceptible to the appeal of prestige – 'the mainspring of all authority' (91).

Le Bon's 'scientific' analysis was influential, because the muckraking journalists 'had alerted an enormous number of people to the excesses of wealth, the corruptions of politics, and the desolation of the urban poor' (Ewen 1996: 67). Simultaneously, they emphasised the need to manage public opinion. With new mass media, 'the texture and dissemination of information' were 'altering the physics of perception' (67) and the ways people experienced their place in the world. No matter which ideology leaders advocated, the crowd had been mobilised and was now a force to be reckoned with.

Le Bon's contemporary, Gabriel Tarde (1843–1904), acknowledged the importance of emerging mass media and reformulated Le Bon's crowd as more expansive, distributed and powerful. The crowd was passé; the public was the social group of the future. The modern public was a 'spiritual collectivity, a dispersion of individuals who are physically separated and whose cohesion is entirely mental' (Tarde 1969: 277). Tarde advanced our understanding of group mind and crowd psychology, in which individuals are unified through imitation and motivation.

Newspapers, periodicals and a transoceanic telegraph service created a new public susceptible to mass media influence. Those who did not read newspapers were influenced by those who did and 'forced to follow the groove of their borrowed thoughts. One pen suffices to set off a million tongues' (1969: 313). Along these grooves of thought, public consciousness could be influenced and managed, perhaps even reasoned with. The addition of film and radio to the mass media repertoire in the early decades of the century dramatically increased opportunities for reaching a mass audience. The stage was set for the great technicians of consent to wage their battles for mind share.

Lippmann's democratic realism

From 1914 to 1917, British Government propaganda was coordinated by a secret bureau run by Charles Masterman at Wellington House (home of the Foreign Office). Most members of Parliament did not know the bureau existed (Taylor 1995: 177). A private organisation, the Central Committee for National Patriotic Associations, was established to promote the war effort within Britain and within Commonwealth countries, such as Canada and Australia. British propaganda was designed to censor German messages and promote the war effort to the neutral United States. During the war, a British naval ship cut the transoceanic cables connecting Germany to North America. While government communications were persuasive, subtle and indirect, British newspapers took every opportunity to report German atrocities and subterfuge.

When the US entered the war in 1917, President Wilson immediately set up the Committee on Public Information (CPI) 'to sell the war to America' under the direction of journalist George Creel: '[I]t was a plain publicity proposition, a vast enterprise in salesmanship, the world's greatest adventure in advertising' (Creel 1920: 4). This propaganda laboratory produced a cohort of experienced publicity practitioners – notably, Walter Lippmann and Edward Bernays, who both worked for the CPI and used new insights from sociology and psychology to influence the public mind.

Ambiguous feelings regarding the use of wartime propaganda complicated their task. While its triumphs were spectacular, there was a strong counter-narrative that propaganda had manipulated the public, created conflict among nations and profit for industrialists, and encouraged corruption and secrecy by the system.

> Indeed, as they learned more and more about the outright lies, exaggerations and half-truths used on them by their own governments, both [British and American] populations came, understandably, to see 'propaganda' as a weapon even more perfidious than they had thought when they had not perceived themselves as its real target. (Miller 2005: 15)

British and Canadian soldiers returning from Western Front horrors were disillusioned to discover how effectively propaganda had hidden those realities to preserve morale on the home front (Davis 2011). Two separate wars had been waged: one simulated, one deadly real.

The success of propaganda in WWI illustrated Le Bon's and Tarde's conviction that sentiments and symbols moved the public more predictably than reason. Influenced by Le Bon and Tarde, Lippmann's thinking evolved from democratic romanticism – where popular sovereignty is based on rational political discourse – to democratic realism – where people are governed by 'enlightened and responsible elites' (Ewen 1996: 147). Just as American Telephone and Telegraph (AT&T) had to convince Americans that monopoly was in their best interests, democratic realists had to convince them that affairs of state were best left to elites operating behind the scenes. Obscuring the practice of democratic realism is one of propaganda's great triumphs, and Lippmann's prophetic insights in *Public Opinion* (1922) still apply to current democratic realities.

Lippmann describes modern society as increasingly complicated by competing national and international interests, emerging media and new sources of news and opinion. Even the literate public does not understand political and social issues sufficiently to make informed decisions. This maelstrom of information requires 'stereotypes' as short cuts to decision-making:

> In the great blooming, buzzing confusion of the outer world we pick out what our culture has already defined for us, and we tend to perceive that which we have picked out in the form stereotyped for us by our culture. (Lippmann [1922] 1997: 54–5)

As a photographer, I experience this when I travel to a new country, look at the postcards on the racks and see that my own 'fresh' observations are already clichés and stereotypes. Lippmann comments: 'We imagine most things before we experience them. And those preconceptions . . . govern deeply the whole process of perception' (59). A culture's shared repertoire of stereotypes provides a common language of images and contributes to social cohesion. Attacking those stereotypes threatens that cohesion.

Drawing on Plato's allegory of the cave, Lippmann argues that, thanks to modern media systems, most people experience the world at a distance. Instead of seeing things as they occur, we experience events as 'pictures in our heads' – simplified, compressed, framed and stereotyped. The mediated pictures merge with our own images and memories to create a 'pseudo-environment' (28), an idea that anticipates Baudrillard's simulacrum and Debord's spectacle. Lippmann's experience of wartime censorship led him to think that without 'some form of censorship, propaganda in the strict sense of the word is impossible . . . Access to the real environment must be limited, before anyone can create a pseudo-environment' (28).

For Lippmann, photography and film are powerful instruments for constructing pseudo-environments. Photographs surpass words in their ability to communicate meaning quickly, without the intervention of rational analysis. In film, 'the whole process of observing, describing, reporting, and then imagining, has been accomplished for you . . . The shadowy idea becomes vivid' (61). Horkheimer and Adorno similarly criticise sound films, 'so constructed that their adequate comprehension requires a quick, observant, knowledgeable cast of mind but positively debars the spectator from thinking' ([1944] 2006: 45). Symbols separate emotion from thinking, bypassing rational analysis to communicate directly to the unconscious. Leaders, Lippmann argued, must use symbols to guide an unthinking public toward reasonable action. The use of images, symbols and stereotypes to bypass rational thought is commonplace today, but in the 1920s Lippmann's insights were a revelation to publicists and leaders alike.

Bernays and engineering consent

> The engineering of consent is the very essence of the democratic process, the freedom to persuade and suggest. (Bernays 1947: 113)

Edward Bernays – nephew of Sigmund Freud, journalist, publicist and veteran WWI propagandist – was deeply influenced by Lippmann's psychological approach to public opinion, though he considered Lippmann too academic. While Lippmann's influence is obvious in Bernays' *Propaganda* (1928) and other writings, Bernays casts himself as being more pragmatic by framing the insights of Le Bon, Tarde and Lippmann for a ruling elite. Bernays was 'a propagandist for propaganda' (Miller 2005: 20), and his 1928 text was both an ad for public relations and an accessible how-to manual for influencing public opinion.

> The conscious and intelligent manipulation of the organised habits and opinions of the masses is an important element in democratic society. Those who manipulate this unseen mechanism of society constitute an invisible government which is the true ruling power of our country. (Bernays [1928] 2005: 37)

This is not a conspiracy, he insisted, but the result of loosely coordinated efforts by intelligent elites merely trying to make the system work: 'They govern us by their qualities of natural leadership, their ability to supply needed ideas and by their key position in the social structure' (37). The public relations counsel, who knows the public mind and how to influence it, mediates between the invisible governors and their public. Significantly, these elites gain status 'by their key position in the social structure'.

As Adam Curtis documents in *Century of the Self* (2002), Bernays applied the psychoanalytic insights of his uncle Sigmund Freud to the practice of public relations. Bernays' synthesis of psychoanalysis and publicity, Curtis argues, informed a whole century of pitches aimed at the self's deep, perhaps guilty, desires. Object cathexis, where inner desires are projected onto an external object or person, and motivation by suppressed desires became two useful concepts for marketing and persuasion. Bernays did not sell pianos; he sold the desire to play beautiful music. He did not market cigarettes to young women; he sold them 'torches of freedom'. The 'new salesmanship' removed sales resistance, instead of mounting a 'direct attack' ([1928] 2005: 77). Above all, the public relations counsel appeals to enlightened self-interest: the point where client interests coincide with audience interests – a win-win solution.

The public relations counsel presents evidence casting a favourable light on the client, a technique Bernays called 'dramatisation by high-spotting' (89). In 1929, he staged 'Light's Golden Jubilee' as a celebration of the fiftieth anniversary of Edison's invention of the light bulb. This publicity event was, in fact, an opportunity to showcase General Electric and its cover organisation, the National Electric Light Association, which had successfully campaigned to keep utilities in private hands. In an example of political high-spotting, in 1953 Bernays promoted the incipient fear that Guatemala was threatened by communists, then represented the United Fruit Company in its efforts to have the CIA topple the democratic government of Jacobo Arbenz, an event that never became a public issue in the US (Miller 2005: 27). For Bernays, propaganda is a 'modern instrument' used to 'fight for productive ends and help to bring order out of chaos' ([1928] 2005: 168). To make the unruly public more productive and orderly, publicists first need to discover what that public thinks and feels.

Statistical polling: giving voice to public opinion

> Polls are now the best way to influence public opinion, largely because they're treated (much like the BBC) as impartial oracles of the truth by most people who read them. (Hitchens 2007: n.p.)

The rapid growth of public relations in the 1930s stimulated the publicists' use of polls and surveys to construct a 'two-way street' between clients and their public. Print, film and radio increasingly accelerated communication with a mass audience; and growing use of electric sorting and calculating machines – the precursors of computers – made it easier to study large audiences. Market research and polling would, it was claimed, give the people a voice and thereby strengthen democracy.

From the beginning, however, critics feared that polling would not only measure public opinion, it would create it. American sociologist Robert Lynd questioned the way polls had become news, 'useful manipulative devices on the level of propaganda', and an example of democracy 'working in reverse' (Ewen 1996: 189). With 'numerical eloquence', polls communicated 'silent civics lessons' (190) by defining what questions were important, how the public was behaving and what the consequences would be of taking action in the public sphere.

Polling issues that persist to the present include the demographic and psychographic models used to define representative samples and the influence exerted by the questions, their order in the survey and the survey's length. Carefully worded questions encourage desired responses, which are then announced as evidence of consensus. Through polling and market surveys, the public becomes a commodity (of statistics) to be sold, and some publics are more valuable than others. The polling organisation's neutrality is a significant question, but even more significant are the client's identity and reasons for polling.

Many countries have questioned the influence of political polls on elections. In his Canadian Government report, Emery (1994) confirms the importance of political polling: 'Although governments have other means of gauging public sentiment . . . polls are now acknowledged to be one of the most significant communication links between governments and the governed' (n.p.). He states that polling has significant direct impact on the election process. When they emphasise who is leading, polls shift the focus away from issues to spotlight the contest – who is winning the horse race. This encourages media fixation on leaders and their performance. Polls affect the morale of party workers and contributors. They influence both a campaign's momentum and voting decisions. Emery concludes that pollsters have become a 'new breed of political advisor', and the popularity of polls rests on their 'apparent ability to quantify something which by its nature is not easily quantifiable'. Polls remain a powerful tool for those communicating with the public, but are significantly less useful for a public trying to communicate what it wants to those in power.

Public relations and journalism

In 1957, Vance Packard worried that the convergence of market research and image management would lead to media manipulation and disinformation – misleading information spread deliberately. Michie (1998) updates Packard's concerns for the 1990s, and Davies (2008) makes a similar argument that declining resources for journalism leave a void to be filled by public relations and spin. Davies comments that public relations is

... not simply about holding press conferences and putting out press releases, but also about constructing pseudo-events to generate coverage, creating phony front groups to make news on specific issues, supplying apparently independent experts who speak to an undisclosed PR agenda, and coordinating campaigns of media coverage with direct lobbying in order to shift government policy. ([2008] 2009: 85)

Now, journalists and public relations consultants routinely collaborate to make the news. The result is 'churnalism', producing 'Flat Earth news': 'A story appears to be true. It is widely accepted as true. It becomes a heresy to suggest that it is not true – even if it is riddled with falsehood, distortion and propaganda' (Davies [2008] 2009: 12).

From 1980 to 2008, the number of US journalists declined by 30 per cent, while public relations numbers doubled to arrive at a ratio of one journalist for every three public relations practitioners, the latter of which were also 'better equipped, better financed' (Sullivan 2011: n.p.). Public relations revenues almost tripled from 1997 to 2007, while newspaper advertising revenue declined significantly during that same period. 'The dangers are clear. As PR becomes ascendant, private and government interests become more able to generate, filter, distort, and dominate the public debate, and to do so without the public knowing it' (Sullivan 2011: n.p.). In the UK, political parties led the PR offensive:

When Margaret Thatcher took office in 1979, the British government was spending £27 million on the Central Office of Information, which runs its PR departments. In less than ten years, that figure rose more than 500%, to £150 million in 1988 ... The Blair government simply took over where they left off, hiring a further 310 press officers in its first two years, increasing its annual output of press releases by 80% to some 20,000 a year, and continuing to give multiple millions of public money to outside PR agencies. (Davies [2008] 2009: 86)

Michie estimates that 80 per cent of business news and up to 50 per cent of general news is 'produced or directly influenced by PR practitioners' (1998: 2). Research on selected British newspapers found that an average of only 12 per cent of stories involved material 'generated by the reporters themselves' (Davies [2008] 2009: 52). The rest were either taken directly from, or influenced by, press releases or news service copy (mainly from Associated Press or Thomson Reuters).

Publicists appropriate the protocols of professional journalism to blur the lines between promotion and unbiased reporting. As a matter of media ethics, journalism and public relations are separated by an imaginary firewall of objectivity. Journalists are ideally expected to be fair and balanced in their reporting; and publicists are expected to represent client interests, hopefully within ethical guidelines. The Public Relations Society of America asks members to 'adhere to the highest standards of accuracy and truth in advancing the interests of those we represent and in communicating with the public'. Journalism is defined by its honesty, insists Davies ([2008] 2009: 22), and it is not enough to quote accurately what someone says to be fair and balanced. News becomes a matter of opinion when journalists looking for balance provide opportunities for 'experts' and representatives to confuse issues and promote uncertainty. National Public Radio reporter Brooke Gladstone says that objectivity in news reporting can be a handicap when trying to locate the truth and may not even be possible. '[H]ypersensitivity to the appearance of objectivity can lead to some lousy reporting. A reporter should be able to call a lie a lie' (Gladstone and Neufeld 2011: 110). Journalists, and their readers after them, need to question misleading or ambiguous statements or any narrative gaps. To do this, journalists need time and resources to check the facts and not merely pass on the neatly packaged promotional message.

Spin doctors and pseudo-events

> I would rather be called a spin doctor than a hidden persuader. Actually I rather like the term. After all, doctors are qualified professionals, and putting the right spin on things is exactly what we do. (Sir Tim Bell, qtd in Michie 1998: 48)

> As the owner of a successful Vancouver public relations firm, I think that PR is a good thing. It connects people and builds understanding . . . It's true that there have always been bad actors in my business – the tobacco apologists and the partisan political spin doctors – but I have always regarded them as obvious exceptions. In my career, examples of spin-doctoring seem episodic, not epidemic. (Hoggan 2009: 2)

Public relations consultants assert that freedom of expression includes the right to persuade. They compare their work not to doctors, but to lawyers, who present their clients' interests in the best possible light (Bernays [1928] 2005: 64, 69–70). Their role is not to make the prosecution's case. The analogy between publicists and lawyers is misleading, however, because lawyers are visible in their advocacy and must provide evidence acceptable to a judge and jury. Public relations advisors are often invisible or acting through proxy organisations and do not have to prove anything, as long as assertions are framed as opinions. But the two professions do share common ground: they protect their client's interests, suppress incriminating evidence, dispute conflicting evidence and foster doubt. Without a prosecutor – or inquisitive journalist – to challenge evidence, truth claims often remain in limbo.

Both lawyers and spin doctors stage their arguments for an audience. In the early 1960s, Boorstin observed the growing number of 'manufactured' events in America and warned: 'In a democratic society like ours ... the people can be flooded by pseudo-events. For us, freedom of speech and of the press and of broadcasting includes the freedom to create pseudo-events' ([1961] 1992: 35). In May 2003, for example, President Bush appeared on an aircraft carrier off the coast of California. He was dressed as a fighter pilot to announce the end of combat operations in Iraq. Behind him, a banner announced 'Mission Accomplished' – the perfect photo op at the time, but premature. In another example, journalists who covered the evacuation of Israeli settlers from Gaza in 2005 suspected the whole thing had been staged to show the settlers' suffering to international audiences (Davies [2008] 2009: 168).

These staged performances are not limited to corporations and governments. In its early days as a small activist organisation operating out of Vancouver, Greenpeace made international news with its media stunts. Greenpeace activists used a variety of tactics to block nuclear testing on Amchitka Island in 1971; interfere with the harp seal hunt in eastern Canada; and harass whaling vessels in the South Pacific. Greenpeace tactics acted as 'mindbombs' – 'simple images, delivered by the media, that would "explode in people's minds" and create a new understanding of the world' (Wyler 2004: 73). Similarly sensational, People for the Ethical Treatment of Animals (PETA), renowned for their dramatic media stunts, threw money soaked in fake blood into the audience at the International Fur Fair in Japan (Specter 2003).

Boorstin defines propaganda as 'information intentionally biased' to distinguish it from pseudo-events: 'While a pseudo-event is an ambiguous truth, propaganda is an appealing falsehood ... While propaganda substitutes opinion for facts, pseudo-events are synthetic facts which move people indirectly' ([1961] 1992: 34). Despite these differences, both pseudo-events and propaganda exploit conventions of popular culture to further their illusions. For example, video news releases (VNRs) are mainly corporate success stories prepared by PR firms and government agencies for submission to broadcasters. They are often broadcast without changes as news. Farsetta and Price (2006) describe the use of VNRs as 'fake news', because they present the 'client's message, using a format and tone that mimic actual TV news'. The PR firm and its sponsor are rarely identified in the broadcast. Video news releases became common practice for firms such as Microsoft, Intel, Pfizer and General Motors among others, but their use came to increased prominence when the US Office of National Drug Control Policy aired VNRs on 300 television stations in 2004. In 2005, the General Accounting Office ruled that the unacknowledged use of video news releases produced by government agencies was a form of 'covert propaganda', because the agency 'did not identify itself to the viewing audience as the producer and distributor of these pre-packaged news stories' (Farsetta and Price 2006: n.p.).

Implementing public relations strategies

PR makes a broad distinction between discovery and implementation. Discovery starts with client interviews and continues with market research, focus groups, surveys and polls to assess existing public opinion. In the implementation stage, PR uses a toolkit of strategies to advance client interests:

- pseudo-events, including press releases, press conferences, media coverage, video news releases;
- publicity, branding and advertising;
- online viral marketing;
- interest groups, associations, grassroots and 'astro-turf' organisations;
- think tanks: reports, websites, conferences, speakers panels, experts;
- political lobbying, political action committees (PACs), campaign contributions, personal leverage, policy and legislation; and
- crisis management and litigation.

PR interventions try to protect an organisation's interests, reputation and assets from threat or crisis. Protecting stockholder investments can be an overriding motivation for corporations, but strategies for crisis management must be adapted to the perceived threat and sensitive to public opinion.

Organisations, corporations and advocacy groups of all persuasions use the mass media to promote their views, often calling in experts to present an authoritative opinion on issues. Frequently, these experts have a hidden agenda. Barstow (2008) reported that a 'Pentagon information apparatus' disseminates news stories supporting government military policy and performance, presented by retired officers now working for defence contractors. Rampton and Stauber (1995) cite many examples of experts and authorities endorsing products, promoting scientific findings and offering advice on domestic and foreign policy. The climate change 'denial industry' (Monbiot 2006) engages in greenwashing – publicity campaigns designed to reposition products and industries as being more healthy and sustainable than can reasonably be claimed.

In extreme situations, PR firms and their clients attempt to suppress the most compromising aspects of a news event with counter-narratives, court injunctions and threatened legal action. SLAPP suits – strategic lawsuits against public participation – attempt to silence critics with the threat of expensive legal costs. Monsanto took out a SLAPP in 1998 against activists from genetiX snowball engaged in direct action against genetically modified (GM) crop use in the UK (corporatewatch.org). In 2009, oil trading giant Trafigura obtained a gag order from a British high court to prevent *The Guardian* and other newspapers from mentioning a report on the company's toxic dumping in the Ivory Coast. When a British MP referred to the report in Parliament – thus making it exempt from libel in the UK – *The Guardian* was able to report on Trafigura's suppression tactics (Leigh 2009).

Since the right to petition is considered a key legal concept of democracy, courts must distinguish between libellous, unfounded criticism and attempts by the plaintiff to silence legitimate opposition. In a famous example of corporate opposition to criticism known as the McLibel case, environmental activists Helen Steel and David Morris were found guilty in 1994 by a UK court of libelling McDonald's restaurants in a leaflet they distributed. In 2005, the European Court of Human Rights ruled they were denied a fair trial, because they did not have access to legal aid and this compromised their freedom of expression. In effect, the greater financial resources of McDonald's gave the corporation unfair advantage in the justice system. Despite McDonald's initial victory in court, the McLibel case is considered 'the biggest corporate PR disaster in history' (Oliver 2005: n.p.).

Case study: PR and climate change

For most of the last two decades, while scientists were growing more convinced about the proof and more concerned about the risks of climate change, members of the general public were drifting into confusion, led there by conflicting stories that minimised the state of the problem and exaggerated the cost of solutions. (Hoggan 2009: 22)

The climate change debate is a contentious public relations battle-ground, where the opinions of experts have played a decisive role in crisis management. When the UN produced its first report on anthro-pogenic (human-created) climate change in 1989, Exxon and other energy corporations set up the Global Climate Coalition (1989–2002) to present their arguments and dispute the consensus of scientists. Following the 1997 Kyoto Protocol to reduce carbon emissions, Exxon supported forty-three different front groups in a sophisticated disinformation campaign using strategies similar to tobacco compa-nies' efforts to obscure the dangers of smoking.

To counter the energy companies' narrative, the Union of Concerned Scientists identified climate change deniers, such as Steven Milloy, Sallie Baliunas, Patrick Michaels, Timothy Ball and S. Fred Singer, who were willing to support the suspect arguments of energy compa-nies. It also advanced its own experts willing to testify to the dangers of global warming. Naomi Oreskes researched peer-reviewed articles published in scientific journals between 1993 and 2003 to assess the extent of scientific uncertainty. She found that not one of 928 arti-cles disputed the consensus that global climate change had human causes. 'Politicians, economists, journalists may have the impression of confusion, disagreement, or discord among climate scientists, but that impression is incorrect' (Oreskes 2005: 1686). Jules and Max Boykoff analysed climate change coverage in the US 'prestige' press between 1998 and 2002. They found that 53 per cent of the articles 'balanced' the statements of scientists with quotes by representatives and 'experts' disputing the evidence (Boykoff and Boykoff 2004). They concluded that attempts at journalistic balance had actually resulted in bias toward climate change uncertainty. Where there had been widespread agreement on climate change in the 1980s, by 2004 the scientific consensus had effectively been undermined in the court of popular opinion. Decisive action on climate change was delayed for at least twenty years.

Advocacy campaigns are often coordinated with direct lobbying of legislators or bureaucrats to influence government policy. The oil lobby is particularly active in the US, UK and Canada to counter pres-sure from the developing world to take action on climate change. In Canada, the government itself is an active lobbyist. Under the leader-ship of Prime Minister Stephen Harper, the Canadian Government and its lobbyists promote what it calls 'ethical oil' from the Alberta tar sands. (The phrase 'ethical oil' originates from Levant's 2010 book and increasingly gained traction in the conservative echo chamber.) They argue that this oil is ethical because Canada is not a repressive regime like Saudi Arabia or Venezuela; it pays its workers well; and it provides a secure energy resource for North America. Critics challenge these arguments by observing that Alberta tar sands oil is a heavy carbon polluter and adds to greenhouse gas emissions far in excess of Kyoto Protocol targets. Under Harper's leadership, Canada withdrew from its Kyoto Protocol commitments in 2012.

US Senator Sheldon Whitehouse describes the 'climate denial beast' as a complex network of sponsors, organisations and corporations acting as one body – 'a whole carefully built apparatus of lies' (2014: n.p.). Money from this network has purchased the compliance of his elected colleagues. In his speech to Congress, Whitehouse names think tanks involved in climate change denial. Think tanks emerged in the 1970s after consumer advocate Ralph Nader created a series of associations to promote his proposed reforms. Nader's model was so successful that corporations responded with their own think tanks to advance business interests through reports, publications, press releases and testimonials. In the US, the Heartland Institute questions climate science and promotes so-called experts, 'who have done little, if any, peer-reviewed climate research' (Oreskes and Conway 2010: 234). Many of the same experts cited by the Heartland Institute previously denied the dangers of smoking, acid rain and ozone layer depletion. When the UN's Intergovernmental Panel on Climate Change reported in 2007 on the 'unequivocal' evidence of human-made climate change, Canada's Fraser Institute – which receives funding from ExxonMobil – responded within forty-eight hours, claiming that 'there is no compelling evidence that dangerous or unprecedented changes are under way' (Davies [2008] 2009: 194).

Public relations efforts to minimise the consequences of climate change are challenged by an informed and concerned public through websites, NGOs and demonstrations. There is sustained grassroots opposition to the Keystone XL pipeline project to bring Alberta tar sands oil to the Gulf of Mexico (Snyder 2013). Grassroots movements emerge when independent citizens organise to raise issues of common concern. When they are authentic, grassroots movements are an important form of democratic expression. Berry (2000) found that grassroots organisations are more effective than interest groups funded by industry and play a significant role in promoting 'postmaterialist', quality-of-life issues, such as environmental protection and civil rights.

Powerful interest groups try to gain credibility by creating fake grassroots movements and engaging in 'astro-turf' lobbying. Astro-turf campaigns establish artificial front groups to communicate opinions, without their unseen sponsors being visible or accountable. The National Smokers Alliance was an astro-turf group set up by public relations firm Burson-Marsteller to promote smoker's rights for Philip Morris. PR giant APCO Worldwide established The Advancement of Sound Science Coalition (TASSC) to dispute the dangers of second-hand smoke (Hoggan 2009: 370). In the 1990s, APCO proposed to expand TASSC efforts to undermine the regulation of global warming, nuclear waste disposal, biotechnology and the labelling of genetically modified foods. Science historians Oreskes and Conway (2010) chronicle the efforts of these 'merchants of doubt' to discredit scientific research, delay action and protect corporate interests. 'It is fair to say that the professional denial industry has delayed effective global action on climate change by years, just as it helped to delay action against the tobacco companies' (Monbiot 2006: n.p.).

In 2010, journalist Jane Mayer reported that wealthy entrepreneurs David and Charles Koch secretly bankrolled the Tea Party movement and other conservative initiatives to discredit the Obama administration and 'destroy progressivism' (Mayer 2010: n.p.). 'The Kochs are long time libertarians who believe in drastically lower personal and corporate taxes, minimal social services for the needy, and much less oversight of industry – especially environmental regulation'. Australian filmmaker Taki Oldham investigates the funding sources of the Tea Party in his 2010 film *(Astro) Turf Wars* and reaches a similar conclusion. In 2013, Pew Research found that Tea Party Republicans were the 'biggest climate change deniers', with only 25 per cent agreeing there is 'solid evidence of global warming' ('GOP Deeply Divided Over Climate Change'). The Kochs are heavily invested in Alberta tar sands properties, with much at stake in the Keystone XL pipeline project. Besides trading in carbon-based energy, the Kochs have made it part of their business plan to influence elite decision-makers by funding politicians and think tanks like Canada's Fraser Institute to dispute the science of climate change (Caplan 2012).

Astro-turf lobbying moves online

Under a variety of guises, astro-turf lobbying thrives in social media. Interest groups and PR firms use internet review sites, discussion forums, blogs and social media to advance their interests, post fake reviews and challenge opponents and critics. The ability to post anonymously or with pseudonyms allows individuals to obscure their identities and locations. In China, '50 cent bloggers' – the 'internet water army' – are paid to post opinions, reviews and recommendations in discussion forums and websites (Chen et al. 2011). 'Sockpuppets' are multiple, false online identities used by individuals, corporations and governments to infiltrate social media communities, where they promote products, uncertainty or ideology ('Sockpuppet' 2013; Flood 2012). In its efforts to monitor and influence anti-American online discussions, the US Air Force developed 'persona' software to manage multiple identities and give the appearance that posters are in different locations around the world. Operation Earnest Voice (OEV) continues persona technology research for its psychological warfare against suspected terrorists. General David Petraeus claimed the operation would 'counter extremist ideology and propaganda and . . . ensure that credible voices in the region are heard', making the US military the 'first with the truth' (Fielding and Cobain 2011: n.p.). Monbiot concludes that 'software like this has the potential to destroy the internet as a forum for constructive debate' and is 'a bonanza for corporate lobbyists, viral marketers and government spin doctors, who can operate in cyberspace without regulation, accountability or fear of detection' (2011: n.p.).

Astro-turf lobbying and other deceptive publicity strategies routinely exploit the internet as a communications medium, but the internet also provides opportunities for genuine grassroots advocacy. For example, the Food Democracy Now website (www.fooddemocracynow.org/) warns about the health and environmental impacts of Monsanto's Roundup Ready™ seeds. Food Democracy Now is able to challenge the aggressive Monsanto publicity machine and chip away at its reputation. It is one of many online sources of complaint against the controversial global corporation.

Bivings – a public relations firm who represented Monsanto in the 1990s – concluded that protests against the agribusiness giant had spread like wildfire on the internet. They decided to undermine dialogue by posting their own firestorm of messages challenging anyone expressing criticism towards genetically modified crops (Monbiot 2002). Monsanto later hired Total Intelligence Solutions (TIS) – a subsidiary of US security contractor Blackwater (now called Academi) – to infiltrate groups opposing the company and monitor their blogs and websites. TIS claims it had 'a rapidly growing, worldwide network of folks that can do everything from surveillance to ground truth to disruption operations', further assuring its clients that 'deniability is built in and should be a big plus' (Scahill 2010: n.p.). Monsanto's online offensive against its critics is learning from the military how to protect its reputation.

Reputation capital and whistle-blowing

'Reputation capital' is valuable to governments, corporations and NGOs and is worth defending, since it translates into trust, profits and influence (Klewes and Wreschniok 2009). Reputation is propagated or destroyed by word-of-mouth, print, radio or television, but the rules have changed since the advent of the internet and social networking. The internet redefines notions of privacy and reputation by dramatically extending the reach and permanence of gossip, rumour and compromising information, whether true or false (Solove 2007). The image-protecting activities of public relations firms and marketers now face an unruly 'smart mob' (Rheingold 2003) of bloggers, email activists and web-savvy hackers such as Anonymous, ready to challenge those who transgress social norms. While the internet is not as free and libertarian as many imagine – it is constrained by codes, protocols, service providers and surveillance – it provides an accessible and influential communication medium. Individuals and small organisations on limited budgets can challenge more expensive efforts at image management. Grassroots advocacy websites, such as Avaaz and 350.org, organise individual citizens into an informed, articulate and authoritative virtual public. Since the mid-1990s, PR firms have increasingly been forced to respond to this networked public. Internet dialogue – whether rumour, gossip or information – is archived and aggregated over time, creating a searchable record of impressions and a growing indictment of perceived wrongdoing.

Internet whistle-blowing sites are transforming the rules of engagement for the public relations industry and forging new relationships between mainstream media and hacker culture. In 2010, Private Chelsea (Bradley) Manning was arrested for leaking classified US military and diplomatic documents to WikiLeaks. Manning was held in isolation for treason, while Julian Assange, founder of WikiLeaks, brokered a publication agreement with five major press organisations – *The Guardian, The New York Times, Der Spiegel, Le Monde* and *El País* – to release over 250,000 documents received from Manning. News of the leak prompted threats by US politicians and counter-charges by Assange that he had been implicated in a sex scandal to discredit his character. Once the documents were published, the WikiLeaks website was hit by denial of service (DoS) attacks by hackers hoping to silence embarrassing revelations about conflict in Iraq and Afghanistan and a variety of other diplomatic activities.

Supporters credit Assange with creating a new form of news agency, providing greater transparency to a diplomatic world cloaked in secrecy. New alliances are forged when corporate media report on the leaks, in effect reversing the trend toward churnalism. At their best, the corporate media provide resources to sift through massive amounts of data, add a compelling narrative, redact the original files to protect those who might be endangered and contribute greater authority and credibility (Leigh and Harding 2011). 'The material that resided in the leaked documents, no matter how voluminous, was not "the truth". It was often just a signpost pointing to some of the truth, requiring careful interpretation' (108). In the first decade of the twenty-first century, public relations entered a new era, in which secrecy and reputation suddenly became harder to manage.

As the example of WikiLeaks shows, it is not as easy to control the message and engineer consent when multiple media channels present contradictory views. Desmogblog.com, 350.org and Insideclimatenews.org challenge the climate change denial industry with the help of journalists in the mainstream press. In Monsanto's case, corporate spin about using chemicals and genetically modified seeds for food security is contradicted by numerous articles and websites that spotlight Monsanto's aggressive marketing, lawsuits and misrepresentations. For example, Leahy (2011) argues that world hunger since 2007 has not been caused by weather events, but by government policy and market speculation, conclusions confirmed by the UN Food and Agriculture Organisation. Leahy's independent reporting (stephenleahy.net/) triangulates reliably with articles by Monbiot (2002), focusing on the role of PR firm Bivings in presenting GM food in a favourable light. Ironically, in 2011 the hacker group Anonymous claimed credit for 'ending' the PR efforts of the now-defunct Bivings Group (Pangburn 2011).

Converging information streams require a new type of news consumer – the 'monitorial citizen' who keeps an eye on events, without always knowing what to do (Schudson [1984] 1986; Jenkins 2006: 226). News is 'discovered through active hashing through competing accounts' and not merely 'digested from authoritative sources' (Jenkins 2006: 227). The advocacy website Avaaz (avaaz.org) is, like WikiLeaks, a new kind of news organisation bringing issues of importance to a global, online community of citizens and asks them to take action on a common cause simply by signing an online petition. Avaaz aggregates public opinion on a global scale. The public relations industry will have to respond to this monitorial public, just as authoritarian regimes in the Middle East have had to respond to networked citizens with greater awareness of system abuses. While corporate media power increasingly goes global, shared information fosters new ad hoc communities, smart mobs and political protests in authoritarian regimes. Since the new citizens/consumers are more active, migratory, connected and expressive, those seeking power will look for new ways to safeguard their reputation capital. In this emerging communications environment, narrative replaces command, and empathy tempers the authoritative voice. Monitorial citizens will use their social capital and digital media to make the manufacturing of consent less invisible, while the public relations industry, and its clients, will respond as required to manage risk, control damage and safeguard reputations.

Exercise questions

1. What are the important symbols and stereotypes of your culture, and what do they mean?
2. How do you define 'the public'? What are your thoughts on managing this public?
3. Describe the staging of a pseudo-event within the last twelve months. Who was sponsoring the event, and what was its purpose?
4. Imagine you work for a public relations firm and are assigned to handle damage control for an influential public figure. Describe the situation and then propose a strategy, a core message and your media of choice. Time is of the essence.
5. What, in your view, has been a significant triumph of public relations over the last ten years?
6. Describe an astro-turf organisation. What outcomes does it promote? If possible, identify how this organisation is supported and funded.
7. Conduct a survey – either online or in person – to determine your learning group's opinions about an issue of importance to you. Discuss the results with your group.
8. Describe/document a media stunt that demonstrated effective public relations.

Figure 5 'Submit: you must obey your passions'. Photo: M. Soules, San Francisco, 1991.

4 Advertising and Consumer Culture

The spirit of capitalism

Advertising and consumer culture flourish under capitalism. Advertising promotes capitalism's benefits, and its art and language express capitalism's values and promises. In 1904, German sociologist Max Weber visited the United States to study the Protestant work ethic and 'rational' capitalism at its source. Weber distinguishes between 'traditional' capitalism – practiced throughout history by diverse cultures involved in buying, selling, trading and plundering ('booty' capitalism) – and rational capitalism, based on Protestant beliefs and attitudes. For Weber, the clearest expression of rational capitalism came from Benjamin Franklin, whose homespun sayings express a philosophy of work, wealth and ethics: 'Time is money'; 'Money can beget money, and its offspring can beget more' (Weber [1904] 1998: 48–50). Franklin believed that increasing his capital was an 'end in itself', and failure to practice rational capitalism was 'forgetfulness of duty' (51). People are taught to embody the spirit of capitalism, much as they are instructed to hold religious beliefs: through 'a long and arduous process of education' (62).

Weber traces the Protestant work ethic to Calvinism, which originated in Switzerland in the 1530s, spread to the Netherlands and England and was brought to New England by Puritans in the 1620s. Weber observes that Protestant belief in predestination – only God knows who will be saved or damned – creates a deep anxiety about the afterlife, only remedied by hard work, frugal living and ethical conduct. Believers must do something redemptive, just in case God is watching, since there is no way of knowing who will be saved. Catholic belief in the forgiveness of sin through confession, ritual and good works removed a source of anxiety that Protestants harnessed as a redeeming work ethic. Calvinism's rational capitalism included 'honest dealings in business, rather than greedy search for maximal profit; reliable, steady production and sales, turning into a system of mass production; and continuous savings and reinvestment into further business growth' (Collins 1998: xiii). A disciplined, frugal life joined with the bureaucratic state and growing democratic rights to form the 'predictable social order within which mass-production capitalism can flourish' (xxiii). 'God helps those who help themselves', and thus the frugal Puritan capitalists grew wealthy.

Weber also reflects on 'the secularising influence of wealth' ([1904] 1998: 170). Like the Catholic monks before them, wealthy Protestants were tempted by wealth and the luxuries it could buy. While wealth is an expression of divine will, luxuries represent 'idolatry of the flesh' (170). Unequal distribution of wealth is the result of divine providence and therefore out of human hands. Calvin believed that the working classes remained obedient to divine will only as long as they stayed poor, thereby justifying low wages. For Protestants, work is a calling and materialism brings responsibilities. In a memorable analogy, Weber describes materialism worn by the saint as 'a light cloak, which can be thrown aside at any moment', but threatens to become an 'iron cage' (181) when pursued without restraint. He concludes: 'In the field of its highest development, in the United States, the pursuit of wealth, stripped of its religious and ethical meaning, tends to become associated with purely mundane passions, which actually give it the character of sport' (182).

Only a few cultures embrace the Protestant work ethic and the same spirit of capitalism, but Weber's analysis illustrates that attitudes towards materialism and prestige are powerful motivators and important arenas of influence. In this chapter, we explore advertising and consumer culture as informed by an ethos, a set of beliefs and values with analogies to religion. This ethos is complicated by ambiguities and tensions regarding materialism's role in the pursuit of happiness. Advertising and marketing constantly tread an ambiguous line between promise and its fulfilment. A sales proposition always involves a contract, a *quid pro quo*, expressed in terms of future redemption and personal salvation similar to religious promises. But when capitalism loses its ethical bearings and becomes amoral, observes Weber, it becomes merely competitive.

Culture and consumption: instruments of instruction and politics

The consumer revolution is a strange chapter in the ethnographic history of the species. For what may have been the first time in history, a human community willingly harboured a nonreligious agent of social change, and permitted it to transform on a continual and systematic basis virtually every feature of social life. (McCracken [1988] 1990: 30)

Grant McCracken says that consumer goods are paradoxically agents of both change and continuity, because they are invested with symbolic meaning. People use objects to express their status and identity – important for social stability – in the context of changing fashions and the spectacle of progress. Consumers 'use the meaning of consumer goods to express cultural categories and principles, cultivate ideals, create and sustain lifestyles, construct notions of the self, and create (and survive) social change' ([1988] 1990: xi). He argues that Weber's 'Protestant ethic' hypothesis is insufficient to explain the appeal of consumer goods.

In McCracken's narrative, there are three significant historical moments in the evolution of consumer culture. Elizabeth I consolidated power over her subjects in the last quarter of the sixteenth century by requiring nobles to attend the royal court and seek her favour. They played a material role in displaying the pomp, ceremony and legitimacy required of a world power: 'The supercharged symbolism of the monarch's court, hospitality, and clothing became the opportunity for political instruction and persuasion' (11). And, in a stroke of political cunning, Elizabeth persuaded her nobles to 'spend conspicuously' and 'squander vast resources' on her behalf (12). The nobles, closely watched by their local dependents, returned from court with the newest fashions and aristocratic tastes, increasingly dependent on Elizabeth for favours and increasingly competitive in their spending.

The trends initiated by the Elizabethans accelerated in the eighteenth century with the opening of new global markets and the Romantic emphasis on individual uniqueness. British and European societies were competitive and status-conscious, and these anxieties were expressed through consumer choices, where style and fashion replaced utility as motives for purchasing. Consumer goods became an investment in status: the right goods could conceal unfavourable origins and aid social mobility. 'This connection between consumption and individualism . . . is one of the great cultural fusions of the modern world. Each of these ideologies could now use the other as a powerful engine for its own advancement' (20).

By the late nineteenth century, conspicuous consumption had become commonplace, with objects taking on new symbolic readings to add value. Social elites were defined by their belongings, creating new patterns of social hierarchy, such as the *nouveaux riches*. The decorative arts movement brought the pleasures of consumption to the middle class with objects that were 'accessible, modest, and dignified' (23). The emergence of the department store, the trade fair and world exposition, film and other spaces for the observation of consumer goods further transformed relations between people and objects. The consumer was constantly exposed to a 'range of persuasive and informational stimuli without any expectation that this stimuli would result in immediate purchase' (26). Wandering through the halls of materialism, 'passive' consumers were stimulated by 'free-floating desire' (26). New credit schemes and layaway plans allowed them to buy now, pay later. McCracken concludes that 'the goods in department stores became instruments of instruction and politics' (28).

McCracken does not criticise the excess, waste, debt and distraction of consumerism, but instead observes that material goods symbolically express taste, status and identity. This symbolic expression is an ancient and transcultural human trait not limited to the capitalist West. Twitchell (1996) agrees that 'Adcult' – the ubiquitous culture of advertising – is an important channel for communicating cultural values: 'Although advertising cannot create desire, it can channel it. And what is drawn down that channel, what travels with the commercial, is our culture' (4). In this view, advertising is the new scripture instilling beliefs and values, looking for converts, turning eyeballs skyward. 'For whatever else advertising does, one thing is certain: by adding value to material, by adding meaning to objects, by branding things, advertising performs a role historically associated with religion' (12). In a more secular analysis, Schudson (1984) introduces the concept of 'capitalist realism' to compare Western advertising practices and their social effects to the socialist realism of Soviet propaganda imposed under Stalin. Capitalist realism, unlike its Soviet counterpart, emphasises consumption, individualism and private ownership over public achievements and cooperative problem solving. In both religious and secular interpretations, advertising and its art channel cultural values and promises.

Properties of advertising

It was the amusement business – first the circus and the medicine show, then the theatre – which taught the rudiments of advertising to industry and commerce. (Bernays [1928] 2005: 107)

A tragedy of the commons occurs when private interests take more than their share of common resources and rivalry develops for what remains (Hardin 1968). From overgrazing common grasslands to polluting public water systems or monopolising the airwaves, human civilisation has witnessed many of these tragedies. Advertising is a tragedy of the commons to the extent that innovations in communication technologies have contributed to the growing saturation of public space with promotional messages. As the commons becomes more crowded with rhetoric and symbolic communication, rivalry for attention increases and advertisers look for new strategies and places to find their audiences.

As much as newspapers and magazines, the telegraph contributed to ubiquitous advertising by allowing producers to purchase ads quickly and directly from newspapers across the country. In its turn, radio carried the advertiser's message to mass audiences and became a national, even international, loudspeaker system: '[R]adio ads reverberated through people's homes on the broadcaster's own schedule, adding the evocative nuances of voice and personality, and the subconscious power of music, to the language of persuasion' (O'Reilly and Tennant [2009] 2010: xxi). Radio pioneered the 'unwritten contract' (xxii) by exchanging programming – music, comedy, drama and information – for the advertiser's message, a model followed by television and the commercial internet.

Since the late nineteenth century, advertising strategies have evolved from straightforward descriptions of products and services, to reason-why pitches, to entertainment, branding, product placement, celebrity endorsement, viral marketing, cross promotion and other strategies for layering messages. In consumer cultures, the sensory environment has become heavily layered to allow multiple messages to play out at the same time. Branding athletes and their arenas with sponsors' logos is an example of layering, but layering also occurs in product placement, celebrity endorsement, benefit performances and public service announcements, where more than one sales message is communicated. O'Reilly and Tennant ([2009] 2010) believe message layering will have a cognitive impact on whole generations who are learning to 'stack' entertainment and communications experiences by multitasking on their digital devices. In turn, advertisers use 'fully-integrated marketing' to promote products on television, mobile phones and the internet 'in the hope that every touch point will converge in one single, sit-down, "stacking" experience' (19). In cultures with widespread cellular and Wi-Fi service, people routinely socialise while computing or communicating with people not present in their physical space. Managing stacking is a survival skill in persuasive environments and a kind of sport.

Advertising is immediate, compelling, accessible and deeply embedded in everyday culture. It exploits and shapes vernacular language to provide the ring of familiarity, constantly adding new catchphrases to the language. From 'Just do it' (Nike) to 'We never forget who we're working for' (defence contractor Lockheed Martin), advertising language is layered in meaning, often relying on symbolic resonance expressed in deceptively simple language. For all these reasons, propaganda appropriates the catchy vernacular language of advertising. In 2011, the British Army was 'Committed to Success' (www.army.mod.uk/), while the Canadian Army encouraged recruitment in 2006 with the forceful and controversial slogan 'Fight Fear, Fight Distress, and Fight Chaos' (Canadian Forces 2006).

Marcuse (1964) observed that the 'voice of command' used by priests, managers, educators, experts and politicians shares its compelling effect with advertising. Syntax is abridged and condensed, giving the language directness and assertiveness. It uses an emphatic concreteness (despite its frequent abstraction), repeats 'you' and 'your' and replays images to fix them in people's minds. Marcuse believed this style of rhetoric creates the 'one-dimensional' citizen incapable of protest or refusal. Similarly, Rutherford argues that advertising and propaganda are instruments of domination, in that they 'express the wishes of the powerful' (2000: 10) and confirm social hierarchy by typically being a monologue from those 'on high' to those below them in status (11).

Althusser (1971) identifies the origins of this authoritative voice as coming from religion, education, family, law, political systems and parties, trade unions and media. Ideology 'recruits' and 'transforms' individuals into followers by 'interpellation' (or hailing). Interpellation can be expressed in everyday language as 'Hey, you there!' Althusser imagines an individual in the street turning around in response to the hailing, thus becoming a subject of the ideology (86). He goes further to suggest that ideology never announces itself as anything but common sense, the way things are meant to be for the subject. With advertising, we are hailed with the sales message 'Listen up! You need this!' and then told what would be best for us. Our conformity to the message is a hidden assumption, never identified, but often described in terms of our future freedom.

Once advertisers gain their audiences through hailing, ads try to resonate with audience memories and experiences – thus, the compelling influence of popular music – while playing on anchors and stereotypes to offer solutions to problems. This interaction is often aesthetic; appreciated for its artistry, cleverness and playfulness; and more memorable for the emotions invoked. Advertising invests objects with symbolic meaning, invoking common myths and cultural narratives to give objects distinction in the marketplace. It displaces previous forms of authoritative discourse by defining standards of cleanliness, body image, behaviour, style and success. Word-of-mouth is effective advertising, because it comes with a familiar personal endorsement and taps into the community-building properties of orality. Movie buzz, investment tips, public relations spin and political gossip all remind us of the power of orality in advertising.

> Advertising is . . .
> - *Ubiquitous*: it is everywhere, adding the clutter of product placement and branding of athletes, celebrities, buildings, and events.
> - *Anonymous*: no authors are identified.
> - *Syncretic*: layers cultures, adapts pagan and religious rituals, and revives mythic heroes, folklore and literature.
> - *Symbiotic*: shares the style, techniques, and meaning of other cultural forms such as music, film, literature, sports, and religion. Advertising is a dialogue with culture.
> - *Profane*: appeals to the senses, the body, and pleasure.
> - *Repetitive*: gains memorability and substance by multiple exposures. Reputation is repetition.
> - *Magical*: animates objects, identifies products with animals, gives them an aura; charms consumers with music and spells, creates new worlds, transfers power from technology to people, and from people to technology; identifies taboos and banishes evil (body odour, wrinkles and cellulite, erectile dysfunction). (Twitchell 1996: 16–32)

As noted earlier, persuasion mystifies by advancing through a hierarchy of values, either upward or downward, to arrive at a state that exists only in the abstract: salvation, damnation, immortality, extinction, patriotism, exile, freedom, slavery. These mystifications are political commonplaces and provide the subtext for most advertising. Following the lead of Weber, Twitchell argues that the early advertisers 'were steeped in the Christian tradition' (1996: 33): 'They understood the nature of yearning and how to franchise it. They knew the language of sincerity. They knew the power of promise, large promise' (33). Ads give thanks, shower praise, confirm self-worth, answer prayers, express devotion, foster hope and inspire belief. Advertising fills the air with optimism for a better world. Twitchell flatly rejects the argument that advertising manipulates audiences. Instead, audiences engage with advertising 'texts' to arrive at their own interpretations. 'We create our own advertising as we create news, religion, politics, law, or entertainment' (51). In the end, we buy the advertising, not the product, because it promises something we want.

Figure 6 'Cuba sells the revolution'. Photo: M. Soules, 2006–8.

Case study: Cuba's revolutionary landscape

Advertising is so commonplace in developed countries that much of it enters individual and public consciousness below the threshold of awareness. Once imprinted, advertising operates like mental wallpaper, layering over our thoughts and feelings about the world. Visiting the socialist country of Cuba is instructive, because commercial messages announcing consumerism's triumph are virtually absent. From one end of the Caribbean island to the other, commercial billboards, signs and posters are replaced by billboard-sized *murales* announcing the values, heroes and challenges of Cuba's socialist revolution. Taken together, the *murales* tell the epic narrative of a people working to change their destiny against the odds.

This national narrative is symbolised around the world by images of the guerrilla freedom fighter epitomised by Ernesto 'Che' Guevara, Fidel Castro, Camilo Cienfuegos and others. The iconic image of Che Guevara – captured by Alberto Korda in 1960 – carries Cuba's message on T-shirts and posters around the world: 'Che appears as the ultimate revolutionary icon, his eyes seeming to stare boldly into the future, his very face symbolising a virile embodiment of outrage at social injustice' (Anderson 1997: 465). Che is a Cuban brand and a symbol of resistance against oppression.

The Cuban Revolution began as an independence movement from Spain in the 1860s and achieved a landmark victory by overthrowing the dictator Fulgencio Batista in January 1959. Many *murales* depict heroes of the earlier wars of independence, especially the philosopher, writer and martyr José Martí, whose image is as recognisable in Cuba as that of Guevara and Fidel Castro. In addition to heroic portraits and revolutionary sentiments, the billboards identify challenges and threats to Cuba, particularly from the United States.

Cuban billboards are produced under the direction of the Interior Ministry of the Communist Party (PCC) in Havana and in its provincial propaganda agencies. Propaganda is transparent and unapologetic in Cuba: *murales* remind the Cuban people of their history and values and educate tourists about socialism's virtues and Cuba's struggle to retain its independence. Following a theory of revolution articulated by Che Guevara – who borrowed freely from Lenin – the Cuban leadership considers itself to be the 'vanguard', forging a revolutionary path in advance of the people. Guevara believed the guerrilla struggle 'developed in two distinct environments: the people, the still sleeping mass that had to be mobilised; and its vanguard, the guerrillas, the motor force of the mobilisation, the generator of revolutionary consciousness and militant enthusiasm' ([1965] 2003: 213). For Guevara, the vanguard acts as a 'catalysing agent' to create the 'subjective conditions necessary for victory' (213). The masses are not a mindless herd; they are merely dormant.

Since 1960, Cuba has survived an economic embargo (blockade) imposed by successive US governments. Billboards remind citizens that their desperate material conditions result from the embargo and not from lack of planning by the government. Cuba has been subject to terrorist attacks, including the Bay of Pigs invasion by the US in 1961. Orlando Bosch and José Posada Carriles are reviled in Cuba for organising the bombing of Cubana Flight 455 in 1976, killing all seventy-three people on board. Along with Bosch and Posada Carriles, George W. Bush was demonised by Cuban propaganda as a threat to Cuban social security and education. The 'Bush Plan' – Commission for Assistance to a Free Cuba – anticipates the demise of Fidel and Raul Castro as leaders and calls for the reconstruction of the Cuban economy along capitalist lines. The detention of Cuban counterterrorism agents, known as the Cuban 5, in US prisons is widely memorialised and another reminder of US hypocrisy concerning terrorism.

Ortega (2006) says that the *murales* displayed across the landscape remind the Cuban people that they are under constant surveillance and simultaneously promote timocracy. In a timocracy, leaders are known for their 'honour, worth, competence, and esteem as opposed to class, heredity, power, [and] privilege' (2006: n.p.). The promotion of timocratic ideals illustrates the shift of values seen in Cuban culture. If social values are based not on class, power and prestige, but rather on honour, loyalty and competence, the basis for determining success and happiness is turned on its head. The Cuban *murales* tell a different story than the commercial billboards of the developed world and announce very different aspirations for the Cuban people.

Branding and reputation

Fundamentally, branding is a profound manifestation of the human condition. It is about belonging: belonging to a tribe, to a religion, to a family . . . It has this function for both the people who are part of the same group and also for the people who don't belong. (Wally Olins, qtd in Millman 2013: 11)

While branding has roots in the human need to belong to a tribe, religion or family, marketing guru Wally Olins says that branding in the contemporary sense is more concerned with differentiating 'fast-moving' products in a cluttered marketplace. Advertising casts a spotlight of distinction on a product or service by making a unique selling proposition. Differentiation is especially important with products difficult to distinguish from their rivals: soap, beer, jeans, cola, water, cars and banks. While branding has been a central fixture of advertising since its earliest days, Naomi Klein (2000) identifies a new threshold of branding activity, when a 'global web of logos and products' (xvii) emerged in the 1980s.

Following financial and trade deregulation, acquisitions and mergers, media consolidation and internet expansion, corporations discovered it was more profitable to market an image of their products – the brand and its associated meaning – than to produce goods and services. Nike shifted its focus from making athletic shoes to marketing the value of sport. The Body Shop morphed into an international franchise marketing consciousness about our bodies and the environment. These and other companies 'fostered powerful identities by making their brand concept into a virus and sending it out into the culture via a variety of channels: cultural sponsorship, political controversy, the consumer experience and brand extensions' (Klein 2000: 20). Much of this branding was accomplished without spending on conventional advertising.

Brands mystify products by adding abstract value, belief and conviction. Material things branded with symbolic meaning cease to be physical objects and aspire to pure information. The branding boom in the 1980s was partly a product of the emerging information revolution, when atoms were being translated into bits and everyone was 'being digital' (Negroponte [1995] 1996). In his analysis of the digital economy, Tapscott asserted that '[k]nowledge work becomes the basis of value, revenue, and profit' (1996: 68). Brands are forms of knowledge that need protection by their owners.

In 2000, Klein predicted an 'anti-corporate backlash' (xviii), anticipated by the Seattle riots in 1999 and growing consumer opposition to aggressive corporate marketing on university campuses. She identified four conditions that would enflame anti-corporate sentiment:

- *No Space*: As corporate branding seeks new spaces to colonise with its commercial messages, we will increasingly see the 'surrender of culture and education to marketing' (xxi).
- *No Choice*: Mergers, consolidation, acquisitions, franchises, monopolies and corporate censorship will diminish real choice and diversity in the marketplace.
- *No Jobs*: Outsourcing manufacturing to developing countries will increase lay-offs and unemployment in the developed nations.

McJobs (low-paying jobs with little or no security) and temporary jobs will become more common.
- *No Logo*: The assault on employment, civil liberties and civic
  space will contribute to anti-corporate activism. (Klein 2000: xxi)

When asked about the 'No Logo' movement, Olins said: 'What people
are really attacking is the capitalist system. Brands are the symbols of
the capitalist system' and it 'has terrible faults' (Millman 2013: 16–17).

In the decade following the publication of *No Logo*, the internet
provided a medium for monitoring corporate activity – CorpWatch,
PR Watch, Amnesty International and SpinWatch are a few examples of those involved – but corporate public relations efforts have
increased to protect the capitalist brand. Corporate lobbyists and
conservative politicians resist demands for higher taxes and government regulation and argue instead for deficit reduction by cutting
spending on education, healthcare and social services. Corporate
publicity keeps economic growth at the top of the news agenda, with
the threat that higher taxes and increased regulation will result in
economic slowdown and fewer jobs, despite evidence to the contrary
(Linden 2011). The success of this corporate narrative is one of the
great propaganda successes of the late twentieth century (Carey 1997;
Gutstein 2009; Hedges 2010). Nonetheless, Klein argues that corporations are sowing the seeds of their own downfall: 'By abandoning their traditional role as direct, secure employers to pursue their
branding dreams, they have lost the loyalty that once protected them
from citizen rage' (2000: 441).

By 2010, Klein was noting Barack Obama's ability to market his
own brand and its contribution to his 2008 election success. Shortly
before he was elected president, Obama was named Marketer of
the Year, beating Nike, Apple, Coors and Zappos for the top award
(Klein 2010; Creamer 2008). After a few years in office, however,
the Obama brand – like the Tony Blair and New Labour brand in
the UK before it – became tarnished by an inability to deliver on
election promises. Rather than feel betrayed by Obama, Klein recalls
that super brands like Apple, Google, Benetton and Diesel, with
their borrowed language of social revolution and change, had awak-
ened 'a longing in people for something more than shopping – for
social change, for public space, for greater equality and diversity'. If
Obama the product is not able to deliver on its promise, Obama the
brand reveals 'a tremendous appetite for progressive change' (Klein
2010: n.p.). Like religions everywhere, advertising and branding
keep hope alive.

Digital advertising: big data, metrics, algorithms

In 1989, Tim Berners-Lee, inventor of the World Wide Web, imagined an unbounded 'web of knowledge' that would bring 'the workings of society closer to the workings of our minds' (Carr [2008] 2009: 109). Rapid internet commercialisation after 1994 illustrates that new communication technologies quickly move beyond their early visionary promise to stimulate unexpected creativity and provide new marketing opportunities. The imprecise idea of Web 2.0 first expressed by Darcy DiNucci in 1999 predicted an evolution of the existing web, consisting mainly of static page views and banner ads, into a media-rich, interactive and immersive environment competing with other media for attention (DiNucci 1999). Active doing, making and connecting would replace passive viewing. While Berners-Lee claimed the term Web 2.0 was 'jargon' (Laningham 2006) – since the existing web was already 'a collaborative space where people can interact' – the original architecture of the internet was evolving, with increased bandwidth and transmission speed; new layers of code and more powerful algorithms; massive increases in storage and database capacity; greater ability to track online activities of users (analytics); increased surveillance; and a dramatic increase in the ability to aggregate bits of information into patterns of behaviour – 'the workings of our minds'.

Whether jargon or not, the term Web 2.0 signifies an evolving emphasis on internet collaboration, user input and creation and social networking (O'Reilly 2005). The proprietary encyclopaedias built by experts (*Microsoft Encarta*, *Encyclopedia Britannica*) were dethroned by the open-source *Wikipedia*, built and edited by voluntary contributors. Social networking, podcasting, blogging, tagging, Twittering, crowd-sourcing, bookmarking, reviewing and sharing all act as new channels of advertising, while contributing social capital to internet communities (Shirky 2008, 2009). Search technologies successfully commercialised by Google, Yahoo and Amazon transform how people research, learn, purchase and collaborate. Google's PageRank algorithm determines the relevance – and value – of search queries by measuring the number of links to a given site. Every search is now delivered with targeted ads related to search terms. Amazon became one of the world's largest online retailers with a commitment to speed, customer service and recommendation algorithms. In this 'culture of metrics', algorithms turn purchasing decisions into advice for other customers (Anders 2012). Amazon's Mechanical Turk service (www.mturk.com/) pays online workers small amounts for completing repetitive tasks only humans can perform, creating a kind of digital sweatshop (Zittrain 2009). One of those tasks is writing product reviews.

Online reviews and other forms of user-generated content – on YouTube, Flickr, Amazon, Trip Advisor and on blogs and social networking websites – shifts content creation from professionals to amateurs and creates niche markets described as the 'long tail' (C. Anderson 2006). A graph of the long tail phenomenon (en.wikipedia. org/wiki/Long_tail) illustrates that a few popular products attract more people per unit, while an equal number of people are attracted to a wide diversity of less popular products. For example, only a few bands are popular enough to receive radio airtime, and the rest must be content with smaller audiences and different marketing strategies. The internet's ability to aggregate audiences over broad geographical areas allows niche products and services to find large enough audiences to be commercially viable (C. Anderson 2006). Fans of obscure bands, out-of-print books, independent documentaries or quirky potential partners can now go online and search for their less-than-popular product. Recommendations and user reviews push demand down the long tail. This power distribution model has as much significance for social organisation, collaboration and dialogue as it does for marketing (Shirky 2008).

In her 2009 report to the US Congress on advertising in the digital age, Kirchhoff identified the main issues confronting the industry at the time: tax deductions for advertising expenses; tracking the movements and preferences of internet users; privacy; advertising to children; financial losses to newspapers; false testimonials on blogs and in consumer reviews; and marketing in social networks. She reports a 400 per cent growth in internet advertising over the past decade, projected to be US$40 billion by 2014 (2009: 5). Mobile technologies provide opportunities for advertisers to target consumers wherever they are. Messages are increasingly delivered to a variety of screens (desktops, tablets and smartphones); websites are being optimised for smartphones; and smartphone and tablet users conduct on-the-spot research and comparative shopping, including the practise of 'showrooming' – viewing products in physical stores before purchasing online.

Social networking sites like MySpace, Facebook and VK provide new spaces for promotion, though Kirchhoff warns that advertising in social networking sites is like 'gate-crashing a party' (2009: 13). In online gaming, product placement and virtual ads are common. YouTube has become a repository for video advertising, whether as archives of vintage television ads or promoted as controversial, funniest or 'best of' collections. Kirchhoff concludes that 'technological advances are forcing media companies and advertisers to refine and reshape their messages to reach consumers in new venues, from mobile phones to handheld readers to online gaming networks'. Companies are attempting 'to become part of the conversation on social networks or part of the landscape by embedding products in news and entertainment programming' (21). Advertisers still need to capture attention, differentiate and brand, but they also need to encourage consumer participation, track and analyse behaviour and serve up customised recommendations.

Data collection and customer recommendations are one of the synergies Jenkins predicts for convergence culture. He uses the term 'affective economics' (2006: 20) to describe the emotional engagement that blurs boundaries between entertainment and branding when audience members join the brand community. The Amazon Kindle eBook reader is just one of many proprietary digital technologies where the brand (Kindle) is inseparable from the content. Marketers include targeted ads with searches, collect customer metrics and integrate product placement into social networking sites to foster brand communities equivalent to fan cultures. Affective economics and social networking become indistinguishable in the metrics of internet commerce. The film *Terms and Conditions May Apply* (2013) documents that internet users virtually sign away all their rights to privacy and ownership when they agree to the terms of software use or contribute to social networking websites, write product reviews or add comments to discussion forums. Increasingly, corporations and governments are sharing information collected online, and the boundaries between public and private information are blurring (Bennett et al. 2014).

Internet activity produces market research – a significant and lucrative by-product. Cookies – small scripts downloaded to a user's computer – automatically customise browsing experiences and – the *quid pro quo* – track internet activity. New methods of determining 'viewable impressions' – what ads people actually pay attention to online – are replacing the more primitive click-through measurement. In 2000, Google shifted from click-through banner ads to the more targeted approach of AdWords, where advertising is pushed to users based on their location, navigation and search choices. Real-time bidding (RTB) allows advertisers to bid on and deliver their ads to particular users, all within milliseconds. Google launched AdX in 2009 and Facebook soon followed with AdExchange to manage delivery of targeted ads at speeds faster than humans can make decisions (Auerbach 2013). Social media provide more than access to like-minded consumers (Facebook's 'custom audiences'); these consumers join the marketing chain by contributing their own recommendations and media buzz. Larry Page and

Sergey Brin, the founders of Google, think of the internet as an evolving system, which will eventually not only supplement intelligence, but surpass it: 'For us, working on search is a way to work on artificial intelligence', says Page (Carr [2008] 2009: 213). In their world, artificial intelligence is a global market asking questions about itself.

The internet operates as a global focus group generating market research. When information is selected and collected as data, it becomes rhetorical, an argument. The convergence of searching, information gathering and advertising into a single delivery platform predicts that all information will have a persuasive bias or hook with which to attach a promotional message. Auerbach (2013) notes with alarm the tendency of online marketing giants to aggregate user profiles, preferences and online activities to 'microtarget' potential consumers. Acxiom Corporation, one of the world's largest consumer databases with over 500 million profiles, aggregates billions of data points to deliver 'actionable consumer insights' (Singer 2012). Alibaba, China's e-commerce giant, was positioned in 2014 to become the global leader in online sales, data collection and market research: 'It knows more than anyone about the spending habits and creditworthiness of the Chinese middle class, plus millions of Chinese merchants' ('The Alibaba Phenomenon' 2013: n.p.).

Jointly, big data and real-time bidding are creating a powerful means of communicating with audiences. Jenkins cites Lisa Gitelman's definition of media as 'layers within an ever more complicated information and entertainment stratum', governed by technical and cultural protocols (2006: 18–19). Search technology is one of those layers and has its own style for blending information and persuasion. Publicly, marketers frame their activities not as attempts to find and influence audiences, but to increase knowledge, engagement, interaction and immersion. A Microsoft marketing executive writes:

> We live in a devices and services world, where experiences are connected across screens and online engagement happens anywhere and at all times. This is empowering a new generation of consumers who are active critics, fact-finders, content creators, buzz-marketers and user-innovators. They demand highly personalized, socially relevant experiences. (Holland 2013: n.p.)

Notice the rhetorical transformation and ascent toward mystification in this analysis. While Frank Holland of Microsoft is primarily concerned with ad delivery to active consumers in a crowded marketplace, his explanation is reframed as a 'socially relevant' benefit to consumers. Carr ([2008] 2009) warns that many users are naïve about the extent of internet tracking, and that they leave a spider web of clues that can be assembled into detailed profiles by those with access to data. Acxiom, BlueKai and Xaxis collect many data points about online consumers and are capable of 'reidentification': converting anonymous users into identifiable people. Issenberg (2012) describes how the Obama Democrats used big data to build voter support one individual at a time and then predict election results months in advance. 'While the internet offers people a new medium for discovering information and voicing opinions, it also provides bureaucrats with a powerful new tool for monitoring speech, identifying dissidents, and disseminating propaganda' (Carr [2008] 2009: 200). In 2013, Edward Snowden came forward to journalist Glenn Greenwald and filmmaker Laura Poitras with details of covert – and apparently illegal – mass electronic surveillance. Snowden, a computer specialist working on contract for the National Security Agency (NSA) in Hawaii, copied classified documents to support his claims and set off a deluge of denial and protest with his revelations that the NSA, Government Communications Headquarters (GCHQ) in the UK and the Communications Security Establishment Canada (CSEC) are spying on citizens and high-ranking government officials alike without their knowledge (Greenwald et al. 2013). Between them, national security agencies and large commercial data miners share powerful new tools for influencing audiences, whether to sell products or promote ideologies.

Exercise questions

1. Describe your approach to materialism by considering your attitudes to work, wealth, status and happiness.
2. What role does advertising play in a given sport? Try to go behind the scenes to account for advertising revenues, their effect on player salaries, sport venues and ticket prices.
3. Illustrate Twitchell's characteristics of advertising with examples from contemporary ads. Create a blog or website to share your examples with your learning group.
4. What are your thoughts on the comparison of advertising and religion?
5. Create an ad to sell a product or service to your class. Use audio, video or presentation software for this thirty- to sixty-second production. Provide a short written explanation (400 words or less) of your approach and unique selling proposition.
6. Discuss a political party in terms of branding.
7. Describe an online community you belong to, paying particular

attention to the presence of advertising and marketing in this community.

8. As a class or learning group, discuss your attitudes about internet privacy, data collection and information sharing between governments and corporations. Summarise your conclusions as a series of recommendations to your political representative.

Figure 7 'The well-armed brain'. Photo: M. Soules, Toronto, 2007.

5 Psychology of Influence

Since the mid-1800s, capitalist societies have provided a mass market laboratory for marketers, advertisers, publicists, politicians and propagandists to test their persuasive powers. Market research, surveys, focus groups, clinical experiments, studies of spending habits and trends and data analysis have all contributed to our understanding of motivation and behaviour in the material world and in the broader context of human culture. Robert Cialdini's applied approach to persuasion provides a core focus for this chapter. Cialdini emphasises that uncertainty and ambiguity are key elements in persuasion psychology. They provide openings for creative – possibly misleading – communication, again reminding us of the trickster's *modus operandi*. Recent advances in neuroscience reveal that reason alone is often unable to remove ambiguity, inspire trust and support optimum decision-making. We need our emotions to point us in the right direction.

Persuasion in the spectrum of influence

Persuasion wears many masks across a spectrum of influence that ranges from giving advice and gaining compliance, to education, promotion, propaganda and physical coercion. These masks disguise persuasion and make it difficult to define without adding numerous qualifications. Gass and Seiter ([1999] 2007) try to balance competing claims to arrive at a definition of persuasion as 'the activity of creating, reinforcing, modifying or extinguishing beliefs, attitudes, intentions, motivations, and/or behaviours within . . . a given communication context' (33–4). Their catalogue of actions and outcomes illustrates the difficulty of defining persuasion easily. Like fish in water, we are immersed in persuasion before we know we are swimming.

Persuasion is

- either 'pure' or 'borderline': persuasion can be mixed with other intentions (borderline), so it does not always announce itself clearly. Often, it is disguised as something else such as 'mere' information;
- interpersonal (extrinsic) or intrapersonal (intrinsic);
- intentional or unintentional: people are not always conscious of persuasive intent, just as they are not always aware of being deceptive;
- successful or not;
- coercive or non-coercive;
- symbolic or non-symbolic communication;
- influenced by media and context;
- adapted for face-to-face, public and mass media delivery;
- sometimes spontaneous and improvised; and
- influenced by socio-cultural factors. (Gass and Seiter [1999] 2007: 22–35)

Persuasion is routinely improvised to fit given circumstances, adjusted for the medium and crafted specifically for an audience whose reception of the message determines its success. Evaluating persuasive messages involves a complex decoding process to distinguish the central persuasive elements – what we are asked to believe or do – from peripheral issues not directly related to compliance. Persuasion is often embedded in friendly banter or humorous anecdotes. Salience – why the message is important to us – determines how the message is decoded or if it is decoded at all. Pratkanis and Aronson conclude that 'the mass media may not tell you what to think, but they do tell you what to think *about* and *how to do it*' ([1992] 2001: 28).

Persuasion is 'a communicative process to influence others. A persuasive message has a point of view or desired behaviour for the recipient to adopt in a voluntary fashion' (Jowett and O'Donnell 2006: 31). There is room for negotiation: persuasion is 'transactional' in its 'continuous and dynamic process of co-creating meaning', but it does attempt 'to evoke a specific change in the attitudes or behaviours of an audience' (32). The desired changes are 'anchored' to beliefs, values, attitudes or norms already held by an audience. The persuasive force of the message seems to originate from within individuals as something already agreed upon, especially when affirmed by a surrounding crowd. Asking an audience to abandon existing anchors can set them adrift and confuse the argument. When accepting the message no longer seems voluntary, persuasion moves toward coercion, threats and intimidation.

Lakoff's theory of 'neural recruitment' proposes that repetition – of talking points, phrases, metaphors and other figures of speech – comes to dominate thinking. Constant repetition establishes familiar neural pathways for arguments to travel along. Examples of neural recruitment include 'war on terror', 'liberal media', 'lower taxes', 'declining markets' and 'global warming'. These phrases frame issues and set agendas for discussion. 'As the same circuit is activated day after day, the synapses on the neurons in the circuit get stronger until a permanent circuit is formed' ([2008] 2009: 83). A 'recruited circuit' becomes the physical embodiment of the metaphor (84) and, in the absence of deeper and slower thinking, is accepted without resistance. Hegemonic thinking depends on neural recruitment at the level of mass society. Persuasive communicators use common social metaphors and analogies as anchors to build understanding and empathy with audiences.

Empathy is activated when 'mirror neurons' recreate in one mind what is occurring in another mind. We intuitively feel we understand the goals and motivations of another person (Keysers 2011: 49). The neuroscience slogan '[n]eurons that fire together, wire together' means that empathy and intuition depend on the operations of mirror neurons. Keysers comments:

> While we witness the actions of others, our own premotor cortex resonates as if it was [sic] doing the actions we observe. The mirror system builds a bridge between the minds of two people and shows us that our brains are deeply social. (62)

This experimental finding adds substance to the Theory of Mind first advanced by Premack and Woodruff in 1978 to describe how we assign mental states to others, allowing us to predict their behaviour. Without this capacity, humans would be unable to anticipate responses to their persuasive efforts, especially useful when the goal is to gain compliance.

Gaining compliance

Gaining compliance is a subset of persuasion primarily 'aimed at getting others to do something or to act in a particular way' (Gass and Seiter [1999] 2007: 227). Most research on compliance gaining focuses on what people do when they want to get something from others. Sociologists Marwell and Schmitt (1967) set the stage for research in compliance gaining with their list of strategies:

1. Promise: You will be rewarded if you comply.
2. Threat: You will be punished if you do not comply.
3. Expertise (positive): You will (eventually) be rewarded for your effort and expertise if you comply.
4. Expertise (negative): You will (eventually) suffer for your lack of skill if you do not comply.
5. Liking: Friendly behaviour prepares the subject to accept your request.
6. Pregiving: Reward the subject before requesting compliance. Foot-in-the-door variant: Give a small token gift before asking for a larger contribution.
7. Aversive stimulation: Punish the subject continuously until compliance is gained. Torture.
8. Debt: Compliance is owed for past favours.
9. Moral appeal: Compliance rests on moral duty or obligation.
10. Self-feeling (positive): You will feel better about yourself if you comply.
11. Self-feeling (negative): You will feel disappointed about yourself if you do not comply.
12. Altercasting (positive): A good person would comply.
13. Altercasting (negative): Only an inadequate person would not comply.
14. Altruism: Other people desperately need your compliance.
15. Esteem (positive): If you comply, people you value will think better of you.
16. Esteem (negative): If you do not comply, people you value will think less highly of you. (Adapted from Marwell and Schmitt 1967: 350–64; and from Gass and Seiter [1999] 2007: 229)

These strategies are context-sensitive, often decided pragmatically and on-the-fly. In general, gaining compliance leverages human relationships using promises of reward or threats of consequence.

Power imbalances directly affect compliance gaining. In their widely cited study, French and Raven (1960) identified five foundations of power:

- *Reward power* is based on control over something of value, such as a raise or promotion.
- *Coercive power* depends on the ability to punish. 'You're fired!'

- *Expert power* is based on expertise, knowledge, or skill, and is regularly practiced by trades workers, doctors, lawyers, architects, engineers, priests, and financial advisors.
- *Legitimate power* depends on formal rank or position: presidents, CEOs, law enforcement officers, judges, and guards.
- *Referent power* results when the subject emulates those asking for compliance such as coaches, teachers, trainers, or gurus. (French and Raven [1960] 1968: 607–23)

More powerful people tend to be more direct in their compliance negotiations. Those with a power deficit can resort to deference and politeness, both of which are closely linked to face-saving. As reported by Gass and Seiter, Kellerman and Shea (1996) discovered that the 'best way to get compliance is by using direct requests (i.e., explicitly ask for what you want); such requests were among the most efficient strategies and were not considered impolite' (Gass and Seiter [1999] 2007: 236). Compliance strategies are also determined by the persuader's personality, as well as by gender, culture and age (238).

More recently, compliance gaining research has shifted from strategies to goals, since 'goals give meaning to situations' and reflect the personality of the person seeking compliance (Gass and Seiter [1999] 2007: 241). 'I think you should volunteer because together we can make a big difference in this community'. When seeking compliance, people often pursue different goals at the same time. Primary goals are supplemented by secondary goals, such as maintaining integrity and self-definition; creating a good impression or building relationships; and managing the emotional climate. Secondary goals set boundaries for the primary intent or adjust conditions to make agreement more likely.

A final factor in the complex dynamics of gaining compliance depends on the communication style of the actors:

- *Expressive* people prefer to speak from the gut. They say what they think and feel without much forethought of consequences.
- *Conventional* communicators follow social conventions and try to be cooperative. They express their thoughts and feelings, but within norms for appropriate behaviour.
- *Rhetorical* communicators create their own compliance context. Their 'rhetorical performance' is highly sensitive to context and often improvised. They negotiate character, adjust situations, solve problems, and build consensus to foster agreement. Their proactive style and pursuit of multiple goals result in persuasive, competent communications, according to Gass and Seiter ([1999] 2007: 243–4).

As skilful as they are, rhetorical communicators can be insincere and manipulative when acting solely in self-interest. For our own self-defence, we need to understand the psychology of persuasion and its 'weapons of influence'.

Cialdini's weapons of influence

Pavlov's scientific experiments on salivation between 1890 and 1904 initiated a new science of conditioned reflexes. Before Pavlov, digestive glands were thought to produce 'psychic secretions' stimulated by food. Pavlov rejected this interpretation and instead hypothesised that psychic activity is actually a 'conditioned reflex', a physiological response to the environment originating in the cerebral cortex. This discovery 'made it possible to study all psychic activity objectively' as observable behaviours ('Ivan Pavlov' [1904] 1967: n.p.).

Pavlov's theories on conditioned reflexes are significant in Cialdini's widely cited work on persuasion psychology (2007). Cialdini assumes that people are generally acting in their own self-interest in compliance situations – an assumption we examine in more detail later in the chapter. Cialdini says that persuasion has six patterns of motivation that, when turned against us, become 'weapons of influence':

- *Reciprocation*: when we receive a 'gift' from someone, we feel obligated to give back in return.
- *Commitment and Consistency*: our desire to keep agreements and appear consistent in our actions is compelling.
- *Social Proof*: we are influenced by behaviours we see around us.
- *Liking*: we are more likely to be persuaded by someone we like and find attractive.
- *Authority*: deference to authority has deep roots in most cultures.
- *Scarcity*: fear of going without and the value of what is rare are two sides of the same coin. (Cialdini [1984] 2007: xiii)

People often take mental short cuts using rules of thumb (heuristics) to make decisions quickly – what Kahneman (2011) calls 'fast thinking' – leaving themselves vulnerable to abuse by these weapons of influence. Generally, fast thinking produces an appropriate response, but when unique situations require a revised decision-making process, these short cuts can lead us astray. For example, a person we automatically assume to be a trustworthy authority figure may, in fact, be an imposter trying to deceive us or the gift we cheerfully accept may turn out to have strings attached.

Cialdini begins his analysis of influence with examples of animal behaviour to illustrate that 'trigger features' initiate 'fixed-action patterns' – predictable automatic responses that work most of the time to enable survival and nurturance. When scientists played a tape recording of the 'cheep-cheep' sound made by her chicks, a mother turkey approached a stuffed polecat – her natural predator – as if it were one of her offspring. When the tape recording stopped, the turkey ceased her nurturing behaviour and attacked the polecat furiously (Cialdini [1984] 2007: 2). In a parallel example, Cialdini cites research that found people waiting in line to photocopy documents are more likely to let someone go ahead of them if the word 'because' is included in their request, even when no additional reason is given: 'Excuse me, I have five pages. May I use the Xerox machine because I have to make some copies?' (4) Cialdini calls this automatic response 'Click, whirr!' (5) to suggest that fixed-action patterns are like tape loops: push the button (with the trigger feature) and the pre-recorded tape plays as usual. He emphasises that we need short cuts in complex social environments; they work to our advantage most of the time. However, the need to assess risk and make decisions quickly makes people vulnerable to false cues and biases. Compliance professionals know how to mimic trigger features, and Cialdini recommends a form of psychological martial arts to defend against manipulation.

Reciprocation and networks of obligation

The reciprocation rule – 'that we should try to repay, in kind, what another person has provided us' (Cialdini [1984] 2007: 17) – is an ancient and powerful force of influence. The anthropologist Richard Leakey stressed the importance of reciprocation in building societies: 'We are human because our ancestors learned to share their food and skills in an honoured network of obligation' (Cialdini [1984] 2007: 18). As noted earlier, First Nations groups in the Pacific Northwest use a communal celebration called the potlatch to share wealth and create a network of indebtedness.

Reciprocation is the basis for trust, sharing, cooperative action and social cohesion. The rule is regularly engaged by organisations handing out flowers, literature or trinkets before asking for a donation. After we take what is given, it is difficult not to repay the gift. Those who break the rule risk losing their reputation for honesty and becoming social outcasts. Bernard Madoff's massive Ponzi scheme cheated his investors, broke the reciprocation rule and earned him a 150-year prison sentence (Rushe 2010). Reciprocation accounts for the significance of political contributions, lobbying and other promises of political favour (Open Secrets 2011; Lessig 2011). Contract negotiations, trade agreements and international diplomacy are all governed by networks of obligation. Regrettably, the reciprocation rule is betrayed when gifts become bribes or excuses for extortion.

Commitment and consistency

'Once we have made a choice or taken a stand, we will encounter personal and interpersonal pressures to behave consistently with that commitment' (Cialdini [1984] 2007: 57). Acting consistently and keeping commitments are widely viewed as positive character traits associated with reliability, honesty and integrity. Consistency provides the foundation for logic, reasoning and the scientific method. But automatic consistency makes us vulnerable to manipulation and influence. In his 1839 essay 'Self-Reliance', Ralph Waldo Emerson warned that 'a foolish consistency is the hobgoblin of little minds' ([1839] 1957: 153). The expectation to be consistent, he believed, encouraged conformity and limited self-reliance, especially when applied without discernment.

Consistency is particularly difficult when we experience cognitive dissonance: the indecision and anxiety we feel when we are forced to hold contradictory beliefs simultaneously or when our beliefs are contradicted by facts. Tavris and Aronson (2013) build on Festinger's pioneering work on cognitive dissonance (1957) to argue that people attempt to remain consistent with self-justification, face-saving and denial. They will claim that 'mistakes were made, but not by me'. This mechanism is particularly apparent when deep-seated beliefs about religion, science or politics are challenged. As we saw earlier, when people's beliefs are challenged, their resistance to change actually increases – a phenomenon known as backfire (Nyhan and Reifler 2010). In religious or patriotic communities, people risk being seen as outcasts, even traitors, if they are inconsistent in their beliefs. In the 2004 US presidential campaign, John Kerry was aggressively challenged for his apparent lack of patriotism, even though he was a decorated veteran of the Vietnam War. As with reciprocation, the consistency rule engages deep issues of character and social responsibility.

Prior commitment activates the consistency rule. During the Korean conflict, US prisoners of war were more likely to collaborate with their Chinese captors if they had written down their criticisms of US society, even if those criticisms seemed mild. When prisoners signed their names to these confessions, they were, in effect, making a commitment (Cialdini [1984] 2007: 70–1; Marks 1979: 129–30). Writing statements down makes them public and thus more powerful as levers for gaining compliance. Sales agents engage the commitment principle

by asking customers to complete sales agreements, increasing the like-lihood that they will follow through with their decision to purchase.
Commitment and consistency increase with investment of time, effort and money. Initiation rites – and their modern counterparts, hazing rituals and military boot camps – impose stressful challenges to encourage group loyalty. '[C]ommitments are most effective in chang-ing a person's self-image and future behaviour when they are active, public, and effortful' (Cialdini [1984] 2007: 92), requiring participants to take 'inner responsibility' for their actions (93). Questions of char-acter, reputation and status are at stake. Those seeking our compliance often ask us to honour commitments we made casually, automatically and without thinking. If we agree, argues Emerson, our foolish con-sistency betrays a lack of self-reliance.

Social proof

The principle of social proof states that we frequently determine correct behaviour by observing the actions of those around us. Despite its annoying clatter in television comedies, canned laughter has a decisive effect on audience response: audiences not only laugh more, they think the routines are funnier (Cialdini [1984] 2007: 115). Social proof contributes to the bandwagon fallacy when voters, sports fans or technology consumers are urged to 'catch the wave' of popular support. Bandura's important research in social learning theory in the early 1960s showed that children who observed violent and aggressive behaviour by adults became more violent and aggressive themselves (Bandura et al. 1961, 1963). More recently, DeLisi et al. (2013: 132) report that 'violent video game playing is correlated with aggression' and contributes to antisocial behaviour of delinquent youth. Social proof is most influential 'when we are observing the behaviour of people just like us' (Cialdini [1984] 2007: 140) – an insight apparent to anyone who learns a sport alongside their peers. Soap operas and telenovelas are popular, in part because they allow audiences to reflect on appropriate social behaviour. Similarly, movie historians frequently note cinema's role in socialisation and language acquisition.

The need for social proof increases in a climate of uncertainty. Early technology adopters provide an enthusiastic vanguard that can make or break a new technology. Investor confidence, based on social proof, is a subjective valuation of financial markets. 'Pluralistic ignorance' results when uncertain people look around and see other uncertain people not knowing what to do. The contagion of uncertainty can immobilise crowds witnessing public crimes, such as riots, homi-cide, mass suicide and civilian deaths, because the inaction of others contradicts any sense of emergency and reduces personal responsibility. People experiencing a medical emergency in public are more likely to be helped when there are fewer bystanders (Cialdini [1984] 2007: 133). During the mass suicide of Reverend Jim Jones and his Peoples Temple followers in 1978, the combination of uncertainty, an unfamiliar location and actions by similar others resulted in tragedy. Jones' authoritative charisma, combined with the pressures of social proof, contributed to the death of over 900 followers, many of them children (Jonestown Institute 2014).

Liking

We are persuaded more easily by people we know and like and who are similar to us. As with the other weapons of influence, familiarity and liking have deep evolutionary origins. In his study of subliminal influence, Mlodinow (2012) suggests that social interaction 'was the driving force behind the evolution of superior human intelligence' (84). To form their societies, where liking and being liked are important for survival, humans need to make complex calculations about who belongs to the community, who is healthy and capable and who is trustworthy. For insiders, repetition breeds familiarity and enhances liking. But for outsiders, lack of familiarity, combined with ethnic and cultural differences, negatively affect liking. The genetic fallacy – judging others based on their origins, ethnicity, religion, profession or class – is used to defend the tribe and keeps outsiders at bay. Zak (2012) argues that the neurotransmitter oxytocin (the 'moral molecule') affects our affiliations, who we will associate with and who we avoid.

At an everyday level, sales parties in a friend's home exploit the liking rule and combine it with reciprocity (sample gifts), commitment (testimonials) and social proof (seeing other people purchase products). The sponsoring host(ess) is instrumental to the success of these parties, because everyone in the room is a friend. Similarly, social networking sites aggregate 'friends' into virtual communities to sell advertising, promote events and conduct market research, all with the appearance of connecting and empowering people. Corporate retreats gather co-workers together to promote familiarity and liking in the context of gift giving, rewards and testimonials. Once liking has been affirmed, reciprocation is expected in the form of increased employee harmony, motivation and productivity.

The 'halo effect' of physical attractiveness enhances liking. 'A halo effect occurs when one positive characteristic of a person dominates the way that person is viewed by others' (Cialdini [1984] 2007: 171). Kahneman states that the halo effect, or the 'mere exposure effect'

(2011: 67), is based on first impressions and 'exaggerated emotional coherence' – we like everything about a person we find attractive (82–3). Advertisers link products to celebrities and attractive people or to pleasant emotions and experiences. Political candidates receive more votes if they are attractive, even though voters deny that they are influenced by appearances. Attractive people receive more favourable treatment, both in the courts and in recruitment interviews (Cialdini [1984] 2007: 171). Dressing alike contributes to liking; following fashion trends and wearing uniforms exert a powerful influence on perceptions of character and community. Sports fans adopt their team's halo of success and suffer with their defeat. With victory, fans proclaim: 'We're number one!' and 'We won!' But, in defeat, they complain: 'They blew our lead!' and 'They lost!' Liking is a powerful force for community solidarity, but can quickly become polarised in defeat.

Even small preferences for liking accumulate into pronounced differences. Research by economist Thomas Schelling shows that slight preferences to live surrounded by similar others eventually led to fully segregated neighbourhoods (Carr [2008] 2009: 159). Polarisation occurs quickly on the internet, where moving around is easy and small differences of opinion can accumulate to segregate people into communities of interest. Polarised blog networks dedicated to political opinion illustrate this form of 'balkanisation'. In 'Divided They Blog', Adamic and Glance report very little cross-linking between conservative and progressive blogs, less than 10 per cent interaction and most of that name calling (2005; Carr [2008] 2009: 163–4). Political segregation leads to 'ideological amplification'; when people discuss issues with like-minded others, their views become more entrenched and extreme ([2008] 2009: 164). Applied to news-making, ideological amplification leads to biased reporting to partisan audiences, whether progressive or conservative. Circular reasoning is involved: people like this source of news and opinion because they agree with it. It is familiar.

Authority

The Nazi extermination of European Jews is the most extreme instance of abhorrent immoral acts carried out by thousands of people in the name of obedience. Yet in lesser degree this type of thing is constantly recurring: ordinary citizens are ordered to destroy other people, and they do so because they consider it their duty to obey orders. (Milgram [1974] 2009: 2)

Stanley Milgram conducted his famous experiments on obedience to authority at Yale University in the early 1960s during the Nuremberg trials. He initially wanted to understand why the German people obeyed their Nazi leaders in committing 'abhorrent immoral acts'. Instead, Milgram discovered a more general human trait not limited to nationality or gender. He demonstrated that people will carry out orders in deference to authority figures, despite their own moral misgivings. In Milgram's experiments, a research assistant dressed in a lab coat directed volunteers to administer electric shocks of increasing intensity to an actor, who reacted with growing distress to the phantom shocks. Shocks were supposedly administered when the actor answered a series of word-pair questions incorrectly; the more incorrect answers, the higher the voltage. Remarkably, Milgram discovered that over 60 per cent of subjects continued to administer shocks up to the maximum 450 volts, despite their own reservations and the actor's dramatic protests. The experiment was repeated in many locations and confirmed Milgram's original findings. There were no appreciable differences between men and women in their responses or between people from different social backgrounds. Deference to authority – even the trappings of authority – is a powerful compulsion and easily abused.

People who follow orders that violate a moral code reduce cognitive dissonance by transferring responsibility to authority figures. They assign 'the broader tasks of setting goals and assessing morality' to the authority figure ([1974] 2009: 7). Milgram observed that 'binding factors', such as the researcher's politeness (liking), the subject's commitment to participate and the clinical setting helped the volunteers overcome their moral reservations. Following orders is even easier when they travel through a chain of command, 'a dangerously typical situation in a complex society' (11). Milgram cites the example of a US pilot in the Vietnam War, 'who conceded that Americans were bombing Vietnamese men, women, and children but felt that the bombing was for a "noble cause" and thus was justified' (9). Milgram's findings are equally relevant fifty years later, when whistle-blowers are imprisoned as traitors, non-combatants are tortured in rendition sites and civilians on the other side of the world are killed on the orders of generals and politicians.

A 2010 documentary by Christophe Nick, *Le Jeu de la Mort* (*The Game of Death*), restages the Milgram experiment as reality television. Directed by an attractive hostess, contestants in a fake game show administer shocks of increasing intensity to their opponents, while the audience demands 'punishment'. The documentary reveals that 82 per cent of participants – an increase from Milgram's findings of 62 per cent – were willing to shock their rivals, suggesting that the game show setting with cameras and an audience added additional pressure. Initially, participants signed a contract agreeing to follow instructions, adding the power of consistency into the persuasive mix ('Reality TV' 2010).

These experiments testing the power of authority illustrate its excesses and dangers, but deference to legitimate authority is required for social contracts and stable societies. Children learn to navigate authority from their parents and teachers, and religious instruction emphasises obedience to moral codes. Doctors, therapists and other healers use their authority and physical setting to encourage compliance for their patients' benefit (Frank and Frank 1961). Authority figures and experts offer helpful advice and contribute to our safety and well-being, so we are persuaded to follow their direction.

As observed by Milgram and others, however, unthinking obedience to authority makes us vulnerable to manipulation. Kahneman says that it is easier for other people to take advantage of our illusions than it is for us to protect ourselves from those illusions (2011: 28). Cialdini reminds us that 'we are often as vulnerable to the *symbols* of authority as to the *substance*' ([1984] 2007: 220). Titles, uniforms and other trappings of authority can all be staged to achieve the desired effect. When people posing as experts purposely distort evidence – about smoking, energy use, wealth distribution, food security or potential enemies – their authority ceases to be legitimate. Authenticity and trust contribute to credible authority, and we need discernment to assess the performance and motivation of experts and authority figures.

Scarcity and psychological reactance

The scarcity principle states that 'opportunities seem more valuable to us when their availability is limited' (Cialdini [1984] 2007: 238). 'Loss aversion' has evolutionary origins, and we experience potential loss as more compelling than possible gain: 'Organisms that treat threats as more urgent than opportunities have a better chance to survive and reproduce' (Kahneman 2011: 282). The notion that commodity prices are subject to supply and demand is premised on the scarcity principle, since 'scarce' resources are usually more expensive. When oil reserves are down (or controlled by hostile regimes), gas prices go up. Environmental threats, economic prosperity and national security demand costly sacrifices. Collectors pay the cost of scarcity when buying stamps, vintage automobiles, antiques and paintings by the Old Masters. In advertising, phrases such as 'while supplies last' and 'limited edition' imply scarcity and encourage immediate action. The logic of scarcity is pervasive and easily manipulated.

Threats of scarcity also gain power through the principle of 'psychological reactance' (Brehm 1966; Brehm and Brehm 1981). When existing rights are threatened, our desire to retain those rights and our resistance to their loss increase. Authorities attempting to remove existing rights can stimulate behaviour they are trying to suppress. Increased drug use during a 'war on drugs' is an example of psychological reactance to scarcity and a challenge to authority (London School of Economics 2014). Censoring pornography or prosecuting sex trade workers may engage psychological reactance in people who believe their freedoms are threatened. The National Rifle Association (NRA) intensifies lobbying during debates on gun control in the US. In December 2012, gun sales across the US increased dramatically after mass shootings in schools reignited demands for stricter gun control laws. The NRA responded to the threat of gun scarcity by calling for armed guards in all schools to protect the students: 'The only thing that stops a *bad* guy with a *gun* is a *good* guy with a *gun*', claimed the head of the NRA (Lichtblau and Rich 2012: n.p.).

The Recording Industry Association of America (RIAA) prosecuted Napster for illegal peer-to-peer file-sharing in 2000 and managed to shut it down, but unintentionally stimulated a global epidemic of illegal file-sharing: forty billion unauthorised music files were downloaded in 2008; and 70 per cent of all network traffic in Europe in 2008 was attributed to file-sharing (Schulze and Mochalski 2009).

Psychological reactance informs James Davies' theory of revolution and provides insight into mass demonstrations associated with Ukraine's Orange Revolution (2004–5) or Occupy Wall Street protests:

> Revolutions are most likely to occur when a prolonged period of objective economic and social development is followed by a short period of sharp reversal. People then subjectively fear that ground gained with great effort will be quite lost; their mood becomes revolutionary. (1962: 5)

The phrase 'democratic deficit' expresses the idea that democracy has been corrupted by powerful interests, creating a scarcity of good government. Clifford Stott, a specialist in crowd psychology, says that riots are more likely to occur where legitimate authority is questioned (Ryan 2011). When governments and their supporters portray street protests as potential criminal actions or eruptions of irrationality, they reinforce the perception that a democratic deficit exists.

Intrinsic motivation and self-determination

Cialdini's phrase 'weapons of influence' aptly describes the typical stimulus-response pattern of persuasive encounters, but there are limitations to this behaviourist approach. Daniel Pink (2009) reviews research conducted since the 1940s to argue that extrinsic motivation – external rewards and consequences for behaviour, the carrot-and-stick approach – works best for routine tasks, but can be counterproductive for more complex and creative activities. In 1949, Harlow discovered that monkeys readily solved a puzzle without any external motivation, but when they were later given a reward for the same task, they made more errors and solved the puzzles less often (Pink [2009] 2011: 3). Harlow identified 'intrinsic motivation' that was unconnected to biological drives or external rewards as the source of this apparent paradox. His research was contrary to accepted behaviourist theory and remained neglected until Deci and Ryan (1985) applied it to human subjects solving puzzle problems, confirming Harlow's conclusions. Since then, Deci, Ryan and their colleagues have continued to research intrinsic motivation and its relation to self-determination (www.selfdeterminationtheory.org/). Self-determination theory proposes that the human need for autonomy, competence and relatedness drives intrinsic motivation.

External motivation and rewards replace autonomy with control by others. Higher financial incentives for corporate executives actually lower performance, while commissioned artworks were judged in experiments to be less creative than non-commissioned works (Pink [2009] 2011: 39–43). Pink notes that 'extrinsic rewards can be effective for algorithmic tasks – those that depend on following an existing formula to its logical conclusion', but they distract attention from activities that 'demand flexible problem-solving, inventiveness, or conceptual understanding' (44). Intrinsic motivation contributed to the open source software development of Linux, Apache and Mozilla Firefox – all requiring creativity, autonomy, competence and relatedness in the programmer community. Paying for blood donations undermines motivation to donate by removing 'a feeling that money can't buy' (46–7). Volunteer organisations, cooperatives and 'social businesses' based on the model developed by Muhammad Yunus (2008) are motivated more by social benefit than profit. When abused, extrinsic motivation encourages unethical behaviour. People take short cuts to reach quotas and projections or rush products onto the market before they are reliable and/or safe. Policies and practises that use fear and insecurity as external motivations or limit autonomy with excessive controls stifle self-motivation and civic engagement.

Heuristics and biases: thinking, fast and slow

Intrinsic motivation is a central focus in behavioural economics – an emerging field of research combining findings in economics, psychology, sociology and neuroscience to challenge assumptions of classical economics, rational decision-making and risk analysis. Classical economists assume that people act rationally in their own self-interest; they conduct cost-benefit analyses to assess risk and make decisions; and they make choices based on consistent tastes. Behavioural economists are challenging these assumptions with new approaches to rationality, including the role of emotions in decision-making and predictable irrationality. They are discovering that intrinsic motivation competes with – or tempers – extrinsic motivation and is an important factor in persuasion.

Errors in judgement are the new fallacies, though now explained as cognitive illusions and miscalculations. Persuasion does more than appeal to self-interest; it can lead us to make cognitive errors by initiating 'resemblance', 'availability' or 'associative activation' short cuts. In *Thinking, Fast and Slow* (2011), Kahneman describes the reliance of fast thinking – or System 1 thinking – on rules of thumb (heuristics), biases and gut instincts to make decisions quickly. System 1 thinking, honed over millions of years of human adaptation, is frequently adequate to the task of survival, but not always. We can be led astray when our short cuts are inappropriate, as with Cialdini's 'click-whirr' response. For example, we may have a bias that people of a different culture will take advantage of us, so we reject their sincere offers of hospitality. Unthinking rules of thumb determine how people vote, who they associate with, what issues they support.

Complex, unfamiliar decisions require the slower, more deliberate and effortful System 2 thinking to include reason, reflection and calculation conducted in the neocortex. Our decision to use one system or another is influenced by such factors as cognitive load (what we are paying attention to), cognitive ease (how much effort is required), salience (what is important to us), availability (recent exposure), the halo effect (attractive features that influence liking), the influence of experts (authority) and level of risk. Statistical thinking (System 2) is difficult for most people, so they prefer the beliefs and narratives of System 1 (Kahneman 2011: 183).

Kahneman's distinction between System 1 and System 2 thinking follows from the social brain hypothesis that extraordinary human brain development over the last 50,000 years results from the increased complexity of living in large social groups. An enlarged prefrontal cortex supports complex reasoning, reflection and calculation necessary for survival in highly social environments. But this greater capacity comes at the cost of effort, time and response rate. Also,

> System 1 is not prone to doubt. It suppresses ambiguity and spontaneously constructs stories that are as coherent as possible. Unless the message is immediately negated, the associations that it evokes will spread as if the message were true. System 2 is capable of doubt, because it can maintain incompatible possibilities at the same time. However, sustaining doubt is harder work than sliding into certainty. (2011: 114)

System 1 is reactive by nature; it responds quickly and with bias to questions of territory, outsiders, mates, ownership, authority, sharing and scarcity. Many efforts at persuasion appeal to System 1 thinking through coherent, if false, narratives and expressions of certainty.

Confidence is an important survival skill and contributes to self-esteem and optimism, but overconfidence is a cognitive error of estimation. It requires the expert to perform a role. Kahneman's sarcasm is evident in his review of Tetlock's (2005) research on expert political judgement: '[P]eople who spend their time, and earn their living, studying a particular topic produce poorer predictions than dart-throwing monkeys who would have distributed their choices evenly over the options' (219). Confidence is a function of cognitive ease and narrative coherence (239–40): solutions come readily to mind and seem to make sense. Experts are 'often less reliable', because they develop an 'enhanced illusion' of their skill and become 'unrealistically overconfident' (219). In *Trust Us, We're Experts* ([2001] 2002), Rampton and Stauber provide many examples of expert overconfidence. In addition, 'the illusions of validity and skill are supported by a powerful professional culture. We know that people maintain an unshakable faith in any proposition, however absurd, when they are sustained by a community of like-minded believers' (217). In many organisational cultures, including political parties, the medical system and corporations, it is often better for career advancement to be certain and wrong, than uncertain and right.

> Experts who acknowledge the full extent of their ignorance may expect to be replaced by more confident competitors, who are better able to gain the trust of clients. An unbiased appreciation of uncertainty is a cornerstone of rationality – but it is not what people and organisations want. (263)

In the previous chapter, we saw that the confident testimony of climate denial 'experts' competes successfully for public acceptance with the qualified certainty of the global scientific community. Slowly, the wisdom of crowds is gaining credibility against the opinions of experts (Surowiecki 2004; Tetlock 2005; Silver 2012).

Prospect Theory (Kahneman and Tversky 1979) provided an important early foundation for behavioural economics, since it challenged the classical economic principle of expected utility. Prospect theory states that most people do not simply consider the expected utility (usefulness) of their decisions, but are often motivated by other factors, such as a baseline reference point (where they are already); diminishing sensitivity to additional gains after a certain threshold is reached; and loss aversion, where 'losses loom larger than corresponding gains' (Kahneman 2011: 297). Because threats loom larger than opportunities in System 1 thinking, references to threats are more likely to gain attention and shape decisions about purchasing products or supporting political decisions. News gains our attention by focusing on threats and crises: 'The brain responds quickly even to purely symbolic threats. Emotionally loaded words quickly attract attention, and bad words (*war*, *crime*) attract attention faster than do happy words (*peace*, *love*)' (301). A perceived threat gains impact through an 'availability cascade' when vivid images are constantly repeated in media and conversations, thus becoming 'highly accessible'. 'The emotional arousal is associative, automatic, and uncontrolled, and it produces an impulse for protective action' (323). With more deliberate System 2 analysis, we can acknowledge the low probability of risk, but the visceral threat has already left its mark on us like a tattoo.

Terrorism and availability cascades

The availability heuristic predicts a tendency to overestimate the probability of events occurring that are more immediate in our experience and to underestimate events more remote from experience:

> In today's world, terrorists are the most significant practitioners of the art of inducing availability cascades. With a few horrible exceptions such as 9/11, the number of casualties from terror attacks is very small relative to other causes of death. Even in countries that have been targets of intensive terror campaigns, such as Israel, the weekly number of casualties almost never came close to the number of traffic deaths. The difference is in the availability of the two risks,

the ease and frequency with which they come to mind. (Kahneman 2011: 144)

Constant repetition and exposure in the news media makes the nebulous terrorism network seem more threatening than the numbers support. Every time people fly an airplane or cross a border, they are reminded of terrorism by the security apparatus they pass through. Lenin stated that 'the purpose of terrorism is to terrorise' (qtd in Silver 2012: 428) to suggest that body count has less impact on changing behaviour than fear. Terrorism is primarily psychological warfare – a form of propaganda aimed at undermining the security and motivation of enemies.

The Global Terrorism Database defines terrorist acts as 'the threatened or actual use of illegal force and violence by a non-state actor to attain a political, economic, religious, or social goal through fear, coercion, or intimidation'. Fear, coercion and intimidation are psychological goals and not primarily concerned with physical casualties. But the spectacle of terrorism broadcast in the media frightens international audiences. Richardson (2006) thinks that the fear of terrorism increases when we do not know what terrorists want. She defines terrorists as 'disaffected individuals' who live in 'enabling communities' with a 'legitimising ideology' (xxii). They are seeking 'revenge, renown, and reaction' – the three Rs of terrorism. '[T]errorists are neither crazy nor amoral but rather rationally seeking to achieve a set of objectives within self-imposed limits' (xxii). Richardson believes that most terrorists deliberate slowly about their objectives, while many nations respond quickly, with insufficient reflection on the actual threat. Silver recommends that those predicting terrorist incidents should look at the big picture by concentrating on the possibility of large-scale attacks with many casualties – spectacular terrorism. 'No Israeli politician would say outright that he tolerates small-scale terrorism, but that's essentially what the country does. It tolerates it because the alternative – having everyone terrorised by fear – is incapacitating and in line with the terrorists' goals' (2012: 441).

The difference between psychological anxiety about terrorism and the statistical probability of an attack on the scale of 9/11 or the London bombings of 2005 is a zone of uncertainty and speculation. 'Where our enemies will strike us is predictable', says Silver: 'it's where we least expect them to' (444). This gap of uncertainty provides fertile ground for propaganda by governments and enterprises responsible for security. In *The Power of Nightmares* (2004), British filmmaker

Adam Curtis argues that politicians in many countries use terrorism's threat to promote fear and win elections. Increasingly, as terrorism becomes a 'fact of life', their fearful messages are not addressed to conscious minds, but to their unconscious depths.

Subliminal seduction revisited

The human mind is designed to be both a scientist and an attorney, both a conscious seeker of objective truth and an unconscious, impassioned advocate for what we want to believe. Together these approaches vie to create our worldview. (Mlodinow 2012: 200)

Packard's *The Hidden Persuaders* (1957) and Key's *Subliminal Seduction* (1973) briefly inflamed the popular imagination with fears that politicians, advertisers and other compliance professionals use subliminal (unconscious) messages to influence audiences. Key's sensationalism likely contributed to a backlash against interest in subliminal techniques, though advances in neuroimaging have stimulated renewed interest. Leonard Mlodinow (2012) focuses on the layering of conscious and unconscious thinking to update notions of subliminal seduction and Freud's theories of the repressed unconscious.

In the new view, mental processes are thought to be unconscious because there are portions of the mind that are inaccessible to consciousness due to the architecture of the brain, rather than because they have been subject to motivational forces like repression. The inaccessibility of the new unconscious is not considered to be a defence mechanism, or unhealthy. It is considered normal. (Mlodinow 2012: 17)

Mlodinow revisits Lippmann's idea that stereotypes help us manage vast amounts of data in everyday experience. Stereotyping gains efficiency by categorising and polarising, transforming 'fuzzy differences and subtle nuances into clear-cut distinctions' (148). Stereotyping is a story we tell ourselves: 'Our subliminal minds take incomplete data, use context or other cues to complete the picture, make educated guesses, and produce a result that is sometimes accurate, sometimes not, but always convincing' (152).

We unconsciously absorb categories and stereotypes through literature, news, films, television, music, computer games and other forms of popular culture. In turn, these categories influence our attitudes and how we act in society. The Implicit Association Test hosted at Harvard (implicit.harvard.edu) reveals that unconscious, 'implicit' stereotyping influences our feelings about affiliation and kinship. For example, membership in groups influences sensitivity to group norms, a willingness to collaborate and liking. People prefer to associate with in-group members they do not like more than with out-group members they do like. In-group members are perceived as more varied and talented than those in out-groups.

Increasingly, cognitive research emphasises the storytelling habit of mind. Both memory and vision are reconstructions made on the fly as we need them. Mlodinow uses the word 'confabulation' to describe 'the replacement of a gap in one's memory by a falsification that one believes to be true' (190). Similarly, the brain fills gaps in vision to construct a seamless illusion of the scene in front of us. We tell stories about what we are feeling and thinking, stitching together content originating from a shared cultural repository. People are predictably overconfident about their own narratives, but only recognise that tendency in others (Ariely [2008] 2010; Tavris and Aronson 2013). One study found that doctors diagnosing pneumonia in their patients were 88 per cent confident in their assessment, but only correct 20 per cent of the time (Mlodinow 2012: 198). Tetlock (2005) researched the accuracy of 284 experts making 28,000 predictions over a twenty-year period. Experts at all levels of experience rarely perform better than random chance in making predictions, yet remain decidedly overconfident, despite their poor record. Remarkably, the higher the forecaster's profile – based on the number of interviews given – the lower the record of success. Overconfidence leads to cognitive errors.

Motivated reasoning justifies a favoured conclusion, while asserting its objectivity (Kunda 1990). While it is biased in its beliefs, motivated reasoning does not consciously misinterpret facts. Belief in the argument is not constructed objectively in the first place and is seldom altered by opposing arguments. People hold tightly to their beliefs about religion, morality or politics not because they are insincere or dishonest. Their beliefs are based on unconscious biases and stereotypes easily recognised in others, but inaccessible to themselves. Motivated reasoning fills gaps of uncertainty to create stories to live by. In the UK, for example, 'half the population believes in heaven, but only about a quarter believes in hell' (Mlodinow 2012: 206). 'We choose the facts that we want to believe', concludes Mlodinow. Our confabulations push 'us in the direction of survival, and even happiness' (218).

Exercise questions

1. Illustrate Cialdini's 'weapons of influence' with examples from your own experience.
2. Write or film a short dialogue in which an expressive person with some form of power tries to gain compliance from a rhetorical communicator, who is polite, but not easily convinced.
3. Group project: identify and discuss the significant risks facing your society today. Try to identify the biases used to prioritise these risks.
4. Take the Implicit Association Test (implicit.harvard.edu/implicit/) and discuss the results in class. What did you learn about your unconscious associations?
5. Describe a situation in which fast thinking (System 1) results in a predictable cognitive error that can be corrected by slow (System 2) thinking.
6. Describe a situation where you see an availability cascade operating.
7. What arguments are used by your government to justify its policies on terrorism and security? Identify any gaps or abstractions in their rationale for these policies.
8. Describe a social group you belong to. How is membership determined? Who is excluded and why? How do you express loyalty to this group? What are the consequences of dissenting from group norms?

Figure 8   'Won't you accept this invitation?' Photo: M. Soules, Freiberg, 1998.

6 Propaganda and War

Leading people to war

> Naturally, the common people don't want war, but after all, it is
> the leaders of a country who determine the policy, and it is always
> a simple matter to drag the people along whether it is a democracy,
> or a fascistic dictatorship, or a parliament, or a communist dictator-
> ship. Voice or no voice, the people can always be brought to do the
> bidding of the leaders. This is easy: All you have to do is tell them
> they are being attacked and denounce the pacifists for lack of pat-
> riotism and exposing the country to danger. It works the same in
> every country. (Hermann Göring, Nuremberg trials 1945–6, qtd in
> Boler 2008: 10)

In his testimony at the Nuremberg trials, Nazi commander Hermann
Göring frankly admitted that leading people to war is a psychological
effort founded in fear and advanced through patriotism and pride.
Philip Taylor's history of propaganda (1995) refers to 'munitions of
the mind' to emphasise the importance of psychological operations
(psyops), both before and during armed conflicts. Taylor defines
propaganda as a 'neutral' concept: 'a process for the sowing, germina-
tion and cultivation of ideas' (1995: 2). It is a 'deliberate attempt to
persuade people, by any available media, to think and then behave in
a manner desired by the source'. Propaganda is an 'additional instrument in the arsenal of power, a psychological instrument' (4) providing an alternative to destruction and killing. 'If war is essentially an
organised communication of violence, propaganda and psychological
warfare are essentially organised processes of persuasion. In wartime,
they attack a part of the body that other weapons cannot reach' (9).

In advance of the Iraq War in 2003, the US and the UK pressed
the United Nations Security Council to pass resolutions authoris-
ing armed intervention, despite lack of evidence for weapons of mass
destruction. US Secretary of State Colin Powell's speech (2003) will be

remembered as diplomatic deception with horrific consequences. At the time, anti-war demonstrations in cities around the globe expressed broad public resistance to military intervention, and the US-UK coalition needed to justify its plan to attack. The Iraq War did not result from failed diplomacy; instead, desire for war trumped dialogue for peace, and weapons of mass deception won the opening battle for mindshare.

It is always useful to ask who hopes to benefit from war. Leading people toward conflict requires propaganda, because the real motives of leaders must be hidden from the people who will only make sacrifices when moved by such motives as fear, pride and duty. Barbara Tuchman chronicles a history of military adventures from Troy to Vietnam, but her history does not celebrate the victors. Instead, she focuses on the 'march of folly', those military campaigns pursued by governments 'contrary to their own interests'. She asks: 'Why do holders of high office so often act contrary to the way reason points and enlightened self-interest suggests?' (1984: 4) In the case of Vietnam, Tuchman observes that the US suffered from illusions of omnipotence, false visions of nation-building and the absence of reflective thought on motives and consequences (374–6). These are not errors of military strategy as much as cognitive errors in the vein of those described in the previous chapter. What will history say about the leaders' motives for taking their nations to war in the Middle East?

Diplomacy as soft power

> More than four centuries ago, Niccolo Machiavelli advised princes in Italy that it was more important to be feared than to be loved. But in today's world, it is best to be both. Winning hearts and minds has always been important, but it is even more so in a global information age. (Nye 2004: 1)

Joseph Nye warns pro-military advocates that hard power is limited in its one-dimensional resort to threats and force. Instead, the road to power must operate along a spectrum of influence, from public diplomacy, to economic inducement (aid, bribes, sanctions), to military force. Public diplomacy, or soft power, secures its goals 'through attraction rather than coercion or payments' and derives 'from the attractiveness of the country's culture, political ideals, and policies' (x).

> The countries that are likely to be more attractive and gain soft power in the information age are those with multiple channels of communication that help to frame issues; whose dominant culture

and ideas are closer to prevailing global norms . . . and whose credibility is enhanced by their domestic and international values and policies. (31–2)

Soft power depends on a national reputation for credibility and legitimacy and requires decades of investment. Tuchman would consider it folly to squander soft power for immediate political gain.

Public diplomacy is 'inseparable' from propaganda (Ellul [1965] 1973: 13n). In her examination of the United States Information Agency (USIA), Nancy Snow uses the terms 'public diplomacy' and 'propaganda' interchangeably ([1998] 2010: 66). She describes USIA engagement in Cold War propaganda through educational exchanges, jazz tours, art exhibits and international visitor programmes with the view of advancing the 'core values of freedom, justice, free enterprise, and open dialogue' (64). Ideally, soft power leads by example, enacting its message of dialogue, understanding and cooperation through the gift of culture. During the late 1940s and 1950s, for example, the CIA secretly funded exhibitions of Abstract Expressionist paintings in Europe to promote US ideals of free expression and modernity (Cockcroft 1974). Throughout the 1950s and 60s, American and Soviet governments both sent ballet companies to Paris and London as part of their Cold War propaganda programmes (Prevots 1998).

Cultural diplomacy can become distorted in the real world of international politics. Snow's definition of propaganda suggests the source of this distortion: '. . . virtually all governments engage in propaganda, defined as those systematic and deliberate attempts to sway mass public opinion in favour of the objectives of the institutions (usually state or corporate) sending the propaganda message' ([1998] 2010: 67). The USIA became increasingly aligned with corporate interests, who used the rhetoric of liberty and freedom to promote capitalism. After the Soviet Union fractured in the 1990s, the USIA's mandate shifted toward free trade advocacy. It became 'a public relations instrument of corporate propaganda which "sells" America's story abroad by integrating business interests with cultural objectives' (86). USIA propaganda targeted educated elites and opinion leaders who would support expanded economic and cultural ties with the US.

Nye asserts that arrogance in international affairs obscures the communication of attractive cultural values. For example, the 'Shock and Awe' campaign in Iraq dramatically displayed US hard power, but resulted in a steep decline in US attractiveness, particularly in Islamic countries (35). Nye cites a 2003 BBC survey, where 65 per cent of respondents from eleven countries considered the US 'an arrogant superpower that poses a greater danger to world peace than North Korea does' (67). Over a decade later, WIN and Gallup International found that 24 per cent of respondents in sixty-five nations thought the US 'is the greatest threat to peace in the world today', far ahead of both Pakistan (8 per cent) and China (6 per cent) (Brown 2014). Van Buren thinks the 2003 invasion of Iraq was 'the single worst foreign policy decision in American history' (2013), both for destabilising the Middle East and eroding sympathy for American values. When hard power is highly visible, soft power loses credibility.

New communications technologies make it increasingly difficult for governments to control their message and frame the diplomatic agenda. Since public trust in governments is low (Pew Research 2013), the credibility vacuum will be filled by other players. Non-governmental actors, such as Médecins Sans Frontières, Human Rights Watch, Amnesty International and a myriad of aid organisations, circulate their own stories of global events, often contradicting official statements. Revelations by WikiLeaks unmasked the secretive face of international diplomacy and global surveillance. Social networking, mobile computing and portable cameras allow citizens to report their version of events. As we will see in a later chapter, investigative journalists are still able to interrupt the spin cycle to report credibly on world events.

Propaganda is, finally, a competition to see whose story triumphs in a crowded global theatre of influence. Edward R. Murrow – a respected broadcaster who became head of the USIA during the Kennedy administration – advised that 'truth is the best propaganda and lies are the worst. To be persuasive we must be believable; to be believable we must be credible; to be credible we must be truthful. It is as simple as that' (qtd in Snow [1998] 2010: 12). Simple in principle, but exceedingly difficult in nations where soft power suffers from a credibility disorder.

Imagined nations

. . . it is useful to remind ourselves that nations inspire love, and often profoundly self-sacrificing love. The cultural products of nationalism – poetry, prose fiction, music, plastic arts – show this love very clearly in thousands of different forms and styles. (Anderson [1983] 2006: 141)

The backbone of both diplomacy and war propaganda is the imaginary construct of nation. Benedict Anderson argues that the decline of nationalism predicted for contemporary globalisation is 'not remotely in sight. Indeed, nation-ness is the most universally legitimate value in the political life of our time' (3). He defines nation as 'an imagined political community', imagined because members of even the smallest nations do not know everyone, 'yet in the minds of each lives the image of their communion' (6). Political leaders conjure up this powerful imaginary construct to justify killing enemies and dying for one's country. War memorials and cenotaphs are constant reminders of the sacrifice needed to sustain the image of nation. Individual citizens do not all think and feel alike, but under the nation's flag their diverse voices resonate as one. Their nation is given a personality and a role to play.

Nationalism's growth in the eighteenth century was a secular response to fading religious conviction and stimulated by widespread print literacy, increased bureaucracy, capitalism and colonial rivalries. The eighteenth century saw the rise of newspapers and the novel, both essential to the imaginings of people seeking the 'confidence of community in anonymity which is the hallmark of modern nations' (Anderson [1983] 2006: 36). Bureaucracy brings organisation, planning, maps, museums, taxes, hierarchies and racism. Capitalism stimulated a restless need for resources, markets and human capital, increasing colonial rivalries.

Hardt and Negri ([2000] 2001) extend this idea of nation by arguing that empires are 'composed of a series of national and supranational organisms united under a single logic of rule' (xii). Nations become empires by building a network of allies: other nations, global corporations, financial institutions, transnational NGOs. Clandestine networks are equally important. In 2014, US Special Operations forces were deployed in over one hundred countries (Turse 2014). The previous year, the secret US 'black budget' was estimated to be US$52.6 billion by Washington Post researchers (Andrews and Lindeman 2013). Funding for covert action, surveillance, counter-intelligence, data collection and analysis increased dramatically after September 2001 and is building a network of influence 'united under a single logic of rule'.

In his complex and nuanced *The Invention of the Jewish People*, Israeli historian Shlomo Sand traces a particular instance of imagined community, which 'rests on the active myth of an eternal nation that must ultimately forgather in its ancestral land' ([2009] 2010: 22). Sand argues that the construct of a Jewish people and a Jewish state in Israel (Zionism) is a grand narrative that contributes to conflict in the Middle East. Hedges ([2002] 2003) confirms this view:

There is an emotional barrier, a desire not to tarnish the creation myth, which makes it difficult for many Israeli Jews, including some of the most liberal and progressive, to acknowledge the profound injustice the creation of the state of Israel meant for Palestinians. (47)

Matthew Cassel (2013), an American Jew working for Al Jazeera, says it is difficult to support Jewish culture without endorsing an exclusionary Jewish state.

Regrettably, the consequences of this invention are significant. In one of his 'messages to the world', Osama bin Laden described his view of the conflict:

> We swore that America could never dream of safety, until safety becomes a reality for us living in Palestine . . . So the situation is straightforward: America won't be able to leave this ordeal until it pulls out of the Arabian peninsula, and it ceases its meddling in Palestine, and throughout the Islamic world. (2005: 127)

Anderson and Sand both approach the idea of nation as a confabulation, a story constructed to bind chosen peoples into a community of shared origins and values. These narratives lead to conflict when diplomacy fails or adversaries such as bin Laden intervene with their own stories of nation-building. In 2014, the Russian ambassador to Britain defended Crimea's decision to join Russia instead of the Ukraine by saying that Crimea's people 'heard the British Government's argument in the Scotland referendum campaign that it is by far better to be part of a bigger and stable nation' (Freeman 2014: n.p.).

A gesture of imperial redemption by a desperate nation

In his grand narrative of a nation at war, Wade Davis (2011) describes the horrific conditions of trench warfare during WWI and the folly of military leaders, such as General Douglas Haig:

> In four years at the head of the largest army the British Empire had ever placed in the field, a force that would suffer 2,568,834 casualties in France and Belgium alone, Haig never once saw the front; nor did he visit the wounded. (29)

In 1916, Prime Minister Lloyd George observed that the 'terrible losses without appreciable results had spread a general sense of disillusionment and war weariness throughout the nation' (Lloyd George, qtd in Davis 2011: 94–5). When peace was declared in 1918, 'two million parents in Britain woke to the realisation that their sons were dead, even as the first of some three million veterans returned to a land socially and politically dominated by those who had not served' (93). Captain Herbert Read experienced the alienating barrier dividing those who fought and those who stayed behind: 'It was not that I despised them, I even envied them', said Read.

> But between us was a dark screen of horror and violation; the knowledge of the reality of war. Across that screen I could not communicate. Nor could any of my friends who had the same experience. We could only stand on one side, like exiles in a strange country. (Herbert Read, qtd in Davis 2011: 93)

Read describes the gap between imagining and experiencing the realities of war – a gap both created and obscured by propaganda and the construct of nation.

British propaganda was equally directed at the home front, the Axis powers and isolationist Americans. As head of the British Propaganda Bureau, John Buchan's mandate was to 'quell and counteract pacifist sentiment and maintain the fantasy that the war remained something honourable' (Davis 2011: 95). Buchan's allies in this task were influential British newspapers: 'Censorship [of actual casualties] left journalists at the mercy of their imaginations. Anything might be written as long as it vilified the enemy and propped up morale . . . The truth itself became a casualty' (95).

After the war, Buchan managed the media for the proposed assault on Mount Everest – a project abandoned when war was declared. The aristocratic George Mallory – a disillusioned survivor of trench warfare – was the most high profile of the mountaineers. After his tragic death in 1922 close to the summit of Everest, Mallory become the iconic embodiment of British courage following the Great War's tragic losses. The assault on Everest became a 'gesture of imperial redemption' by a 'desperate nation' (Davis 2011: 95). The non-combatant Buchan rationalised the Everest expedition by claiming:

> The war had called forth the finest qualities of human nature, and with the advent of peace there seemed the risk of the world slipping back into a dull materialism. To embark on something which had no material value was a vindication of the essential idealism of the human spirit. (95)

The Everest expeditions of the early 1920s were propaganda by other means – a role taken up by the Olympics and other spectacles of sport pitting nation against nation.

Talking about war

> Even with its destruction and carnage [war] can give us what we long
> for in life. It can give us purpose, meaning, a reason for living . . .
> Trivia dominates our conversations and increasingly our airwaves.
> And war is an enticing elixir. It gives us resolve, a cause. It allows us
> to be noble. (Hedges [2002] 2003: 3)

In times of war, a debate takes place about national identity, homeland,
duty, patriotism and spirituality. Those who dissent from the official
narrative are unpatriotic, failing in their duty, traitors. When nations
talk about war, they talk about who they are and who they are not.
Paradoxically, war divides nations and gives them meaning and purpose.

As Fussell (1989), Hedges (2002), Richler (2012) and many others
argue, however, the purpose and nobility of war are mostly illusions
for the home front crafted from corrupt language. When nations go
to war as a *crusade* or a *jihad*, they go to war 'not against a state but
against a phantom' (Hedges [2002] 2003: 4). War propaganda uses
false dichotomies, such as *good* versus *evil* or *civilisation* versus *bar-
barism*, to identify threats and prop up morale with national myths:
divine providence, defence of empire, manifest destiny, duty to allies,
responsibility to protect.

> That the myths are lies . . . is carefully hidden from public view.
> The tension between those who know combat, and thus know the
> public lie, and those who propagate the myth, usually ends with the
> mythmakers working to silence the witnesses of war. (Hedges [2002]
> 2003: 11)

Phillip Knightley (1975) chronicles tales of war correspondents who
faced a stark choice between acting as cheerleaders for the conflict
or risking censorship. Looking back at his reporting of WWII, the
Canadian Reuters correspondent Charles Lynch recalled:

> It's humiliating to look back at what we wrote during the war. It
> was crap . . . We were a propaganda arm of our governments. At
> the start the censors enforced that, but by the end we were our
> own censors. We were cheerleaders . . . It wasn't journalism at all.
> (Knightley 1975: 333)

When journalists reported atrocities, such as the 1968 My Lai massacre during the Vietnam War, they brought an awareness of civilian
deaths into American homes and undermined the national appetite for
war. It became

a war with no front line, no easily identifiable enemy, no simply explained cause, no clearly designated villain on whom to focus the nation's hate, no menace to the homeland, no need for general sacrifice, and, therefore, no nation-wide fervour of patriotism. (Knightley 1975: 381)

In response, US leaders used denial and distortion to create 'a torrent of questionable statistics, a bewildering range of euphemisms, and a vocabulary of specially created words that debased the English language . . . to get over its version of the war' (381–2). US newspapers refused to print reporter Martha Gellhorn's stories about orphaned children, refugees and other casualties of war. Her stories were eventually published by *The Guardian* in the UK, but she was never able to get a visa to return to Vietnam and thus concluded she must have been blacklisted at embassies around the world (390).

Noah Richler (2012) examines Canadian participation in Afghanistan and provides a case study of how nations talk about war. In Canada's case, after fifty years as a *peacekeeping* nation acting *multilaterally* through the United Nations, the government and opinion-makers of the day decided to refashion the national myth for a *warrior nation* prepared to sacrifice lives for a *just* cause, but more particularly to fulfil a *duty* to its allies: the US and the UK. 'Between September 2001 and 2006, the recalibration of Canadian ideas about the importance of the military and its role in foreign policy was massive' (47). Historic battles were resurrected to portray the bravery, skill and self-sacrifice of *our troops*. Recent experiences in Somalia, the Balkans and Rwanda had tarnished the Canadian peacekeeping reputation, and a new myth was promoted by the government, pro-military academics, military leaders and think tanks such as Historica Canada, all attacking Canada's peacekeeping role or rewriting history for a warrior nation. Peacekeeping was a *hollow façade*; *hard force* should replace *soft power*. Canada needed to be *punching above its weight* in the *global war on terror*. One journalist wrote of her desire 'to be among people who love soldiers, who do not go all timorous and squeamish at the very mention of the word "war"' (Blatchford, qtd in Richler 2012: 99).

Richler thinks of this collective revision as 'epic storytelling', where 'history bolsters the tribe' (137). The story cannot be confusing or ambiguous. General Rick Hillier said: 'It doesn't matter whether we are in Afghanistan or anywhere else in the world . . . They detest our freedoms. They detest our society. They detest our liberties. They want to break our society' (151). A profound overgeneralisation, Hillier's assertion brooks no contradiction, entertains no ambiguity, polarises public opinion and sends soldiers into combat. Richler describes the ritual 'ramp' ceremony, where dead soldiers are returned to their families, as 'an occasion of mourning but also a galvanising public relations opportunity' (163) for those promoting war.

Since WWI, euphemisms to describe conflict have softened the blow on the home front. From WWII came *precision bombing* to describe massive dumping of bombs onto civilian targets; and from Vietnam came *collateral damage* to describe civilian deaths and property destruction. Now, collateral damage is *proportional* when measured against military gains. *Friendly fire* mistakenly kills one's allies. In the Gulf Wars, *surgical strikes* updated *precision bombing*. Journalists who take the military's point of view are *embedded*. *Extraordinary rendition* sends terror suspects to secret locations where they are interrogated and tortured; prisoners are *detainees*, subjected to *enhanced interrogation* (torture), sometimes by *waterboarding* (threatened drowning). Popular uprisings are *insurgencies* if the intent is to suppress them, while *regime change* overthrows a government by force. *Mission creep* describes increased conflict, because the war is not going well. War is not organised murder; it is a *crusade*, a *jihad*.

Euphemisms are a form of censorship to safeguard public support, but they also create the moral distance necessary for justifying war. But

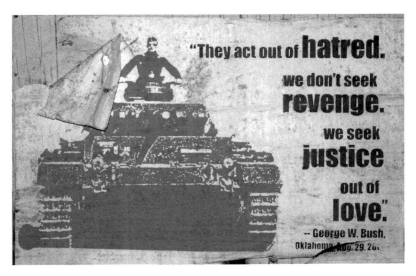

Figure 9 'They act out of hatred'. Photo: M. Soules, Toronto, 2009.

the euphemisms of conflict can be morally corrupting, both personally and for entire nations. Paul Fussell writes with some bitterness about WWII, a conflict he participated in:

> The damage the war visited upon bodies and buildings, planes and tanks and ships, is obvious. Less obvious is the damage it did to the intellect, discrimination, honesty, individuality, complexity, ambiguity, and irony, not to mention privacy and wit. For the past fifty years the Allied war has been sanitised and romanticised almost beyond recognition by the sentimental, the loony patriotic, the ignorant, and the bloodthirsty. ([1989] 1990: xi)

The euphemisms, myths and narratives of war propaganda are designed to bind nations together and boost their confidence for an epic struggle. Whether inspired by propaganda or true threats, fear provides the most direct route to public mobilisation. In 2002, as the UK debated joining the US in an attack against Saddam Hussein, Tony Blair asserted: 'He is a threat to his own people and to the region and, if allowed to develop these weapons [of mass destruction], a threat to us also' ('Timeline' 2009: n.p.). In this case, the threat was a noble lie.

Noble lies and pious fraud

In *The Republic*, Socrates relates a myth about the origin of social classes: god endowed future rulers with gold, their assistants with silver and farmers and other craftsmen with iron and brass. If people believe this myth, asserts Socrates, they will be more inclined to accept state rule and its hierarchical organisation. This tale traversed the centuries as a defence of the 'noble lie' – a myth necessary to justify state priorities and decision-making.

Plato's concept of the noble lie informs a political philosophy articulated by Leo Strauss in the 1940s. Strauss believed that noble lies are useful in propaganda campaigns. Enduring myths we see today include the polarised conflict between good and evil empires, the godly versus the godless, freedom lovers versus totalitarian tyrants – all useful for waging war. Shadia Drury (2007) notes that followers of Strauss continue to exert influence on US foreign policy. Straussians are politically conservative and consider progressives to be 'simpletons who could not grasp the harsh realities of political existence', which requires 'unquestioning belief, unswerving commitment and resolute devotion' (Drury 2007: n.p.).

The conservative think tank Project for a New American Century issued a 'Statement of Principles' in 1997 in a letter to the Clinton administration. Under the direction of William Kristol, the Statement was signed by prominent neo-conservatives, many of whom became senior advisors in the G. W. Bush administration. This group advocated a bold, militaristic and decisive approach to American foreign policy and regime change. With the Soviet Union no longer a world power, America had a unique opportunity to achieve global dominance. Specifically, the US should increase defence spending significantly; strengthen ties to democratic allies; challenge regimes hostile to US interests; promote political and economic freedom abroad; and preserve and extend an international order friendly to US security, prosperity and principles. They felt that political will at the time was lacking and predicted, in a subsequent report (Stockbauer 2003), that some horrendous catastrophe would be required to jolt the liberal public into combat readiness. The attacks of 11 September 2001 provided the necessary crisis and initiated a new era of political history.

Many neo-conservatives are atheists (as was Strauss himself), but they believe religion is a 'pious fraud', 'indispensable for cultivating deference to authority, undermining hedonism, instilling discipline and making people ready to die for their country. Religion was vital to prepare people for death, tragedy and horrors of war' (Drury 2007: n.p.). Irving Kristol defends this 'double standard of truth' by arguing:

Let men believe in the lies of religion since they cannot do without them, and let the handful of sages, who know the truth and can live with it, keep it among themselves. Men are then divided into the wise and the foolish, the philosophers and the common men, and atheism becomes a guarded esoteric doctrine – for if the illusions of religion were to be discredited, there is no telling with what madness men would be seized, with what uncontrollable anguish. (Kristol 1995, qtd in Drury 2007: n.p.)

In this view, manipulation of public opinion is noble, because the masses are incapable of perceiving the truth. They need wise leaders touched with gold to show that the state's political interests are aligned with universal principles of justice, goodness and truth. Following Strauss, these leaders believe deception is the norm in politics and war.

Tellingly, Adolf Hitler explored the philosophical ground for this approach to propaganda in his autobiographical manifesto *Mein Kampf*, first published in 1926. Hitler based his propaganda methods on a few basic propositions: appeal to emotions and avoid intellectual abstractions; use constant repetition of a few ideas using stereotypes; present one side of the argument; demonise enemies of the state; and identify one particular enemy for vilification (Jowett and O'Donnell 2006: 230).

Let the storm break loose: the propaganda of Joseph Goebbels

On 1 May 1945, after attending to the suicide and funeral of Hitler and his new wife Eva Braun, Joseph Goebbels and his wife Magda killed their six young children, before taking their own lives in the Führer's bunker. British, American and Russian troops were converging on Berlin, and much of Germany was bombed-out ruins. In a final letter to his stepson, written on 28 April, Goebbels made a prediction and offered his version of the noble lie:

> One day the lies will crumble away of themselves and truth will triumph once more. That will be the moment when we shall tower over all, clean and spotless, as we have always striven to be and believed ourselves to be. (Goebbels 1978: 330)

As Hitler's Minister of Propaganda from 1933 to 1945, Goebbels excelled at censorship and tight media control. In his diaries, he congratulates himself on his ability to play like a conductor on the German people's emotions. He was considered a radical in the party, both an opportunist and a skilful administrator. His public eloquence and passion betrayed an 'inner emptiness' filled by his loyalty to Hitler (Trevor-Roper 1978: xvii). Goebbels eventually took control of Germany's press, radio, film, theatre and arts, including its public ceremonies and rallies, and he used them to propagate the Third Reich's message of nation, race and triumph. In his role as 'master of the media . . . he saw to it that nothing was heard or seen on party platforms, on the radio, in the cinema, or in the press, except what he judged useful for immediate political purposes' (xv). Reports from the front were censored at the news agencies, before being released to newspaper editors and journalists, who were then free to write what they wanted.

Goebbels was an eloquent orator and master of theatrics, but had few beliefs of his own not borrowed from Hitler. His most powerful speeches are tainted with hatred and resentment against communists, Jews and the bourgeoisie. Goebbels' approach illustrates Ellul's comment that 'the aim of modern propaganda is no longer to modify ideas, but to provoke action' ([1965] 1973: 25). Goebbels distinguished between behaviour (*Haltung*) and morale (*Stimmung*) when provoking his audiences. Their morale might be low, but he expected their behaviour to remain steadfast. Ellul credits Goebbels with the rule that:

> the propagandist must find the optimum degree of tension and anxiety . . . Too much tension can produce panic, demoralisation, disorderly and impulsive action; too little tension does not push people to act; they remain complacent and seek to adapt themselves passively. (188)

Goebbels displayed the Reich's power through frequent rallies and demonstrations, including inflammatory rituals, such as book burning in May 1933 and the infamous *Kristallnacht* in November 1938 when Jewish shop windows in Berlin were 'spontaneously' smashed. Goebbels claimed there was little point trying to convert intellectuals. Instead, arguments must be kept simple and direct for the common people, who, he claimed, are moved by passion, not reason. Influenced by Le Bon, Goebbels thought of the crowd as 'brutal, violent, emotional, corrupt, and corruptible' (Taylor 1995: 241). Both Hitler and Goebbels – like Churchill, Roosevelt, Stalin and Mussolini – admired films and respected their power of persuasion, especially when woven seamlessly into the fabric of popular culture. Films did not require reading and could play directly on audience emotions.

Goebbels' preferred medium, however, was radio. Radio extends the human voice, turning it into a loudspeaker capable of communicating passion, justification and insults. The Nazis produced millions of 'people's receivers' (*Volksempfänger*), nicknamed *Goebbels-Schnauze* (Goebbels' snout) by the German public. At the Nuremberg trials, Albert Speer, Hitler's architect and Minister for Armaments and War Production, claimed that Hitler's dictatorship was unique in history, because it

> made the complete use of all technical means for domination of its own country. Through technical devices like the radio and loudspeaker, 80 million people were deprived of independent thought. It was thereby possible to subject them to the will of one man. (Snell 1959: 7)

In February 1943, Goebbels delivered an impassioned speech on the theme of total war. Russia was humiliating the German Army during the Battle of Stalingrad, and only a miracle could salvage victory. In ringing commandments, Goebbels called on the German people to work harder, increase production and make greater sacrifices not out of desperation, but as necessary for victory. His final words proved prophetic: 'Now, Nation, arise and let the storm break loose' (Taylor 1995: 247).

Why We Fight

> Now, Capra, I want to nail down with you a plan to make a series of documented, factual-information films – the first in our history – that will explain to our boys in the Army why we are fighting, and the principles for which we are fighting . . . (General George Marshall to Frank Capra, qtd in Capra 1971: 326)

Leni Riefenstahl's monumental Nazi propaganda film *Triumph of the Will* (1935) set a new benchmark for persuasive cinema and inspired Hollywood director Frank Capra when he made a series of propaganda films called *Why We Fight*. Capra described Riefenstahl's film as 'the ominous prelude of Hitler's holocaust of hate. Satan couldn't have devised a more blood-chilling super-spectacle' (Capra 1971: 328). After the US declared war in December 1941, the US Army and Office of War Information produced seven films to explain the conflict to military personnel. Eventually, the films were shown to a public reluctant to intervene in the European conflict, especially with the Soviets as allies.

The fifth film in the series – *The Battle of Russia* (1944) – uses archival footage from Russian and German films to explain the motives on both sides, with a voice-of-god narration driving the message home. Disney Studios contributed animations and graphics, and the War Department supervised military re-enactments to fill gaps in the archival footage.

All references to the attacking German forces are derogatory and scornful. They are misguided in their quest for domination; they are cruel; they kill civilians and rape women; they destroy the vibrant Russian culture and despoil its land. In stark contrast, the Soviets are culturally diverse, but united through their industrious spirit and love of the land. They are courageous, determined and resourceful. Their cause is a noble one. Their defence of Russia is strategic and clever and, ultimately, successful after great hardship and sacrifice. The Soviets swear revenge against their invaders and pledge 'blood for blood, death for death'. The film ends on a triumphant note by repeating that the legendary German invincibility has been shattered by Soviet allies.

Remarkably, the film does not mention socialism or communism and portrays Stalin as an effective and popular leader. Inconvenient facts – such as the Nazi-Soviet Pact (Molotov–Ribbentrop Agreement, 1939) and the Soviet invasion of Poland – are absent in *The Battle of Russia*. Stalin was so pleased with this film he had it screened in theatres across the nation. But when the war ended, the US Government rigorously suppressed *The Battle of Russia* well into the 1950s, due to its sympathetic depiction of the Soviet Union.

The Pentagon and Hollywood

War is hell, but for Hollywood it has been a Godsend, providing the perfect dramatic setting against which courageous heroes win the hearts and minds of the movie going public. (*Hollywood and the War Machine* 2012)

Capra's successful series shows that film had become the medium of choice for war propaganda, eclipsing public speeches and newspaper editorials due to its ability to combine image, sound, argument and emotion into one dramatic presentation. By WWII, film had become deeply embedded in popular culture, and propaganda films could effectively play on cinematic narrative conventions. War propaganda looked just like another action-packed adventure with villains and heroes.

Al Jazeera's 2012 documentary *Hollywood and the War Machine* examines cooperation between the Pentagon and Hollywood to make war films. The Pentagon's Film Liaison Unit wanted Hollywood's help with recruitment and personnel retention and to justify America's involvement in conflicts around the globe. The Pentagon provides advisors, locations and weaponry in exchange for positive portrayals of soldiers and their motivations. The 1986 film *Top Gun* (directed by Tony Scott) was so successful in glorifying military training that recruitment centres were set up in theatre lobbies.

Pentagon requirements – and threats to deny support – often result in films that are inaccurate historical records. Recent examples include *Pearl Harbor* (2000), *Black Hawk Down* (2001), *Rendition* (2007) and *The Hurt Locker* (2008), all of which justify military operations and the actions of soldiers. Hollywood producers and directors are faced with a stark decision: either lose independence in telling the story or lose funding and support. For example, a series of films critical of the Vietnam War (*Apocalypse Now* 1979; *Platoon* 1986; *Full Metal Jacket*

1987) were denied military support. *Charlie Wilson's War* (2007) was edited to remove any suggestion that the abrupt withdrawal of US support for the Mujahedeen after the Soviet departure left a power vacuum in Afghanistan that allowed Osama bin Laden and the Taliban to gain influence.

Hollywood and the War Machine concludes with a discussion of Kathryn Bigelow's Oscar-winning *The Hurt Locker* – a gripping story about soldiers who risk their lives to defuse explosive devices. Michael Moore calls the film 'war pornography' for its celebration of the addiction to war, without explaining motivations or consequences. The film does not try to explain why bombs are being set or why Iraqis are fighting against US 'invaders'. The Iraqis in the film are never personalised. The message that 'war is a drug' fails to comment meaningfully on the conflict's origins. In contrast, the documentary praises *The Green Zone* (2010) for its portrayal of Iraqis as 'real people'. Even though it was marketed as an action adventure, only four people were shown being killed in the film.

Why We Fight redux

In 2005, filmmaker Eugene Jarecki released a challenging rebuttal to the Capra series with his own version of *Why We Fight*. Quite unlike the rousing patriotism and militant sense of destiny conveyed by the original series, Jarecki's version begins with President Dwight Eisenhower's prophetic warning in his 'Farewell Address' to the American people in 1961. Eisenhower warns Americans of three related dangers: the military-industrial complex, research driven by profit and a lack of vision regarding resources: 'Only an alert and knowledgeable citizenry can compel the proper meshing of the huge industrial and military machinery of defence with our peaceful methods and goals, so that security and liberty may prosper together' (Eisenhower 1961: n.p.). Eisenhower's warning sets the stage for Jarecki's quietly outraged dissection of why America fights. His subjects tell their own version of the truth; there is no voice-of-god narration leading the audience to patriotic conclusions. Interviewees – both supportive and critical – comment on recent US conflicts, especially the Iraq War.

Senator John McCann and President George W. Bush reiterate claims that US military intervention promotes democracy and freedom. Wilton Sekser, a retired New York City police sergeant, tells an emotional story about losing his son in the World Trade Center collapse. Chalmers Johnson is a former CIA operative and self-confessed cold warrior, who was once dedicated to communism's defeat. He introduces the concept of 'blowback', defined as the unintended consequences of keeping covert operations hidden from the public. When retaliation comes, citizens cannot understand why. Joseph Cirincione notes that global public opinion was largely sympathetic to the US after 9/11, but that sympathy was squandered with the pre-emptive attack on Iraq in 2003.

The architects of the Project for a New American Century – Wolfowitz, Cheney, Rumsfeld, Perle, Kristol and others – advance their vision of the United States as the new Rome, the undisputed superpower with a mandate to extend its interests globally through the doctrine of pre-emptive military strikes. Perle asks: 'If you know someone is about to attack you, wouldn't you strike first?' Using archival footage, Jarecki reminds his audience that Eisenhower opposed dropping atomic bombs on Japan – which was attempting to surrender at the time – merely to warn Stalin. This was a pre-emptive strike policy in the making.

These narratives are intercut with the commentary of two stealth bomber pilots – identified only as 'Fuji' and 'Tooms' – who recall their mission to bomb Baghdad in the opening salvo of 'Shock and Awe'. These two pilots are instruments of impersonal destruction.

Jarecki revises Eisenhower's warning and identifies a military-industrial-congressional complex where lobbyists pressure politicians to approve military spending and provide jobs. Few in Congress are willing to cut defence funding and jeopardise electoral support. Congress failed to debate or explain the Iraq conflict, because representatives wanted military contracts. Jarecki also notes Dick Cheney's involvement in Halliburton and its subsidiary Kellogg Brown Root – corporations profiting from US military contracts during the Bush presidency. Though Cheney and his supporters deny any conflict of interest, one commentator observes that voters 'elected a government contractor as vice president'. When war becomes this profitable, the film argues, stakeholders will push for war when opportunities arise. The narrative of a nation fighting for freedom, democracy and peace has been a durable myth, despite a recent history of military intervention for financial gain and strategic influence.

The film's various narrative threads increasingly add evidence of the deception and betrayal necessary to engage in war. The patriot Wilton Sekzer finally concludes that his president has lied to him about the reasons for going to war. There was, apparently, no connection between 9/11 and the Iraq War. Stealth bombers drop their precision payload in Operation Iraqi Freedom, while subsequent medical records confirm that 90 per cent of bombing casualties are civilians. Jarecki's message of betrayal and indignation is palpable, while echoes of Eisenhower's repeated warning close the film. The people have not been vigilant.

Case study: the power of nightmares

In *The Power of Nightmares* (2004), British filmmaker Adam Curtis argues that the global war on terror is based on a myth providing politicians with their power to govern. His claim applies equally to conservative, militaristic Western and Islamic leaders who use fear to further their political goals. Both groups see liberal democracy as a decadent system, undermining traditional values and promoting hedonism. Each group promotes the story of a secret, global network of terror threatening the world. Instead of selling dreams for a better future, politicians with the darkest visions now hold sway.

Curtis traces the rise of contemporary Islamic fundamentalism from the teachings of Egyptian Sayyid Qutb – a founder of the Muslim Brotherhood and fierce critic of US influence in the Muslim world. In 1966, Qutb became a martyr when he was tried for treason against the Egyptian Government and executed. One of his disciples was the Egyptian physician Ayman al-Zawahiri. Following the assassination of Egyptian President Anwar Sadat in 1981, al-Zawahiri was arrested, imprisoned and tortured. During this experience, al-Zawahiri came to believe that terrorism for the fundamentalist Islamic cause was justified. He eventually became a mentor for Osama bin Laden and, in June 2011, was proclaimed leader of al-Qaeda, following bin Laden's assassination in Pakistan ('Ayman al-Zawahiri' 2011).

Curtis compares the beliefs of Qutb and his followers with those of neo-conservative political philosopher Leo Strauss, who also believed that liberal America was decadent and contained the seeds of its own destruction. Like Bernays, Strauss thought political elites needed to foster necessary illusions to control a wayward populace. Mythic stories with clear values – such as the founding of the nation, the imposition of justice on a lawless frontier and the triumph of good over evil – provided direction for the masses, led by a vanguard of political elites.

Strauss inspired neo-conservatives to promote their vision of America as engaged in a life-and-death battle against evil. Rumsfeld, Wolfowitz and Cheney – all highly placed in the Ford administration – manufactured evidence in the 1970s to convince Americans that the

USSR was arming itself with secret weapons. America was in danger of immanent attack. The Committee on the Present Danger produced and promoted the propaganda film *The Price of Peace and Freedom* (1976). With their Christian allies, neo-conservatives set out to reform American values through 'culture wars' (Hunter 1991), remarkably similar in intent to Islamic fundamentalism: remove moral relativism and replace it with moral certainty; tell a 'noble lie' to promote social order.

With the fall of the USSR in 1989, the US needed a new threat to replace the evils of communism. When al-Zawahiri and bin Laden orchestrated bombings of US embassies in Tanzania and Kenya, the US found its new enemy. US prosecutors invented the secretive al-Qaeda network, dedicated to waging global jihad on America and its allies. In fact, al-Qaeda did not exist as an organised terror network at the time, but was a loose-knit, decentralised, largely ad hoc collection of people with a common animosity towards the US. After 9/11, Britain joined in the hunt for bin Laden, but also found no evidence of terrorist strongholds. Following the London transit bombings in 2005, a government inquiry determined that the terrorists had no affiliation with al-Qaeda and had acted independently (Townsend 2006). However, the bombings provided an opportunity for Blair and his US allies to make a compelling argument for a global Islamic network. The battle of good and evil would be epic, of Biblical proportions.

A new political strategy called the 'precautionary principle' was borrowed from the environmental movement. Environmentalists had argued that governments could not wait for conclusive evidence of global warming; they had to anticipate the worst case scenario. Politicians adopted this precautionary principle to justify the surveillance and imprisonment of people not for what they had done, but for what they might do in the future. This principle set the stage for the 'dirty wars' of torture, rendition, extra-judicial murders, special ops and drone attacks. 'The war on terror had become a self-fulfilling prophecy' (Scahill 2013: 521).

Curtis concludes that politicians with the darkest vision of threats to national security are awarded the most power and influence. Those who once promised visions of a better future now promise to protect us from terror, no matter the cost.

Exercise questions

1. Describe your country as an 'imagined nation'. What myths, beliefs and values bind the nation together? What forces threaten its survival?
2. Group project: you belong to an advisory group whose task is to make recommendations for improving the global reputation of your country, its 'soft power'. Research the characteristics and reputation of your country using a variety of sources; identify and prioritise your recommendations; and consider how best to advance your agenda in the international media.
3. Compare two military conflicts in recent decades: one that you feel was justified, and one that was not. Under what circumstances is military conflict justified?
4. Describe the language used to report a conflict from at least two sources with divergent ideological perspectives.
5. Illustrate the concept of the noble lie with current examples.
6. Discuss the treatment of conflict and war in a recent film. What explanations are given for the conflict's origins? What values are at stake? If the film is based on actual events, compare it with the historical record.
7. Write a 600-word human interest story on 'the costs of war' for a national newspaper.
8. You have been invited to give a ten-minute panel presentation on the theme of 'conflict, propaganda and new media'. What would you say? If possible, have someone film your presentation.

Figure 10   'Tired of men. I want God'. Photo: M. Soules, San Francisco, 1991. Between reality and perception lies room for argument.

7 Toward a Rhetoric of Film

Moving images moving the world

> If we could tell a film, then why make a film?
> (*This Is Not A Film* 2011)

Since the mid-nineteenth century, global culture has produced a flood of images through photography, print, film, television, digital video, the internet and mobile computing. Frames and screens are everywhere. Digital networks and storage media have accelerated image production and distribution and shifted the balance of production toward 'amateurs'. Manovich says in *The Language of New Media* (2001) that visual culture is progressively replacing print culture; increasingly, messages are delivered as 'audiovisual moving image sequences, rather than as text'. As people become more conversant with computers and screen culture, they come to 'favour cinematic language over the language of print' (78). Manovich identifies film as a direct influence on emerging computer-based culture, and in this chapter we will follow his lead by seeking out the protocols and rhetorics of moving images to see what makes them persuasive.

The ability to distribute still images digitally, to display them online in repositories of image banks, was soon followed by the production and distribution of digital video as bandwidth increased. It is commonplace today for individuals to shoot digital video with a cellphone and upload it to the internet anywhere within range of a cellular tower or satellite uplink. The convergence of cellular telephony, digital video compression, database storage and internet distribution profoundly realigns access to perception management opportunities. Online news and entertainment sites seamlessly embed video streams into stories; advertisers entice the eye away from surrounding text with moving images; and people around the world broadcast everything, from amateur pornography to reports on political or environmental disasters.

Cizek and Wintonick's 2003 documentary *Seeing is Believing* argues that the digital camcorder reconfigured electronic news gathering (ENG) and armed citizen journalists and activists with tools to film their stories. The non-profit Witness.org gives cameras to activists who want to bring attention to human rights abuses. In *Burma VJ: Reporting from a Closed Country*, Anders Østergaard used smuggled footage and dramatisations to document events occurring in 2007 inside Burma, where reporters were banned. Undercover video journalists with camcorders risk jail and torture to smuggle video reports out of the country, where they are then offered to international media organisations and broadcast back to Burma via satellite.

Jafar Panahi, an Iranian film director under house arrest for making 'propaganda against the regime', was banned from making films for twenty years. In the confines of his apartment, with a Persian carpet as his stage, Panahi made his 'non-film' by filming himself with an iPhone and with the assistance of Mojtaba Mirtahmasb recording on digital video. *This is Not A Film* (2011) was smuggled out of the country on a flash drive hidden inside a cake and went on to become a critical success. The technology and aesthetics of the moving image are changing, but the tension between representation and actuality in film remains as contentious as ever.

The noise of amateurism

The Zapruder footage of JFK's assassination illustrates the persuasive authenticity of the 'noise of amateurism' (Chanan 2000: n.p.). The one-minute clip clearly shows President Kennedy being shot from the front and thus contradicts the Warren Commission findings. Though 'shaky and poorly framed', Zapruder's amateur video footage is the 'principle visual material evidence of the event' (Chanan 2000: n.p.). The culture-shaping news stories of the past decade – terrorist attacks in New York, London and Madrid; hurricanes and tsunamis; populist revolutions and civil wars – are documented by people on the scene with the ability to record events as they happen and upload results within minutes. The use of amateur video is increasingly familiar on mainstream news broadcasts, as local eyewitnesses are often the first to experience breaking stories. This trend is partly driven by twenty-four hour news cycles and reduced budgets for news offices, but ubiquitous video cameras and digital distribution networks are the enabling technologies.

YouTube, Vimeo and other aggregators have become significant repositories of digital video, amateur or otherwise, making them new sources of information and propaganda. McChesney (2013) notes the impressive growth of YouTube as a medium for distributing video:

> By 2012 the amount of video being uploaded to YouTube had *doubled* since 2010, to the equivalent of 180,000 feature-length movies per week. Put another way, in less than a week, YouTube generates more content than all the films and television programs Hollywood has produced in its entire history. (2013: 1)

The persuasive potential is enormous. When it can be found, some of that video will be newsworthy. In 2013, Syrian rebels used cameras to tell their version of the civil war to dispute government versions, which were broadcast through state-controlled media and by the online Syrian Electronic Army ('Syria's Media War' 2013).

While not generally spotlighted in discussions of the moving image, surveillance video and remote sensing as used in military drones or exploration devices are quickly expanding notions of documentary evidence (Lyons 2007; Ball et al. 2012). As with amateur video, surveillance video increasingly appears in news broadcasts, where its grainy, low-resolution images have come to signify the direct recording of actual events. WikiLeaks' remarkable *Collateral Murder* (2010) is 'a classified US military video . . . shot from an Apache helicopter gun-sight' and records twelve people being killed, including two journalists, and leaving two children wounded in a Baghdad suburb (www.collateralmurder.com/). Google Earth and Google Street View literally place global surveillance on civilian computers, while Google Earth Pro adds geographic information system (GIS) data to provide a tool powerful enough for risk assessment and homeland security. In the UK – a global leader in public surveillance using closed circuit television (CCTV) systems – an estimated 1.85 million cameras are watching public and private spaces (Lewis 2011). At the same time, squadrons of cellphone camera users are making short movies of public demonstrations, political rallies, police activities, suicide bombings and cultural events. They are transforming the look and feel of the mediasphere many of us operate in.

Significantly, these innovations are not limited to the developed world. Quite the contrary: the 'asymmetry of power of the surveillance gaze' is the newest colonising eye (European Parliament 2009: 18). Millions of manufactured eyes are watching the planet, with profound implications for security, secrecy, privacy, control and public expression. Under the guise of protecting security and property, governments and corporations are watching the public, and the electronic citizen armies are watching back in a process called 'sousveillance' (Mann et al. 2003). Many amateur filmmakers want their images and films to make a difference. They are the new documentarians and propagandists wanting to provide evidence, make an argument and move viewers to take action.

Rhetoric of film: identification and association

Cinematic rhetoric mainly aims to entice and persuade and is only secondarily concerned with evidence, clarity and truth: '[B]efore anything, it is intended to *move* us by means of verbal skill, bodily eloquence, spectacle, colour, performance, and all the well-known elements of cosmetics, stagecraft, and *mise en scène*' (Naremore 2000: n.p.). Naremore begins his search for the rhetoric of film with first principles: film rhetoric is theatrical, a performance to persuade, and needs to engage audience emotions using all the tools of stagecraft. He echoes Aristotle's analysis of Greek tragedy in its emphasis on 'arousing the passions' through a process of identification and empathy, then using catharsis to purge spectators of unruly emotions.

Identification is a significant rhetorical strategy (Perez 2000) and is often accomplished through association. When workers are filmed walking through city streets on their way home, as in Vertov's *Man with a Movie Camera* (1929), viewers will identify them with urban rather than rural living. Identification becomes ideological when the filmmaker wants viewers to think of these urban workers as more sophisticated than their rural counterparts. In *The Birth of a Nation* (1915), director D. W. Griffith suggests that the love between a southern white man and northern white woman is natural by associating them with nature and polite society. His strategy becomes ideological in a film that dramatises the evils of miscegenation, the mixing of racial groups. This relationship between white people is the way it should be, the film asserts, even though they are on opposite sides of the Civil War. The identification is a rhetorical feint, because, in another time and place, the naturalness of their love would not be taken for granted.

Perez acknowledges his debt to Kenneth Burke's *A Rhetoric of Motives*, where Burke argues, in Perez's words, that 'persuasion rests on identification: a speaker persuades an audience by identifying his cause with their interests, by identifying himself with something that appeals to them, that has their approval' (Perez 2000: n.p.). In this sense, identification takes advantage of anchors. In film, identification is especially influenced by visual associations and juxtapositions and explains the importance of montage, where series of shots are edited into a sequence to concentrate time, space and narrative flow.

When viewing a film with ideological messages, discerning viewers pay attention to ways the film leads them to identify with characters and what those characters are associated with. Identification with characters often hinges on a distinction between alignment and allegiance. Alignment merely places spectators 'in relation to characters', while allegiance depends on 'the moral and ideological evaluation of characters' (Smith 1994: 41). We may understand the actions and motivations of characters (alignment), but we may not necessarily agree with them. 'Allegiance means approval, taking sides with the character in a moral sense, rooting for the hero against the villain' (Perez 2000: n.p.).

Viewing a documentary film, we can follow the argument and understand it, but we may not feel an allegiance to it and thus reserve our moral approval. In *The Fog of War* (2003), filmmaker Errol Morris asks us to align ourselves with his controversial subject, Robert McNamara, but the film also suggests that withholding our allegiance for moral reasons is justified. As US Secretary of Defense during the Vietnam War, McNamara was required to make difficult ethical decisions, resulting in heavy military and civilian casualties. Morris devised the Interrotron (interview + terror) – a type of teleprompter, where a live video feed of Morris as interviewer replaces the usual text to allow McNamara to make eye contact with his audience. 'We all know when someone makes eye contact with us. It is a moment of drama . . . And yet, it is lost in standard interviews on film' (Morris 2004: n.p.). This innovation allows Morris to adjust his subject's credibility – and viewers' empathy – by capturing these dramatic moments.

One distinction between fiction and documentary films is the general taboo in fiction against actors addressing the camera directly, thus preserving the illusion of the camera as unseen witness. The fourth wall convention in dramatic realism achieves a similar purpose of isolating the performance in its own stage space, separate from an audience cast as voyeurs. The fourth wall convention heightens the illusion of psychological realism and encourages scopophilia – the (guilty) pleasure of looking. Mulvey's 'Visual Pleasure and Narrative Cinema' (1975) remains an important manifesto on the camera's control of audience gaze and gender differences in cinematic viewing. By controlling the viewer's gaze, the camera and its director also control what reality looks like on the screen and how it compares to the real thing. In documentary, there is no such prohibition, because direct address to the camera communicates 'a sense of actuality, of testimony, and of the presence of the camera as a witness in the same space as the events unfolding' (Chanan 2000: n.p.).

Representation and reality

Fiction or narrative films are a staple of popular culture from Hollywood to Bollywood, and their stories range from psychological realism to science fiction, fantasy and animation. In contrast, documentaries claim to show something happening to non-actors in front of the camera: 'The genre of documentary always has two crucial elements that are in tension: representation and reality. Their makers manipulate and distort reality like all filmmakers but they still make a claim for making a truthful representation of reality' (Aufderheide 2007: 9). Barnouw ([1974] 1993) says the central concern of documentary is 'its ability to open our eyes to worlds available to us, but for one reason or another, not perceived' (3). Like novels, fiction films can make legitimate claims to represent reality, and the distinction between the two genres remains as contested as ever. *The Hurt Locker* (2008) and *Zero Dark Thirty* (2012) are both based in reality, but their commitment to factuality is not as sustained and convincing as *The War Tapes* (2006), *Restrepo* (2010) or *The Dirty Wars* (2013). Documentaries have to present two kinds of evidence: one validates the film's argument and the other claims credibility based on the filmmaking process. Documentary depends on the 'disposition to believe', while fiction requires the 'suspension of disbelief', concludes Chanan (2000: n.p.).

Documentary films use expository, narrative or poetic rhetorics (Steven 1993). Exposition cites examples, rejects counter-arguments, uses experts and authorities, presents personal testimony and uses reason and emotion to build an argument. The narrative 'crisis structure' follows an extraordinary event, such as a political campaign (*Primary* 1960), a day-in-the-life (*Deadly Currents* 1991), a concert (*Stop Making Sense* 1984), a demonstration (*This is What Democracy Looks Like* 2000) or a political crisis (*Kanehsatake: 270 Years of Resistance* 1993). Finally, some documentaries work through poetic associations, rather than exposition or narrative. In *Suite Habana* (2003), the camera peers into the lives of ten ordinary Cubans throughout their day, from early morning to late at night, and finally comes to rest at day's end. There is no exposition, no compelling narrative; instead, audiences are held in thrall by the melancholy poetry, sounds and rhythms of everyday life in Havana. *Suite Habana* is a unique example of the city symphony film, and Cuban audiences praised it as realistic, convincing and moving ('Raw Side of Havana Life' 2003).

From mimesis to the cut

> All things are beautiful, as long as you've got them in the right order.
> (*Grierson* 1973)

In the *Poetics* (c. 335 BCE), Aristotle identified the formal elements of drama as plot, character, language, theme, music and spectacle. He arranged these elements in a hierarchy of importance, with plot being most significant and spectacle the least. Aristotle was suspicious of spectacle's ability to move emotions by sheer display – as in today's action films – instead of through plot and character. Ultimately, drama's power depends less on plot and character than on mimesis – the ability to imitate life convincingly. Debates about mimesis – including such variations as verisimilitude, realism and naturalism – have a complex history in Western culture, beginning with Plato and continuing through Auerbach (1946), Taussig (1993) and Bhabha (1994). The neuroscientist Donald Merlin (1991) argues that mimesis was the first step in the evolution of human culture and led to expanded cognitive capacity in the neocortex. Ramachandran ([2011] 2012) advances this insight by arguing that language and imitation are the 'core mediums' for humans to participate in culture. Humans can construct 'a mental model of another person's complex thoughts and intentions' (118), allowing them to anticipate and possibly manipulate the actions of others. The ability to imitate life convincingly is a powerful tool, and few media are as adept at mimesis as drama and film.

Persuasive effects in film are communicated through multiple sensory channels acting in concert – an insight central to any analysis of film rhetoric. Editing weaves all those sensory inputs into a gestalt, an organised whole perceived as more than the sum of its parts. Walter Murch, the editor of *Apocalypse Now* and *The English Patient* among many other films, says that the art of editing depends on the 'cut' (or 'join' in the UK), a 'sudden disruption of reality' ([1995] 2001: 16). The cut, which defines most filmic storytelling, introduces discontinuity into what is continuous in our everyday visual experience and potentially interferes with our perception of lifelikeness. The cut radically transforms visual experience and gives film its singular power: discontinuity allows editors to 'choose the best camera angle for each emotion and story point', which can then be edited 'together for a cumulatively greater impact' (8). Murch advises editors to 'produce the greatest effect on the viewer's mind by the least number of things on screen . . . because suggestion is always more effective than exposition'. The more detail, 'the more you encourage the audience to become spectators rather than participants' (15). Participants are more likely to engage reflectively and respond with empathy.

Editors make decisions about when to cut and what to join, and Murch makes his decisions based on the 'rule of six':

1. *Emotion*: stays 'true to the emotion of the moment';
2. *Story*: 'advances the story';
3. *Rhythm*: 'occurs at the moment that is rhythmically interesting';
4. *Eye-trace*: follows 'audience's focus of interest within the frame';
5. *Two-dimensional plane on screen*: adjusts for transposing three dimensions onto two ('planarity'); and
6. *Three-dimensional space of action*: 'respects the three-dimensional continuity of the actual space'. ([1995] 2001: 18)

As an editor, Murch tries to preserve all six criteria whenever possible, but if the ideal solution cannot be found, he recommends selecting from the top down: 'Emotion, at the top of the list, is the thing that you should try to preserve at all costs' (18). Murch confirms that moving emotions is the primary persuasive force of film.

Murch's 'rule of six' revises Aristotle's elements of drama to accommodate the discontinuity of cinematic storytelling. In film, engaging audience emotions occurs in the 'blink of an eye', not through the continuous *mise en scène* (everything placed on stage: set design, lighting, costumes, actors, make-up). What the filmic cut sacrifices in verisimilitude, it gains back in compression, emotion and impact. Significantly, Ondaatje concludes that: 'much of the real editorial influence on the audience . . . is subliminal' (2002: xvi).

Frames, motion and control

The illusion of realism in film derives from another source besides imitation – the camera itself. As noted earlier, Alberti's invention of perspective uses geometry to create the illusion of three dimensions on a two-dimensional surface and to enclose realistic images within a bounding frame. The ability to portray the world realistically within a frame is a triumph of visual convention and was subsequently passed on to photography when science, exploration and industrial practises created a strong demand for visual evidence. The photographic studies of Muybridge in the 1870s and his invention of the zoopraxiscope – a device for displaying pictures in motion – advanced the camera's use for scientific inquiry. In France, Marey's pioneering work in photography contributed to studies in cardiology, aviation, instrumentation and cinematography. Marey's chronophotographic gun recorded the movement of animals and humans and contributed to cinematography's invention.

The image of reality enclosed in a frame and presented as evidence is a fundamental protocol of film and is always a translation, a representation striving for mimetic credibility. The framing of a film and the framing of an argument are related: some elements are included, some excluded. Inside the frame, film distinguishes itself by capturing movement. While the photographic series of Muybridge and Marey were studies in motion, the Lumière brothers are credited with the first projected display of a film to a public audience in December 1895. Their *actualité*, *Arrival of a Train at La Ciotat*, had a profound impact on audiences by creating a powerful illusion of movement that literally impacted spectators' bodies. Today, their footage appears mundane to audiences trained in action film conventions and special effects, but when first shown, the illusion of the locomotive approaching the station and passing through the frame's boundary startled and amazed audiences. This 'discomposition of space' (Littau 2005: 50) violated familiar conventions of painting and photography and imposed a 'strain on the nerves' or caused 'blood fever' (57). Perhaps contemporary audiences experience a similar spatial reorientation while viewing 3D films, such as *Avatar* (2009) and *The Life of Pi* (2012) or the monumental IMAX production of *Everest* (1998). Alfred Hitchcock's *Vertigo* (1958) plays with the disorientation of peering into the abyss – both physical and symbolic – a sensation enhanced by his innovative use of the dolly zoom to accentuate the sensation of precipitous falling.

Audiences of the first Lumière films associated their society with increasing speed and destabilising complexity, an age of proliferating images and sensual bombardment symptomatic of modernity (Littau 2005). Marinetti's 1909 *Futurist Manifesto* rejected the past and celebrated speed, violence, machinery and industry in his definition of an extreme modernist aesthetic. Kracauer ([1926] 1987) observes that in early cinema, 'the stimulation of the senses succeed each other with such rapidity that there is no room left for even the slightest contemplation to squeeze in between them' (94). The production line of still images moving fast enough to create the illusion of movement stimulates the body and emotions well in advance of contemplation and analysis – a criticism often levelled at television (McLuhan 1964; Mander 1978; Postman 1985).

As mediums, film and television are demanding on the brain's processing resources. Film's illusion of motion is created by frame rate (typically twenty-four to thirty frames per second), with a brief interval of blackness between each frame. With analogue television, each complete image is constructed of scan lines generated in two separate passes to 'write' the image on the cathode screen (and the retina of the viewer). For digital television, the screen is refreshed sixty times a second. The illusion of motion depends on the delay or latency of cognitive processing – the brain cannot process individual images faster than the projection rate and thus perceives continuous movement. Neuroimaging research by Hasson and his colleagues (2008) confirms that viewers process film stimuli in similar ways, and this similarity increases with edited and directed film. Filmmakers who construct a film with a carefully planned sequence of images increase their control over spectator response, making film a premier instrument of persuasion.

Action, narrative, ideology

> I found *The Birth of a Nation* to be offensive, poisonous propaganda – and this was a comfort. But I also found it fascinating, gripping and the work of a master. And this was more worrying. Almost a century on, Griffith's rabid, racist tour-de-force has lost none of its voltage . . . It is the original sin that sired a century of dreams. (Brooks 2013: n.p.)

D. W. Griffith's *The Birth of a Nation* (1915) is an epic narrative with didactic moral purpose, making it an early model for propaganda classics, such as *Battleship Potemkin* (1925) and *Triumph of the Will* (1935). Set during the American Civil War and Reconstruction, the narrative follows two upper-class families – the Stonemasons from the north and the Camerons from the south – whose lives are transformed by war and racial politics. Juxtaposing two main narrative threads requires constant intercutting and, when combined with dramatic action and battle scenes, the film delivers an excess of motion and discontinuity for the senses to absorb. Rational reflection is difficult in the emotional heat of the moment, perhaps the real theme of this film. Visually and narratively, this is a complex and busy film of action and reaction.

Griffith based his production on two novels written by Reverend Thomas Dixon, who was sympathetic to the Ku Klux Klan – a white supremacist movement. Stark racial stereotypes collide with the narrative of family fortunes, civil war and political turmoil. Griffith portrays mulattos in a harsh light, since they signify the threat of racial interbreeding to white privilege in the emerging nation. Despite the reality that the 'curious institution' of slavery silently encouraged interbreeding between white men and black women to create mixed race offspring, Griffith treats the Klan as a noble organisation of patriots dedicated to racial purity. When a black man – played by a white actor in blackface – pursues a young white woman until she hurls herself over a cliff to escape his lust, an archetype of racial transgression was etched into American consciousness. The film inflamed audiences, incited demonstrations and closed theatres. It also stimulated a resurgence of membership in the Ku Klux Klan, which used the film for recruitment.

As propaganda, the film treads ambiguously between history and fiction. While rightfully acknowledged for its technical innovations, the combination of powerful narrative, symbolic resonance and moral imperatives anticipates that other propaganda classic, Riefenstahl's *Triumph of the Will*. Both films claim to document actual events, but ideology and master narratives deflect reality towards idealism and abstraction. 'Griffith used historical references to legitimise the artistic decision to represent blackness as bestial or servile and whiteness as superior yet under threat' (Bernardi 2005: 87). *The Birth of a Nation* and films like it illustrate that compelling storytelling and innovative technique can obscure the boundaries between art and propaganda. Historical accuracy is vulnerable to ideology's push and pull, especially when reassuring lifelikeness distorts reality.

Quentin Tarantino's controversial 2012 film *Django Unchained*, set two years before the outbreak of the Civil War, can be viewed as a dialogic response to *The Birth of a Nation*. The eponymous Django is a slave, who has been given his freedom by a German posing as an itinerant dentist, and the two characters enter into a successful partnership as bounty hunters. After Django and Dr King Schultz have raised enough money from collecting bounties, they go in search of Django's wife, now owned by a sadistic Mississippi slave trader and plantation owner.

A highly referential film in the Tarantino style, *Django Unchained* is influenced by spaghetti westerns (including a 1966 Italian film called *Django*), martial arts and revenge films, cartoons and first-person shooter computer games. It is an unapologetic action film with a dark sense of humour. Tarantino mainly portrays his black characters as individual and human in their persecution, while his white characters, again with a few notable exceptions including Schultz, are uncouth, cruel and clannish in their roles as oppressors. The film choreographs violence artfully, and Django executes revenge with no apparent qualms of conscience. Like *The Birth of a Nation*, *Django Unchained* has a compelling story to tell; Tarantino won an Oscar for best screenplay. It is replete with action sequences enhanced by cinematic technique, and it makes a powerful argument about racism, power and destiny. But is it propaganda?

Documentary: film on a mission

The term 'documentary' was first used by the influential Scottish producer and filmmaker John Grierson to describe Robert Flaherty's 1926 film *Moana*. But the term equally applies to Flaherty's earlier and more famous *Nanook of the North* (1922). Grierson defined documentary film as the 'creative treatment of actuality' (Hardy 1966: 13) and argued that film should be used for social purposes, not for escapist fantasies on the Hollywood model. Grierson was a conservative political philosopher influenced by Lippmann's *Public Opinion* (Morris 1987). According to Lippmann, government should be managed by technocratic experts manufacturing consent behind the scenes, since the masses are irrational, acting on stereotypes and 'pictures in their heads'. For Grierson, communicating with this audience was a form of propaganda similar to the church's efforts to propagate the faith. Documentary makers should exercise 'directive statesmanship' (Morris 1987: n.p.) by acting in the state's best interests to balance the demands of selfish individuals. As chief architect of the National Film Board of Canada in 1939, Grierson decisively influenced Canada's wartime propaganda efforts, while continuing his mission to promote documentary film's potential to shape social policy.

For Grierson, communicating with the public was based on instinct and reason, 'giving a pattern of thought and feeling' to predispose and shape the 'mind of the citizen' (Morris 1987: n.p.). Borrowing from Trotsky's oft-cited metaphor about revolutionary art – 'Art . . . is not a mirror, but a hammer: it does not reflect, it shapes' (Trotsky [1925] 2005: 120) – Grierson thought of art as a transformative instrument serving the state:

> They tell us that art is a mirror – a mirror held up to nature. I think this is a false image . . . In a society like ours, art is not a mirror but a hammer. It is a weapon in our hands to see and say what is right and good and beautiful, and hammer it out as the mould and pattern of men's actions. (qtd in Morris 1987: n.p.)

Morris concludes that Grierson is 'an authoritarian with totalitarian tendencies'. While perhaps overstated, this assessment describes the documentary style often associated with Grierson: authoritative and omniscient voice-of-god narration, invariably by men; strong moral viewpoints followed by directive solutions; and an overarching emphasis on individual responsibility and sacrifice to the greater social good.

Aufderheide says 'no documentary is a transparent window onto reality', since 'all meaning-making is motivated' (2007: 77). She sensibly distinguishes between propaganda and other forms of documentary, based on their sponsors and the power they wield:

> Propaganda documentaries differ from other documentaries in their backers, who are agents of the state – the social institution that sets and enforces the rules of society, ultimately through force. Those backers control the message. Those differences ramify the significance of propaganda documentaries, since the portrayal of reality is backed by such enormous power. (77)

Based on this distinction, Grierson can legitimately be called a propagandist, because he produced films using state funding to promote government messages. The same can be claimed for Pare Lorentz and his work for the Roosevelt administration in the 1930s and during WWII or Joris Ivens and his documentaries produced for the Soviet Union, Canada and China. Ivens is best known for his anti-fascist documentary *The Spanish Earth* (1937), though it was funded by an ad hoc group of writers, including Ernest Hemingway. Despite its didactic narration written by Hemingway, and its obvious opposition to Franco's fascism, *The Spanish Earth* is an advocacy film, according to Aufderheide's definition, and not propaganda, based on its sources of funding.

Propaganda or not, documentary filmmaking involves a variable set of cinematic practices and traditions subject to audience reception and expectations. Many documentaries use dramatisations and graphic illustrations, but generally they make claims about reality using archival photographs and film, new footage filmed on location and the testimony of experts and eyewitnesses. Documentary filmmaking assumes that 'images provide evidence of a state of affairs that exists, or once existed, in the world outside the film' (Giannetti and Leach 1998: 317). *The Birth of a Nation* makes claims as evidence, but its revisionism and ideology are distorting lenses. As an historical record, it can usefully be compared to Ken Burns' television series *The Civil War* (1990). Burns uses archival photos, contemporary writing and newspaper articles and the 'Ken Burns effect' – panning the camera slowly across photographs to provide motion and the illusion of discovery. Burns signals his commitment to historical accuracy by using archival evidence to authenticate his narrative.

In addition to the costly issue of copyright management for archival images (Bernard 2005), documentary filmmakers face at least three challenges when collecting their raw footage and turning it into a non-fiction film: camera framing, the impact of filming on subjects and editing. As noted above, something is always excluded from the frame. Filmmakers make decisions about where to point their cameras and what to focus attention on – the problem of perspective or point of view. The act of filming will frequently have an impact on events being documented – notably, on subjects' behaviour. And, finally, the raw footage must be selected, arranged and edited according to creative decisions, involving aesthetics, biases, ideologies and anticipated audience reception. Since every documentary film is a construction with some degree of distortion, questions of authenticity and credibility are significant. This is the reason ethnographers and documentary makers often describe the process and context of their projects so carefully. A documentary's credibility often depends on the commentary surrounding it.

Ethnographic film swallows culture

> There is a widespread saying among American Indians, 'Traders stole our furs, settlers our lands, now missionaries want our souls'. I recently heard an Indian say this on TV. He was on guard against the missionaries; in the meantime he let the media capture & possess his spirit totally. (Carpenter 1972: 162)

Robert Flaherty's reputation as a documentary filmmaker derives mainly from significant technical innovations in *Nanook of the North*, a tale of survival featuring Inuit hunter Nanook and his family in the Canadian north. Flaherty stayed with his subjects for long periods, until they became more comfortable with the camera, and used long takes and deep focus to capture the sense of duration and space experienced by his subjects. He positioned these subjects realistically in a time and place they would have known first-hand. To keep audience interest, Flaherty emphasised action and movement over static images and constructed a story about the struggle for survival in a challenging environment. With a myriad of small decisions about camera placement, focus of attention and selection of details, Flaherty captured a sense of authenticity and eyewitness presence in his romantic treatment of the noble savage archetype.

Grierson criticised Flaherty for his tendency to organise his narratives around a heroic individual and to romanticise exotic cultures. Others have noted that Nanook's real name was Allakariallak, and his clothing in the film was not typical of the region (Geiger 2005: 126).

Claude Massot's *Nanook Revisited* (1988) reveals that the Inuit woman who plays Nanook's partner, Nyla, was Flaherty's mistress (Alia 2014; Rony 1996: 123). Further complicating its credibility, the film had commercial sponsors – French fur company Revillon Frères – with some stake in the fur trade's public image.

Rony (1996) says that *Nanook* is an 'ethnographic spectacle' typical of colonialism – with hints of voyeurism and cultural superiority – despite Flaherty's intent to preserve culture under threat. Flaherty defended the film's authenticity by claiming that Allakariallak died of starvation two years after filming, when, in fact, he died in his home, possibly of tuberculosis (Christopher 2005: 387–8). While documentary filmmakers must try to preserve the 'illusion of authenticity', 'Flaherty never promised absolute authenticity, and early audiences coming to his film were for the most part willing to overlook *Nanook*'s partial truths' (Geiger 2005: 135). Valerie Alia concludes fairly that: 'Flaherty's detractors have focused on *Nanook*'s failure to reproduce life literally, but its ability to convey the spirit and culture of Inuit must also be acknowledged' (1999: 19).

Documentaries merge evidence and storytelling, with raw footage framed by either an embedded narrative or a voice-over to provide context and continuity. Edward Curtis' *In the Land of the Head Hunters* (1914) is an early ethnographic film of the Kwakiutl peoples of coastal British Columbia that used only native subjects as actors. While the film accurately depicts aspects of Kwakiutl culture and technology at the time of filming, its melodramatic plot was based on pre-contact or otherwise fictional practices. Curtis did not present the film as documentary evidence, nor did he call it fiction. Notably, the film records rituals prohibited at the time by the Canadian Government (Glass et al. 2008: 2–3) and so remains an important record of Kwakiutl culture.

In *Oh, What a Blow that Phantom Gave Me!*, filmmakers Bishop and Prins discuss the ethnographic recording practices of anthropologist Edmund Carpenter in the Sepik River region of Papua New Guinea in the late 1960s. In order to observe the impact of new technologies introduced into a culture – a typical concern of Media Ecology – Carpenter gave cameras to the indigenous people and showed them filmed images of themselves. (He was subsequently criticised by anthropologists for tampering with his subjects' 'pristine' state.) Carpenter discovered that the camera imposes its conventions on indigenous people just as having to learn a new language would, and their films of themselves were not especially original. On the other hand, seeing themselves in photographs and film footage appeared to have a profound effect on their self-perception and social ease.

He describes the men's collaborative film project about a sacred initiation ceremony, and their decision to allow a woman filmmaker (Adelaide de Menil) to access the ceremony, because she was identified as the best camera operator. She was allowed to film a scarification ritual previously unseen by any women in the village. Alia (2014) suggests de Menil was permitted to film the ritual, because she was an outsider and temporary visitor permitted to bypass local norms and gain access not available to women insiders. Perhaps the camera became a mask that disguised her presence at the ceremony. This question of access is critical to ethnographic filmmaking, because it informs perceptions of authenticity and the subjects' ease in front of a camera. Is this authentic behaviour? Are they acting? Carpenter recalls that when the men saw the film and heard its soundtrack, they decided to make this the ritual's last performance. He concludes that: '[M]edia are so powerful they swallow cultures. I think of them as invisible environments, which surround and destroy old environments. Sensitivity to problems of culture conflict and conquest becomes meaningless . . . media play no favourites; they conquer all cultures' (*Oh, What a Blow!* 2003). It is difficult to verify the men's motivation for ending the ritual practice, but we now have the film and not the ritual as evidence.

Atanarjuat: The Fast Runner (2001) was advertised as 'the first film written, directed, and acted by Inuit in the ancient oral language of Inuktitut'. It was screened around the world with subtitles and received numerous international awards. To write the screenplay, Paul Apak Angilirq collected versions of the legend of Atanarjuat from Inuit elders and reconstructed the story to reflect a worldview and language quickly fading from collective Inuit memory. The myth provided only the story's bare bones, so Apak and his collaborators had to provide character motivations to flesh out the story of a skilled hunter challenged by rivals, who threaten the community's survival. This reconstruction process revealed the significant impact of Christian values on Inuit spirituality. '[T]he film's writers made a big step forward, since such sympathetic public portrayal of shamanism would have been unthinkable twenty years ago when even discussion of these practices was strictly forbidden by the Church' (Saladin d'Anglure 2002: 203).

In the signature episode, rivals pursue the naked Atanarjuat across the Arctic ice floes after murdering his brother. Leaping across an impossibly wide crack in the ice, Atanarjuat eventually escapes his rivals and returns to avenge his brother's death and restore social order. Even though it reconstructs an Inuit myth, the film convincingly depicts the pre-colonial Arctic and its people and is given additional credibility with the involvement of the Inuit production team, actors and language. In the text written to accompany the film (Angilirq et al. 2002), *The Fast Runner* illustrates that the actuality of film lies in its making – what happens both on and off camera, before and after filming. While a single film will not save Inuit culture and the Inuktitut language from being swallowed whole by media, it contributes to a wider initiative to foster indigenous production and broadcasting – to create a 'new media nation' (Alia [2010] 2012) not dominated by outsider frames, perspectives and associations. Sometimes it takes a revolution for people to reclaim their media representations.

Cinema of revolution: association, montage, agitation

Revolutionary filmmakers in the Soviet Union were decisively influenced by Pavlov's theories of association and conditioning. In one famous editing experiment, filmmaker and theorist Lev Kuleshov combined three identical clips of movie idol Ivan Mosjoukine's expressionless face alternating with shots of a bowl of soup, a girl in a coffin and a woman reclining on a divan. Audiences reported how impressed they were with the actor's changing expression, as it conveyed hunger, sorrow or desire, depending on what he was associated with (see online on YouTube: Kuleshov Effect).

Kuleshov used his experiment as evidence to argue for juxtaposition's expressive power in film editing. Interpretation of meaning is based on association between images and not on the content of a single image. Audiences bring their own associations to screen images, he argued, and trained actors are unnecessary for expressing emotion in film. The Kuleshov Effect, which Hitchcock cites as an example of 'pure editing' (Truffaut 1983: 219), provides an important insight into the rhetorical effects of editing in general and montage, or the rapid juxtaposition of images, in particular. As the previous discussion of the filmic cut suggests, meaning in cinema is not solely communicated by the content of shots, but also by their juxtaposition and arrangement in sequence. Montage is a basic instrument of cinematic narrative and persuasion and is frequently associated with Sergei Eisenstein's revolutionary films.

Eisenstein's 1925 *Battleship Potemkin* remains a classic of agitational propaganda for its use of montage and didactic plot structure to inspire and educate its Soviet audiences. The film tells the story of a mutiny aboard the Russian battleship *Potemkin* in 1905, then shifts to the Odessa funeral of a mutiny leader. In solidarity with the mutineers, the citizens of Odessa come to view the martyr's body. A montage of their waving hands signifies that the people, inspired by the revolutionary vanguard of mutineers, are acting as one body. In the famous Odessa Steps scene, the Tsar's Cossack militia attack the gathering citizens on the steps leading down to the waterfront. Rapid editing between images of massacred men, women and children builds emotional reaction to the violent display of power.

Battleship Potemkin remains a model of political filmmaking, inspiring such films as *The Battle of Algiers* (1966) and *The Hour of Furnaces* (1968) with its didactic approach and innovative use of montage and type characters ('typage') to construct an argument. Eisenstein is closely associated with the Constructivist movement of artists and intellectuals, including Malevich, Rodchenko, Lissitsky, Tatlin and Vertov. Constructivists found inspiration in photomontages by Hannah Höch and John Heartfield, which juxtaposed images for subversion and satire. Eisenstein adopted innovative editing techniques first employed by Griffith in *The Birth of a Nation* and *Intolerance*, especially for their contribution to ideological narration. In 1923, he published 'Montage of Attractions', within which he cited photomontage constructions as models for a new kind of filmmaking. Attractions were, for Eisenstein, similar to circus acts and other popular spectacles designed to galvanise attention. Juxtaposing distinct elements emphasises movement, change and discontinuity to engage attention and raise awareness – 'the only means by which it is possible to make the final ideological conclusion perceptible' (Nichols 2005: 161; Eisenstein 1923 [1957]: 230–1).

Teitelbaum (1992) thinks montage involves 'a degree of narrative breakdown', where discontinuities and ruptures signify modernism (7). Montage illustrates 'radical realignments of power' and 'suggests new paradigms of authority and influence' (8). For example, Riefenstahl's extensive use of montage in *Triumph of the Will* and *Olympia* repositions its subjects (Nazi leaders, Olympic athletes) in their cinematic space to make them larger-than-life super-beings towering above the masses. Montage communicates emotion, because spectators are forced to fill ruptures and gaps with their own meaning. Montage has become familiar to contemporary audiences through advertising and music video.

Vertov's *Kino-Pravda*: two cameras in search of a story

Dziga Vertov's 1929 film *Man with a Movie Camera* includes one of the defining images of revolutionary cinema. In a startling montage sequence early in the film, we see a towering movie camera aimed in our direction, while a man with movie camera and tripod mounts the monumental camera and sets up for the shot. Without film, the scene is impossible. In its search for truth, the camera turns its inquisitive eye on the audience to reveal it watching the film with fascination. The image reminds us there will be two cameras in this film, though we will only see one most of the time. Vertov's self-reflexive gesture announces that everything we are about to see is mediated and made possible by film technology. We now view the film with two minds: one attending to content and the other to process. Vertov's message in this visual manifesto? The first step in grasping this film's truth is to become aware of film's power to guide and shape our perceptions.

The film is an extended version of Vertov's *Kino-Pravda* (Film-Truth) newsreel series produced in the 1920s, with his brother Mikhail Kaufman on camera and his wife Elizaveta Svilova editing. The team's virtuoso performance is still widely esteemed for its cinematic invention: jump cuts, split screens, double exposure, fast and slow motion, freeze frames, Dutch (diagonal) angles, extreme close-ups, tracking shots, reverse footage and stop-motion animation. Its catalogue of effects is uninterrupted by inter-titles; there is no soundtrack; and there is little evidence of traditional plot or character. The unseen camera follows the man with the movie camera as he records urban life in Odessa, Riga and other urban locations, while their citizens go about their lives in the new Soviet Union.

Its self-reflexive style makes the film an experiment in discovery, as well as invention. We see audiences watching the film in a theatre; we see the film being catalogued and edited by Svilova; we see shots being set-up, then we see the results; we see the same scene from different points of view; people are watching, and learning and seeing themselves in others. The film is a masterpiece of sly agitational propaganda – what we might call meta-propaganda – in its argument that the camera can be used as an instrument of instruction and social change.

Manovich calls *Man with a Movie Camera* a 'database movie'. Vertov films all the segments in random order, without any preconception of the story to be told, and hands this collection of clips over to Svilova for editing:

> As the film progresses, straight footage gives way to manipulated footage; newer techniques appear one after another, reaching a roller-coaster intensity by the film's end – a true orgy of cinematography . . . This gradual process of discovery is the film's main narrative, and it is told through a catalogue of discoveries. (Manovich 2001: 243)

Vertov's catalogue of effects is 'motivated by a particular argument, which is that the new techniques of obtaining images and manipulating them . . . can be used to decode the world' (243). Causal narrative is displaced by associational logic, innovation and montage to capture a new society of people in their homes, in the streets, at work and play, productive and attractive, curious and engaged with life. Society is awakening, on the move and in transition. The film documents factories, shops, bars, bridges, transportation systems and mechanical control mechanisms, such as switches and valves. The camera looks into anything and everything, inquisitive and passionate about a brave new world not yet dominated by authoritarian rule, surveillance and bureaucratic corruption. This film is about a new way of seeing, necessary because a new world is being constructed under socialism's banner. Confidence and hope inspire the filmmakers to scale the heights and survey the progress below.

Triumph and hope in war propaganda

Triumph of the Will (1935) and *Olympia* (1938) remain landmarks of ideological propaganda, though filmmaker Riefenstahl steadfastly denied being a Nazi Party member or condoning its practices. In his revealing three-hour biography, *The Wonderful, Horrible Life of Leni Riefenstahl* (1993), Ray Müller presses his subject to account for her collaboration with Nazis, but she insists she just wanted to make beautiful and moving films and was following orders from Hitler. (Despite her denials, Riefenstahl spent four years in prison after the war undergoing 'denazification'.) In the 1970s, however, Riefenstahl asserted to journalist John Pilger that the messages of her films did not follow 'orders from above', but rather exploited the 'submissive void' of the German people (Pilger 2013: n.p.).

Riefenstahl's Germany under Nazi rule was a nation looking for a renewed sense of direction with a deep hunger for former glories (its void), which Hitler and his supporters exploited with their vision of hope, cooperation and unity. The Nuremberg Rally of 1934 was a highly choreographed celebration and ritual for the party faithful to demonstrate their allegiance to Adolf Hitler, who descends from the clouds in the opening scene. *Triumph of the Will* visually and symbolically identifies Hitler with the nation and displays the party as a unified and powerful force. Assisted by thirty cinematographers and the best of equipment at the time, Riefenstahl carefully orchestrated the filming to capture the faces of Germans, young and old, in thrall to the spectacle and their passionate leaders. Telescoped panoramas of crowds in precise formation inspire awe in the cavernous filmic space. And uplifting bombastic music recalls Wagner's total theatre and mythic themes.

'Its key image is the moulding of tens of thousands of human beings into artistic patterns – stationary and solid masses in the huge stadium or moving with deliberation and vigour in endless parades' (Ellis and McLane [2005] 2008: 102). The film avoids political debate – the direction forward is already settled – and instead records the emotional intoxication of participating in mass historic events.

So powerful are its images, *Triumph of the Will* has often been used as counter-propaganda to warn about the dangers of totalitarianism: 'its command over the viewer is imperial; it became a visual demonstration of the will to conquer and crush', writes Aufderheide (2007: 73), who contrasts the film's power to examples of British and American propaganda. *Listen to Britain* (1942), for example, quietly celebrates the British way of life by showing people of all classes going about their lives during wartime, constantly alert, doing what is necessary to survive and without any apparent animosity for the enemy dropping bombs and killing their men and women. It was 'a highly popular, short film that evoked a shared understanding among Britons that they would uncomplainingly do what it took to win, without giving up who they were'. The film appeared 'not to be propagandising at all' (Aufderheide 2007: 69). Ellis and McLane (2008) confirm the general assessment that British documentaries during WWII emphasise 'togetherness' and 'working together to get the job done', while minimising very real issues of class distinction. Much the same attitudes are depicted in the WWI episodes of the popular British television series *Downton Abbey*.

William Wyler takes a similar approach in *Mrs. Miniver* (1942), a popular feature film about the unassuming heroism of a British woman left behind while her husband participates in Dunkirk's evacuation. When a German pilot parachutes into her quiet village not far from London, Mrs Miniver bravely disarms the desperate pilot, after he takes her hostage. At the film's end, a vicar's sermon in a heavily bombed church explains why people have to make sacrifices during war:

Because this is not only a war of soldiers in uniform. It is the war of the people, of all the people. And it must be fought not only on the battlefield but in the cities and in the villages, in the factories and on the farms, in the home and in the heart of every man, woman and child who loves freedom. Well, we have buried our dead, but we shall not forget them. Instead they will inspire us with an unbreakable determination to free ourselves, and those who come after us, from the tyranny and terror that threaten to strike us down.

In this sermon, rhetorical abstractions ascend from tyranny and terror to resistance, hope and freedom. Comparing *Mrs. Miniver* with *Listen to Britain*, we see how propaganda messages circulate in wartime: explicitly as documentaries and news programming and more covertly when embedded in other forms of popular culture. Aufderheide concludes that while 'propaganda films have never been very effective at changing public opinion . . . each documentary forms part of a larger picture of persuasion and agenda-setting, creating expectations and redrawing mental maps of what is normal' (2007: 71).

Cinematic realism

In the 1940s and 50s, André Bazin – the French film critic and exponent of *auteur* theory – articulated a theory of film realism to counterpoint prevailing theories of editing and montage. Bazin argued that photography, film and television, unlike the other arts, record actual images. Reality is already ambiguous and open to personal interpretation, and Bazin admired filmmakers like Flaherty, who approached reality's ambiguity with straightforward curiosity. Montage imposes ideology onto complex reality through the editing process and overdetermines what viewers must pay attention to. Deep focus and long takes control the viewer's gaze less rigidly and allow more time for personal contemplation – a characteristic Bazin found in films by Jean Renoir and Orson Welles.

For Bazin, 'the essence of cinema was situated in the art of *writing the film visually through découpage*' (Barnard 2009: 267). *Découpage* is often translated as 'cutting' or 'editing', but actually refers to the composition process, when the film is being planned and written as a series of scenes. 'In its classical form, *découpage* established the first claim that a film's authorship lay on the side of the script and the *mise en scène*, not on montage and editing' (268). The creative balance of power shifts away from the editor and toward the writer/*auteur*. Barnard notes that Bazin was influenced by Astruc's idea of the *caméra-stylo* – the camera as pen – and suggests that 'breaking down', rather than 'cutting', might be a more appropriate translation to describe how the *auteur* filmmaker writes a film with images.

Bazin observed that major technical innovations improved film's ability to express the realistic ideal: in the 1920s, sound recording allowed actors to use more natural gestures; in the 1930s and 40s, colour and deep-focus photography aligned film more closely with human perception; and in the 1950s, widescreen added context, detail and complexity. Bazin's ideas about cinematic realism decisively influenced film's production and reception, including Italian Neorealism after WWII (Rossellini, de Sica, Visconti, Fellini and others), *cinéma vérité* and direct cinema in the 1950s and the French New Wave (*La Nouvelle Vague*) cinema of Godard, Truffaut, Chabrol, Varda and others. Since realism claims to imitate reality convincingly, it influenced the *cinéma vérité* documentary movement.

Realism and documentary

The *cinéma vérité* movement, beginning in 1950s, was a reaction against the authoritative documentary style promoted by Grierson and illustrated by Capra's *Why We Fight* series. A founder of the *cinéma vérité* movement, the anthropologist and filmmaker Jean Rouch pioneered the ethnofiction film – a blend of documentary footage and fictional elements. Rouch questioned the importance of visual evidence and tried to look beyond the image for meaning. For example, he frequently collaborated with his Nigerien [sic] subjects in the making of films (for example *Moi, un noir* 1958) and felt this collaboration should contribute to the film's authenticity. Rouch soon turned his ethnographic eye onto his own tribe in Paris with his *Chronique d'un Été* (1961).

> The cinema, which is already an art of the double ... presents us with a constant movement from reality to the imaginary ... [T]he last thing to worry about is whether reality as such has been lost in the process of creation. (qtd in Burnett 2008: n.p.)

The NFB documentary *Cinéma Vérité* (1999) skilfully reviews the genre's history, its major practitioners and rhetorical principles. Canadian documentarian Wolf Koenig identifies French photographer Henri Cartier-Bresson and his notion of the 'decisive moment' as a defining influence, since *cinéma vérité* ('direct cinema' in the US) declares itself willing to pursue the moment at the expense of a preconceived script or storyline. Koenig notes a theme running through direct cinema's history: increasing camera mobility and synchronised sound allow for more intimate engagement with subjects. Karel Reisz says that the free cinema movement in the UK set out to challenge the Griersonian documentary style using an unplanned approach, making the film out of what happens and using synchronised sound to record subjects' actual dialogue. His documentaries *Momma Don't Allow* (1955) and *We Are the Lambeth Boys* (1958), and the kitchen-sink drama *Saturday Night and Sunday Morning* (1960) replace exposition and argument with attention to detail. Images and sounds are free to express their own meanings without intrusive narration.

Other influential figures in the movement include Richard Leacock, who worked with Flaherty in the 1940s and is credited with many technical innovations. Leacock collaborated with Robert Drew (*Crisis* 1963), D. A. Pennebaker (*Don't Look Back* 1966) and others to develop a direct cinema style for television news reporting. Drew brought direct cinema's spontaneous approach to US television journalism. In Canada, Tom Daley, Wolf Koenig and Roman Kroiter at the National Film Board (NFB) brought direct cinema innovations to television journalism with their *Candid Eye* series. Michel Brault, esteemed for his technical innovations, contributed creative direction and mobile film technology to Rouch's *Chronique d'un Été*, including a remarkable scene where the character Marceline (playing herself) recalls a reunion with her family after her experiences in a concentration camp, all filmed from a moving automobile.

Other pioneers in the direct cinema movement include Albert and David Maysles (*Salesman* 1968), Fred Wiseman (*Titicut Follies* 1967) and Barbara Kopple (*Harlan County, USA* 1976). The reality television series *Cops* (1989–2013) uses a home video aesthetic to bring 'amateur' eyewitness accounts into contact with law enforcement realities. The films of Jennifer Fox (*Beirut: The Last Home Movie* 1987; *An American Love Story* 1999; *My Reincarnation* 2011) are notable for their intimate and patient portraits of their subjects, combining the best of direct cinema techniques. Other prominent examples of the style include *Horns and Halos* (Galinsky and Hawley 2002), *Restrepo* (Hetherington and Junger 2010) and *Infiltrators* (Jarrar 2012). Velcrow Ripper's films (*Scared Sacred* 2004; *Fierce Light* 2008; *Occupy Love* 2012) find a satisfying balance between the spontaneous happenstance of direct cinema and powerful storytelling emerging from unscripted materials. Direct cinema has had a profound impact on contemporary visual culture, including reality television, music videos, infotainment, talk shows, commercials and television news programming.

Critics of *cinéma vérité* have questioned the assumption of veracity implied by its name. Errol Morris, for example, argues that stylistic manoeuvres are insufficient to represent the complex and ambiguous truths of the real world. Filmmakers must have an epistemology – ideas about how we know things – and must be transparent about how these ideas influence the material (Aufderheide 2007: 52). Godard criticised the movement for downplaying 'the benefit of selection and reflection' (52), of exchanging the camera's 'intelligence and sensibility' for its 'honesty' (52). Allowing the camera to 'write' the story does not mean the person holding the camera is free of intent; the filmmaker might well pursue an ideological message disguised as objective curiosity. 'Cinema verité is no longer revolutionary', concludes Aufderheide. 'It is the default language for music documentaries, and for all kinds of behind-the-scenes and the-making-of-documentaries; it is part of the DNA of cop shows and docusoaps and part of the credibility apparatus of reality TV shows' (55).

Digital media: codes and screens

Manovich says that our 'media became new' following the eventual convergence of two inventions: the *daguerreotype* of Louis Daguerre (1839); and the prototype of modern computers – the Analytical Engine proposed by Charles Babbage in the 1840s. While the *daguerreotype* matured into modern photography before the century's end, digital computers made a dramatic debut with the code-breaking machines of WWII (Gleick [2011] 2012: 213–19). By 1984, the release of the Apple Macintosh, with its graphical user interface (GUI), announced a new era of personal computing and desktop publishing. Apple's '1984' television ad by Ridley Scott remains an advertising landmark, with its narrative of an athletic woman iconoclastically throwing a hammer through a giant screen image of Big Brother. The message? Apple's personal computer will set you free from domination and conformity. By 2014, Apple had become one of the world's most profitable technology companies, by designing a series of personal computing devices – including iPods, iPads and iPhones – that paradoxically tethered users to a controlling military technology (the internet), while enabling mobile multimedia production and display.

Given its genealogy from cameras and computers, digital media share formal characteristics that determine its production methods and rhetorics:

1. *Numerical Representation*: Objects (images, sounds, text) are represented mathematically, as binary code subject to manipulation by algorithms.
2. *Modularity*: New media objects are composed of modules that can be rearranged. A film clip inserted into a webpage remains independent and can be edited by the application that created it.
3. *Automation*: Numerical coding and modularity allow automation of repeated computing tasks. Image or film editing applications can apply filters or adjustments to several images or whole films all at once.
4. *Variability*: The previous three characteristics allow new media objects to be altered easily to produce new versions. Remix culture (Lessig 2008) depends on ease of variability and the widespread availability of digital production methods.

5. *Cultural Transcoding*: While digital media objects resemble their analogue counterparts, they have been constructed from discrete modules (bits, codes, algorithms) and organised in ways appropriate to computers and their conventions. Each object has a cultural layer, familiar to humans, and a machine-readable computer layer. Computer transcoding leads progressively to cultural transcoding or 'reconceptualisation'. (Manovich 2001: 27–48)

While digital media protocols have taken their expressive and rhetorical lead from computers and cameras, the direction of influence is reversing: new media increasingly influence film and television and even our ways of interacting with media more generally.

Laws of media and transforming mirrors

In his final work (*Laws of Media* 1988), Marshall McLuhan and his son Eric reformulated a lifetime's work into four principles for anticipating the effects of a new medium on culture:

- *Extension/Enhancement*: Every technology extends or amplifies some organ or faculty of the user. What does the medium enhance or intensify?
- *Closure/Obsolescence*: Because the senses strive for equilibrium (homeostasis), when one area of experience is heightened or intensified, another is diminished or numbed. What is pushed aside or obsolesced by the new medium?
- *Reversal*: Every medium, pushed to the limit of its potential, reverses its characteristics. How does the medium reverse itself when pushed to its limit?
- *Retrieval*: The content of any medium is an older medium. What older medium is retrieved by the new one?

This tetrad of effects is not sequential, but simultaneous; all four aspects are present from the start; and all are interdependent. Film extends vision and hearing by bringing sights and sounds to our consciousness that would otherwise be unavailable. By emphasising spectacle, film and television push aside (obsolesce) print literacy in certain markets. When film and television saturate our lives, we become numb to their images through reversal and see them as so much visual wallpaper. Film retrieves novels, travel adventures, ethnographic studies, stage plays, musical performances and concerts. In its turn, digital media retrieves archived films and photographs, recycling news reporting, television programming and advertising into documentaries, remixes, compilations, cartoons, computer games and films about film and television.

What can we anticipate for the intersection of camera and computer? David Rokeby is internationally recognised for his interactive installations exploring the boundaries of human perception and technology. His early *Very Nervous System* (1986–90) translates human gestures into music and 'teaches' participants to move in certain ways to produce satisfying compositions. Consider how a new digital device or computer game teaches users to navigate its interface and controls. In Rokeby's immersive *Hand-held* installation (2012), participants' hands become screens for projected images when they are positioned precisely in the display area (vimeo.com/48946545). In his artistic manifesto 'Transforming Mirrors: Subjectivity and Control in Interactive Media' (1996), Rokeby says that interactive technology is a 'transforming mirror':

> A technology is interactive to the degree that it reflects the consequences of our actions or decisions back to us. It follows that an interactive technology is a medium through which we communicate with ourselves . . . a mirror. The medium not only reflects back, but also refracts what it is given; what is returned is ourselves, transformed and processed. (Rokeby 1996: n.p.)

We can make the same observation about film: it is persuasive because it refracts what spectators bring to it and reflects back images of the self – the spectator makes the picture. When documentaries and advertisements include emotional appeals and calls to action, they are playing on our subjectivities and attempting to exert control. But the computer interface (screen, keyboard, cursor, joystick) is a different medium than film and retrieves film and television as content. The interface extends our feeling of control – our agency – over the medium.

The interface provides a degree of control within the computer program's 'navigable structures' – where it allows us to go – but this partial control requires an exchange of freedom with the computing machine. Instead of watching the unmediated world as it unfolds or having face-to-face conversations, we interact through the interface:

> As interactive technologies become increasingly common in our everyday relationships, and as they approach transparency, these simplified representations replace the relationships to which they initially referred. This substitution turns the interesting ambiguities

of control and subjectivity in interactive art into serious issues of control, manipulation and deception. (Rokeby 1996: n.p.)

In his analysis of network protocols, Galloway (2004) confirms Rokeby's warning about control and manipulation: 'nearly all Web traffic must submit to a hierarchical structure [Domain Name System] to gain access to the anarchic and radical horizontal structure of the internet' (9). Every networked computing device has a unique Internet Protocol (IP) address, allowing that device to be tracked and observed by other computers and internet service providers (ISPs). We exchange our privacy and control for the ability to navigate through digital networks. Our digital technologies teach us how to use them and we learn to dance within their protocols.

Screen culture and egocasting

Digital networks and their terminals compete with movie theatres and television as places to watch moving images and provide an alternative to film and television production studios. Films and information about films now circulate together through the same networks. Video streaming websites like YouTube, Vimeo and Netflix offer alternate means of distribution and act as user-driven databases to be searched and played like instruments with vast sample selections. As Negroponte predicted in 1995: 'On the Net each person can be an unlicensed TV station' ([1995] 1996: 176). The internet swallows (retrieves) culture, stores it in a database and loops it. Older material is remixed into newer versions, while ownership and copyright are fiercely debated. Former economic models for creators, producers and distributors become obsolete. New social models emerge: creating, showing and watching through the internet connect us to friends and strangers alike. We can ask: 'How do you like this?'

In her 2012 TED Talk, new media theorist and psychoanalyst Sherry Turkle observes that being connected through our digital devices does not mean we feel less isolated. Turkle refers to Meyrowitz's landmark 1985 study on television's impact on social boundaries and notes that media technologies make interpersonal boundaries more permeable and can leave us with 'no sense of place'. This observation echoes Hayles' concern that virtuality encourages feelings of disembodiment and disconnection from the physical world (1999). Social media, SMS (texting) and email, search engines and news feeds give users the illusion of control over where to place their attention. Posting allows users to refashion themselves, shape their public image and manage their relationships: not too close, not too far, just right – the Goldilocks Effect. Machines offer companionship; they are sociable robots; and we never have to be out of touch. We expect more from technology than we expect from each other, concludes Turkle. But she warns that conversation with others is a two-way mirror and we learn about ourselves from others. If we use our touch screens all the time, we can lose touch with other things that matter. You can watch Sherry Turkle right now if you are connected and have twenty minutes to spare (www.ted.com/talks/sherry_turkle_alone_together.html).

Pariser (2011) observes a shift in online information flows, because 'filter bubbles' use algorithms to personalise and customise searches, news feeds, social media websites and shopping decisions. Internet users increasingly operate within a bubble of their own preferences, but are also influenced by the algorithmic filters and protocols of digital networks. Similarly, Sunstein (2009) warns that civic dialogue is degraded when partisan blogs create information cocoons and echo chambers, exposing people to ideas that merely confirm existing beliefs and values. Taken to extremes, filter bubbles and information cocoons create virtual castles, surrounded by defensive walls and moats.

Christine Rosen (2005) advances a similar argument with her concept of 'egocasting': the 'extremely narrow pursuit of one's personal taste'. She traces this concept's evolution from the advent of television remote controls through to personal video recorders (PVRs), iPods and mobile phones, all of which 'redefined our expectations of mastery over our everyday technologies'. The remote control encourages 'grazing' through television programming, allowing viewers to collage images and (re)mix their own programmes by changing channels frequently. The graphical browser allows people to 'surf' the web, making their own movies of image and text. Users are broadcasting their egos by creating and immersing themselves in their own media productions. Helfand (2001) notes that on the internet 'instead of camera movements, it is mouse movements that induce meaning and trigger changes in visual dynamics' (63). User input 'fundamentally relocates the creative parameters within which design is both constructed and consumed'. Echoing a recurring theme in new media analysis, Helfand concludes that the 'screen succeeds best when understood as a balance of fundamentally opposing forces: it is all about the tension between structure and freedom' (61).

Egocasting creates its own filter bubble. While personal music systems, smartphones and mobile computing provide greater control of the sensory environment, they also encourage a shift toward sensory isolation, where users can avoid stimuli – including expressions of value and belief – they do not want to experience. McLuhan ([1964] 1994: 41ff) uses the term 'narcissus narcosis' to describe a state in which the self-absorbed viewer – Narcissus the 'gadget lover' – mistakes his own reflection for another person (whom he falls in love with). In a case of mistaken identity, Narcissus is numbed into a stupor by his reflected image.

Being watched: Panopticon and sousveillance

Digital media are redefining what it means to be watched. In the world of *Nineteen Eighty-Four*, being watched by Big Brother is a form of control and coercion anticipated by Jeremy Bentham's design for the Panopticon prison (Bentham 1787; en.wikipedia.org/wiki/Panopticon). Guards in the Panopticon prison can look into each cell if they choose to, but the prisoners never know when they are being observed. In effect, the Panopticon architecture imposes self-discipline on prisoners in a manner analogous to government security agencies monitoring citizen internet use.

In 2013, Google began beta-testing its Glass technology – a small screen worn like traditional eyewear and connected to a processor (google.com/glass/start/). Glass can display time and information, take photos and record film, stream live video, record audio, translate foreign languages and recognise faces (although it seems that Google is reluctant to support this last function). Google Glass was anticipated by inventor Steve Mann, who has been refining his wearable computing and EyeTap technology since his graduate work in the MIT Media Lab in the 1990s (www.eyetap.org/research/eyetap.html). Mann's EyeTap technology allows the eye to function as both camera and display. Controlled by a wearable computer, the EyeTap processes what the user sees, augmenting or altering visual perception of the surrounding environment. The technology can, for example, edit out unwanted advertising.

The 2001 film *Cyberman* profiles earlier iterations of Mann's invention and the social issues it raises for both surveillance and sousveillance (filming by a person being filmed). In 2012, Mann was at the centre of controversy when he was physically ejected from a Paris McDonald's restaurant after he refused to remove his EyeTap apparatus, even though he was being filmed by surveillance cameras (Stenovec 2012). Mann is an expert in using wearable digital technology to live in computer-mediated reality – thus, the title *Cyberman* – and has discovered that the watchers do not like being watched back.

Exercise questions

1. Make a five-minute documentary with your cellphone or DV camera and upload it to a video-sharing website.
2. Describe the cuts used in a short scene and how they determine meaning.
3. Evaluate the credibility of a film that presents itself as an accurate representation of something that actually occurred. What claims are made by the film to strengthen its authenticity?
4. Discuss the use of video embedded in an online newspaper of your choice. How does the use of video enhance or compromise the delivery of news?
5. Describe the use of amateur video to break an important news story.
6. Watch a documentary in a group setting, writing down your assessment of the arguments and evidence presented. After viewing the film, share your assessment with the group and debate your differences of opinion, with the (optional) goal of reaching consensus.
7. Write a 400-word review for a film/documentary/television production that you believe your peers should see, because it reveals something they should know about.
8. Discuss the role of documentaries in preserving disappearing cultures, threatened species and compromised landscapes. How do media 'swallow cultures'?
9. Analyse social media using McLuhan's 'laws of media'.

Figure 11   'Slingshots: taking aim at capitalism'. Photo: M. Soules, Toronto, 2003.
Popular opposition to secretive trade negotiations inspired anti-corporate activists.

8 Propaganda and Global Economics

> Since trade ignores national boundaries and the manufacturer insists
> on having the world as a market, the flag of his nation must follow
> him, and the doors of the nations which are closed against him must
> be battered down. Concessions obtained by financiers must be safe-
> guarded by ministers of state, even if the sovereignty of unwilling
> nations be outraged in the process. (Woodrow Wilson 1907, qtd in
> Snow [1998] 2010: 73)

Dr Strangelove: mutual assured destruction

Stanley Kubrick's black comedy *Dr. Strangelove: Or How I Learned
to Stop Worrying and Love the Bomb* (1964) is a satire about nuclear
war, but it is also a story about economic ideologies in conflict. The
weapons of capitalism and socialism are arrayed against one another in
a classic display of diplomatic brinksmanship.

Peter Sellers plays three characters in the film: a British RAF officer,
the US President and Commander-in-Chief and, most famously, Dr
Strangelove – a nuclear war strategist and former Nazi. Strangelove is
confined to a wheelchair and his black-gloved right hand has a mind
of its own. He appears to be a composite of personalities, including
German rocket scientist Wernher von Braun, foreign affairs advisor
and future Secretary of State Henry Kissinger and Herman Kahn,
author of *On Thermonuclear War* (1960). In the early 1960s, Kahn was
a defence strategist famous for devising nuclear war scenarios and presenting them to terrified audiences with his trademark morbid sense of
humour. Following the Cuban Missile Crisis in October 1962, Cold
War propaganda was at its height as the two superpowers showcased
their military might and competed for supremacy in space. From class-
rooms and dinner tables to the highest levels of government, people
debated the merits of bomb shelters and other survivalist preparations
in the event of nuclear Armageddon.

Kubrick had at first intended his script – based on Peter George's

1958 novel *Red Alert* – to be a melodrama; instead, he and Terry Southern wrote a nightmarish comedy of the absurd. Southern recalls that Kubrick read everything he could find on nuclear war and was struck not only by the corruption of language, but by the '"cautious sterility of ideas, the reverence of obsolete national goals, the breeziness of crackpot realism, the paradox of nuclear threatsmanship, the desperately utopian wish fantasies about Soviet intentions, and the terrifying logic of paranoiac fears and suspicions"' (Southern [1963] 2004: n.p.). The talk of pre-emptive strikes, fallout shelters, casualties measured in the millions (megadeaths), mutual assured destruction (MAD) and Doomsday Machines was too terrifying without a mantle of dark humour.

Dr. Strangelove tells the story of a rogue general who orders a pre-emptive strike against the Soviet Union with B-52 bombers, and the subsequent efforts of US and Soviet leaders to avert a nuclear catastrophe. The plot could have been a scenario lifted directly from Kahn's *On Thermonuclear War* (Ghamari-Tabrizi 2005). Despite its apparent absurdity, *Dr. Strangelove* captures the anxiety of the times with considerable realism and remains an enduring Cold War document. Kubrick's unflinching ending shows a US pilot-as-cowboy riding a nuclear bomb toward its Soviet target, cutting to archival footage of actual atomic explosions to trigger audiences' darkest fears. While the film comments on nuclear folly and political brinksmanship, audiences are left alone to question why the Americans and Soviets are so intent on destroying one another and the rest of humanity with them.

The Communist Manifesto: 'workers of the world, unite!'

The nuclear troubles had their origins over a century earlier, when two revolutionary thinkers agreed to write a manifesto for the Communist League – an international association of workers that commissioned the work in 1847. It was to be a 'detailed theoretical and practical programme of the Party' (Marx and Engels [1872] 2011: 23), first published in German in 1848, shortly before the February Revolution in France and a wave of uprisings in other countries. Bloody and largely unsuccessful in their immediate goals, the 1848 revolutions were fuelled by demands for democratic reform and workers' rights, and *The Communist Manifesto* provided vision, soaring rhetoric and a call-to-arms. Almost immediately, its resonant message sent shock waves around the world. It ends with a famous appeal for working class unity and commitment to struggle that echoes down to our own time, though often in parody (Marx and Engels [1848] 2011: 103–4):

The Communists . . . openly declare that their ends can be attained only by the forcible overthrow of all existing social conditions. Let the ruling classes tremble at a Communistic revolution. The proletarians have nothing to lose but their chains. They have a world to win.

WORKING MEN OF ALL COUNTRIES, UNITE!

The 'existing social conditions' were described by Marx and Engels as a class-based oligarchy, where wealthy and privileged elites control economies, legal systems and governments for their own advantage. The central mechanisms of this privilege are private property ownership and inheritance rights that prevent the equitable distribution of wealth and resources. Significantly, the working class does not own the means of production and thus cannot earn surplus from their labour. Transforming wealth distribution will only occur if the bourgeoisie are forcibly overthrown from power. The proletarians – workers exploited for profit – have nothing to lose but their serfdom, defined as poor working conditions, subsistence wages, a lack of social mobility and insecurity. Subsequent communist revolutions in the USSR, China, Cuba, Vietnam, North Korea and numerous socialist variations caused capitalists and ruling elites to arm themselves, since they stood to lose property, privilege and power.

In their commentaries on *The Communist Manifesto*, Berman (2011), Priestland (2009) and others emphasise that Marx was ambiguous about capitalism, criticising it for its predatory exploitation on one hand and admiring its drive, energy and force for change on the other. For Marx, capitalism 'integrated the world and destroyed "backward" institutions and old, primitive ways of life' (Priestland 2009: 29). The bourgeoisie described in the *Manifesto* is itself revolutionary, responsible for building great trade empires and new cities. 'The need for a constantly expanding market for its products chases the bourgeoisie over the whole surface of the globe. It must nestle everywhere, settle everywhere, establish connections everywhere' (Marx and Engels [1848] 2011: 68).

Nevertheless, capitalism is dangerous, because it calculates everything, including human beings, in monetary terms. As Polanyi comments, capitalism depends on a 'fiction' that converts labour, land and money into commodities: 'But labour, land, and money are obviously *not* commodities; the postulate that anything that is bought and sold must have been produced for sale is emphatically untrue' ([1944] 2001: 75). For Marx and Engels, capitalism converts human relationships into 'naked self-interest' and noble human emotion into 'egotistical calculation'. 'Personal value' becomes 'exchange value', and former freedoms are replaced by a 'single unconscionable freedom – Free Trade. In one word, for exploitation, veiled by religious and political illusions, it has substituted naked, shameless, direct, brutal exploitation' ([1848] 2011: 67). These are fighting words to capitalists and have enflamed conflict over economic ideologies from the 1850s to the present. Economic insecurity, anxiety and competitiveness found a potent metonym in the image of the nuclear bomb and its mushrooming cloud.

Agitation propaganda and planning

Social reformers must organise and channel the masses toward revolutionary ends. Lenin faced this monumental task in the early twentieth century, trying to implement the theories of Marx and Engels in Tsarist Russia. In his 1902 pamphlet *What is to be Done?* Lenin emphasises the importance of theory, organisation and planning in guiding a revolutionary party: 'Without revolutionary theory there can be no revolutionary movement', since theory provides the consistency and vision needed to inform both propaganda and agitation. Propaganda is directed at the revolutionary movement's vanguard – its leaders – and is education about communism, while agitation motivates the masses to action with emotional appeals. The revolutionary vanguard faces the difficult task of planning and building an extensive organisation, while avoiding repression by authorities.

Lenin believed the masses are responsive to education and consciousness-raising, therefore not an irrational throng. But they are also susceptible to demagogues, 'the worst enemies of the working class . . . because the unenlightened worker is unable to recognise his enemies in men who represent themselves, and sometimes sincerely so, as his friends'. Lenin was sensitive to criticism that his small group of 'professional revolutionaries' might become elitist and autocratic – a criticism with some merit – but he defended the need for secrecy in the early stages. As propaganda and agitation take effect, 'the membership will promote increasing numbers of the professional revolutionaries from its ranks' to join the vanguard.

Eventually, Lenin's emphasis on planning and organisation led to the Soviet Union's centrally administered command economy and series of five-year economic plans, beginning in 1928. Marx predicted that the transition to communism would require 'technicians and bosses', since 'the main advantage of Communism over capitalism lay in efficiency: rational planning and its ability to end the chaotic booms and busts brought by the free market' (Priestland 2009: 38–9). As we will see later in this chapter, planning – who controls the nation's future – is a major focus of the twentieth century's economic propaganda.

Hayek's *Road to Serfdom*

In the 1940s, the ideas of Marx, Engels and Lenin found an articulate opponent in the Austrian-English economist and philosopher Friedrich Hayek, who eventually became a guiding light for free enterprise advocates occupying positions of power. Both Ronald Reagan and Margaret Thatcher were influenced by Hayek's economic theories, as are political leaders today who advocate liberalised trade, private enterprise, restricted government intervention in market operations, reduced union power and a general emphasis on self-reliance and individual motivation to get ahead.

In *The Road to Serfdom* (1944), Hayek argues that socialism inevitably leads to totalitarianism, whereas democracy, free enterprise and liberal economic policies protect individual freedom and dignity. Writing in London during National Socialism's rule in Germany, Hayek wanted to warn Britain that it was drifting dangerously towards socialism. In particular, he opposed policy recommendations to continue the centralised planning necessary during wartime. In his opinion, the fatal flaw in economic planning is the need for central planners to impose a code of values rationalising their decisions. Why redistribute wealth to this group, impose quotas on this industry or legislate these hiring practices? Even in a democratic society, centralised planning requires a propaganda apparatus of the kind envisioned by Bernays and Lippmann to promote the plan. Hayek observes that proposed reforms rarely include practical implementation plans, with the result that authoritative leadership is increasingly accepted as necessary to accomplish anything and inevitably leads to totalitarianism. Despite obvious differences, the authoritarian style of Hitler, Mussolini and Stalin grew from similar roots in Hayek's view – the planned economy and social engineering required for its implementation.

In his 'pamphlet for the time' ([1944] 2007: 55), Hayek worries that 'we are all socialists now' (59). On a theme promoted by his influential protégé Milton Friedman in *Capitalism and Freedom* (1962), Hayek argues that '[w]e have progressively abandoned that freedom in economic affairs without which personal and political freedom has never existed in the past' (67). While acknowledging the need for planning in times of national crisis, Hayek asserts that capitalist markets must find their own equilibrium, guided by Adam Smith's 'invisible hand', and be free to cross national borders. Economic freedom creates a prosperous marketplace of goods: 'Wherever the barriers of the free exercise of human ingenuity were removed, [humans] became rapidly able to satisfy ever widening ranges of desire' (70). Satisfying these 'ever widening ranges of desire' is the ultimate promise of commodity capitalism and its consumer society.

Capitalism and socialism are distinguished by differing approaches to equality: while capitalists pursue equality through freedom of choice and individual initiative, socialists seek equality through wealth distribution and collective prosperity. Friedman (1962) takes this distinction one step further by arguing that corporations should not be expected to operate with 'social responsibility', because their business is to make a profit, not improve society. Governments who enforce codes of moral responsibility on corporations subvert capitalism's freedoms and move toward totalitarianism. Hayek was sympathetic to socialism's idealistic goals, just as Marx was sympathetic to capitalism's transformative power, but he disputed its means. Socialism's fatal flaw was centralised economic planning, which threatened private enterprise, free markets and profit-taking.

An ideological iron curtain continues to separate free market capitalists from communists and socialists, because key differences remain concerning the control of production, markets and wealth distribution. How do societies support disadvantaged and 'unproductive' citizens? Who protects human and natural resources from exploitation? The questions are difficult and the stakes are high. As we see in the following section, market fundamentalists in Western nations spent vast amounts on propaganda during the twentieth century to promote a familiar agenda: business interests are in the public interest; free enterprise equals democratic freedom and is patriotic; socialism inevitably leads to totalitarianism; unions and intrusive government regulations interfere with free enterprise.

Taking the Risk Out of Democracy

The twentieth century has been characterised by three developments of great political importance: the growth of democracy, the growth of corporate power, and the growth of corporate propaganda as a means of protecting corporate power against democracy. (Carey [1995] 1997: 18)

Figure 12   'Mad cow'. Photo: M. Soules, Manchester, UK, 1990.
Margaret Thatcher's proposed poll tax infuriated Britain's working class.

Democracy is risky for capitalists, because voters are, theoretically, consulted about future planning. Capitalist propaganda is thus an effort to convince voters and governments that economic planning is best left to experts, who know how markets operate and how to make profits for everyone's benefit. In *Taking the Risk Out of Democracy*, Australian scholar Alex Carey says that corporate propaganda took a remarkably consistent approach in celebrating capitalism and condemning socialism. He focuses on the United States, since business interests there formed corporate propaganda's vanguard and these resulting techniques were eventually adopted in Britain, Australia, Canada and other nations. Carey identifies the influence of philosophical pragmatism articulated by Benjamin Franklin, William James, John Dewey and others. For pragmatists, truth depends not on evidence for holding a belief, but on the consequences of holding that belief. Truth is what works. US corporate propaganda constructs a stark dichotomy, where capitalism is identified with efficiency, freedom, opportunity and patriotism, while communism is inefficient, controlling, demoralising and subversive.

Carey observes that cycles of corporate propaganda respond to increasing public resistance to business practises and higher expectations for shared prosperity. The periods 1919–21, 1945–50 and

1976–80 saw intense propaganda efforts to counter public sentiment following major military conflicts:

> For modern wars require the support of everyone; and so wartime propaganda idealises the humane, egalitarian, democratic character of the home society in a way that no elite or business interest has any intention of allowing actually to come about. (Carey [1995] 1997: 137)

The public notices that wars are profitable for business, while wages are kept low as a national priority. These periods also experienced renewed opposition to unions and anxiety about immigrants, foreigners and other 'subversive' elements. 'In every case a massive campaign of business propaganda went into action directed at arousing fear of a communist threat and in the process discrediting liberal and democratic critics of business and corporate interests' (137).

Carey defines propaganda as 'communications where the form and content is selected with the single-minded purpose of bringing some target audience to adopt attitudes and beliefs chosen in advance by the sponsors of the communications' (20). 'Grassroots' propaganda attempts to reach a mass audience to change public opinion – the approach taken by corporations in the 1920s, and then again in the 1940s and 50s, following the success of wartime propaganda. The activism and democratic reforms of the 1960s and 70s, however, prompted business leaders to take a different approach, characterised by Carey as 'treetops' propaganda, directed at legislators, judges, bureaucrats, newspaper editors, journalists and television executives in a position to influence policy (Carey [1995] 1997; Gutstein 2009: 18–19). Grassroots propaganda is less necessary the more treetops propaganda is successful. Treetops propaganda – largely carried out by think tanks through lectures, reports, press releases and books – defines the terms of public discussion, frames issues and establishes talking points favourable to corporate interests.

Typical talking points on the business agenda are presented as common sense assumptions (following Gramsci's definition of hegemony) and, when successfully propagated, form an armature of assumptions explaining the news of the day. Examples of corporate talking points include:

- corporate investment drives economic prosperity;
- business executives deserve high levels of compensation because they earn it;
- increasing taxes for the wealthy is unfair and harms the economy;

- lower taxes contribute to increased investment and more jobs;
- public education and healthcare are broken and need reform;
- restrictive environmental regulations discourage investment;
- welfare creates dependency; employment benefits encourage unemployment;
- unions only look after their own members and increase production costs;
- technology innovation increases productivity and is in the national interest;
- trade liberalisation is good for the economy and good for jobs;
- economic prosperity depends on inexpensive energy; and
- corporate freedom equals democratic freedom equals patriotism.

McChesney (2013) calls these statements a free market 'catechism' (23) to suggest they are largely articles of faith contradicted by empirical evidence. They identify business interests with national interests and claim that opposition comes from 'special' interests: socialists, extremists, even traitors and terrorists.

Two examples illustrate ways that corporate messaging was deeply embedded in American public consciousness. Fourth of July (Independence Day) celebrations in the US were initiated in 1915 by the Committee for Immigrants in America and various Chambers of Commerce as a 'national Americanisation Day', 'a great nationalistic expression of unity and faith in America' (Carey [1995] 1997: 47–8). This annual event converted fear of immigrants – with their cheap labour and subversive ideas – into a celebration of patriotism and free enterprise. In the early 1950s, Senator McCarthy, acting in concert with corporate interests, ruthlessly applied a good-versus-evil narrative during his public purge of anti-American communists. Carey says that a century of anti-communist, pro-capitalist propaganda fostered an 'intense and shallow' patriotism vulnerable to the threat of nuclear annihilation. These sentiments 'are easily exploited by manipulating sacred and satanic symbols in relation to nationalism' (124).

'Powell Manifesto': attack on the American free enterprise system

In 1972, a confidential memorandum from future Supreme Court judge Lewis Powell to the US Chamber of Commerce became a call-to-arms for corporate propaganda efforts. The 'Powell Memorandum' – or 'Manifesto' – asserted that American free enterprise was under attack by forces on the left, and business interests needed to organise under Chamber of Commerce leadership. 'Business and the enterprise system are in deep trouble, and the hour is late', Powell warned (1971: 34). Attacks came not entirely from the Marxist fringes, but 'from perfectly respectable elements of society: from the college campus, the pulpit, the media, the intellectual and literary journals, the arts and sciences, and from politicians' (2–3). He noted that it 'is still Marxist doctrine that the "capitalist" countries are controlled by big business' (24). But, he argued, 'few elements of American society today have as little influence in government' as the business executive, who has truly been 'forgotten' (24).

Powell challenged the enterprise system to advance its interests to the campuses, media, politicians, public and the courts. A 'great truth' must be communicated: 'The threat to the enterprise system is not merely a matter of economics. It is also a threat to individual freedom' (32). Political power 'must be assiduously cultivated . . . it must be used aggressively and with determination . . . characteristic of American business' (26). Since business leaders 'have not been trained or equipped to conduct guerrilla warfare with those who propagandise against the system' and have 'shown little stomach for hard-nosed contest with their critics' (8), they need to prepare for battle.

> [I]ndependent and uncoordinated activity by individual corporations . . . will not be sufficient. Strength lies in organisation, in careful long-range planning and implementation, in consistency of action over an indefinite period of years, in the scale of financing available only through joint effort, and in the political power available through united action and national organisations. (11)

Powell makes it clear that centralised planning by a vanguard of leaders is not limited to socialists.

Powell's 'Memorandum' signalled a sea change in corporate propaganda. The corporate offensive in the 1970s was aggressive and included a dramatic increase in public affairs offices and lobbyists operating in Washington, with an equivalent increase in corporate political action committees (PACs) after 1976 (Hacker and Pierson 2010). The influential Business Roundtable was formed in 1972. Corporations increasingly organised grassroots and treetops campaigns using networks of shareholders, employees and other companies to promote their issues through letters, phone calls, lobbying, publications and films. As election campaign costs increased – largely from television advertising – corporations saw opportunities to support sympathetic candidates.

In another significant development, David Rockefeller and Zbigniew Brzezinski founded the Trilateral Commission in 1973 to promote political and economic cooperation between North America, Western Europe and Japan. Rockefeller selected its 250 members from business, political and media elites. Variously criticised for advancing neoliberal interests and undermining national sovereignty, the Commission sponsored an influential report called *The Crisis of Democracy* (Crozier et al. 1975). The problem identified was an 'excess of democracy', allowing 'special interests' – besides business – to have undue influence. The report identifies 'disintegration of civil order, the breakdown of social discipline, the debility of leaders, and the alienation of citizens' (2) as potential problems for business. 'Adversary intellectuals' pose a 'significant challenge' when they 'assert their disgust with the corruption, materialism, and inefficiency of democracy and with the subservience of democratic government to "monopoly capitalism"' (6). This adversary culture infects faculty, students and the media and poses a threat as potentially dangerous as 'aristocratic cliques, fascist movements, and communist parties' (7). In short, democracy threatens capitalism.

Think tanks and organic intellectuals

Think tanks illustrate Gramsci's idea, expressed in *Prison Notebooks* (1971), of the 'organic intellectuals' (6) of the ruling class. Intellectuals are necessary for spreading ideology, and Gramsci distinguishes between traditional and organic types. (He defines intellectuals broadly and includes anyone capable of informed and credible debate, both inside and outside formal organisations.) Traditional intellectuals consider themselves to be independent thinkers, operating autonomously within the dominant system, though Gramsci is sceptical of their claims to autonomy. They think of themselves as tradition's protectors and tend to be conservative in their views. On the other hand, organic intellectuals are nurtured alongside the dominant class and function for its benefit.

To challenge dominant ideology, Gramsci proposes a programme of 'counter hegemony' using its own organic intellectuals to spread ideology. To be effective, these 'adversarial intellectuals' identified in the Trilateral Commission's report cannot limit their efforts to universities and academic journals, but must take their arguments to the masses and ground them in everyday life. These intellectuals are not merely eloquent, but actively participate 'in practical life, as constructor, organiser, "permanent persuader" and not just a simple orator . . .' (1971: 10). Ultimately, their role is to challenge and discredit illegitimate authority.

Donald Gutstein (donaldgutstein.com/) is an example of Gramsci's adversarial intellectual and offers recommendations for a 'progressive' agenda to counter market fundamentalism. Gutstein suggests, for example, that accusations of media's liberal bias can be countered with an opposing frame – the 'commercial' media (Gutstein 2009: 303). To address the issue of media bias, citizens should become 'defensive news consumers' (305), who question source credibility and ask who these sources speak for.

> As well as a common name, progressives need a common enemy if they are to rally their diverse groupings to a common cause. Historically, the enemies of the left have been poverty, homelessness, inequality, poor health care, racism and sexism. The enemy of the right, in contrast, is the left. Progressives need to make the right – the radical conservatives – the enemy. (309)

He recommends that progressives use the term 'market fundamentalists' to identify classical liberals, neoliberals and libertarians, because they believe that competitive markets will solve all problems when given a free hand (309). The association with religious fundamentalism is not accidental in Gutstein's analysis: dogmatic faith in the market surpasses reason and inspires passionate intensity.

The Washington Consensus

Eventually, Hayek's theories were embedded in the Washington Consensus – a term introduced by John Williamson in 1989 to describe economic principles guiding the International Monetary Fund (IMF), the World Bank and the US Treasury Department, all located in Washington, DC. After 1995, the same principles have informed World Trade Organisation (WTO) policies – the target of numerous populist demonstrations against trade agreements negotiated beyond public scrutiny. Since the term was introduced, the Washington Consensus has become more controversial, but Williamson's original formulation was meant to guide aid provision to developing countries during economic crises. The ten principles include:

- fiscal discipline;
- a redirection of public expenditure priorities toward fields offering both high economic returns and the potential to improve income distribution, such as primary healthcare, primary education and infrastructure;
- tax reform (to lower marginal rates and broaden the tax base);

- interest rate liberalisation;
- a competitive exchange rate;
- trade liberalisation;
- liberalisation of FDI (foreign direct investment) inflows;
- privatisation;
- deregulation (in the sense of abolishing barriers to entry and exit); and
- secure property rights. (Williamson 1990: n.p.)

The Washington Consensus sets the agenda for global market fundamentalism and provides guidelines for lenders, operating through the World Bank and International Monetary Fund, to negotiate with debtor nations. In effect, economic aid comes with ideological strings attached.

Beginning with Occupy Wall Street in September 2011, the various Occupy movements oppose Washington Consensus ideology. Occupy's meme ('We are the 99 per cent') encapsulates the movement's complaint that global neoliberalism may have increased GDP in developing countries, but the net effect has been to concentrate wealth in fewer hands (the 1 per cent) at the expense of the 99 per cent, whose economic prosperity has stagnated since the 1970s. Harvey (2012) traces a thread of continuity in public protest movements around the globe since the late 1990s, largely led by urban youth with diminished economic prospects. Chomsky identifies class conflict between the 'plutonomy' – the wealthiest segment of society – and the 'precariat' – those 'living precarious existences', who are increasingly numerous and insecure (2012: 32–3).

Globalisation and its discontents

Caring about the environment, making sure the poor have a say in the decisions that affect them, promoting democracy and fair trade are necessary if the potential benefits of globalisation are to be achieved. The problem is that the institutions have come to reflect the mindsets of those to whom they are accountable. (Stiglitz 2003: 216)

Joseph Stiglitz was an economic advisor to Bill Clinton in the 1990s, chief economist at the World Bank for three years beginning in 1997 and winner of the Nobel Prize in Economics in 2001. He is the ultimate insider to capitalism's operations and its global propagation under the Washington Consensus banner. Stiglitz defines globalisation as:

- pursuing international trade;
- integrating economies through innovations in transportation and technology, increasing the mobility of goods and services (though not labour);
- removing impediments to trade and investment; and
- increasing activity of global institutions, aid organisations, NGOs and large multinational corporations. (Stiglitz 2003: 4–5)

While a strong proponent of free enterprise, Stiglitz argues that critics of the International Monetary Fund, World Bank and World Trade Organisation are justified in many respects. He believes the IMF 'champions market supremacy with ideological fervour' (2003: 12). Critics of globalisation are not against free trade, but against unfair trade and the hypocrisy of developed nations keeping their own protective tariffs in place, while insisting that developing nations remove their trade barriers (6). Market fundamentalism masks the economic motives of creditor nations, who want access to markets and resources without making the necessary investment in social capital: 'In many cases commercial interests and values have superseded concern for environment, democracy, human rights, and social justice' (20).

Washington Consensus policies may have failed for a large majority in debtor nations, but they succeeded in transferring great wealth to lending nations. Instead of stabilisation during times of economic crisis, its policies lead to destabilisation, resource transfer and indebtedness – the mechanics of the new colonialism. Stiglitz concludes: 'Simplistic free market ideology provided the curtain behind which the real business' of the IMF could be conducted – 'pursuing the interests of the financial community' (206–7).

Shock therapy and disaster capitalism

In 1947, along with Milton Friedman and other market fundamentalists, Hayek founded the Mont Pelerin Society – an economic think tank advocating neoliberal policies. Through Friedman, Hayek became associated with the Chicago School of Economics, and in the 1970s and 80s they advised Chile's Pinochet government on its transition from socialism to a market economy. Hayek had warned that any movement toward socialism would end in totalitarianism, but his support of Pinochet's military dictatorship required him to make a finer distinction between authoritarian and totalitarian regimes. In a 1981 interview, Hayek commented: 'At times it is necessary for a country to have, for a time, some form or other of dictatorial power

... Personally, I prefer a liberal dictator to democratic government lacking in liberalism' (Robin 2012). Pinochet's military coup to overthrow Salvador Allende's elected socialist government was, in Hayek's view, a pragmatic decision to cleanse democracy and make it safe for capitalism. In the 1970s, Hayek, Friedman and the Chicago School had, according to Naomi Klein (2007), its first opportunity to apply their theories of neoliberalism to regime change:

> Friedman advised Pinochet to impose a rapid-fire transformation of the economy – tax cuts, free trade, privatised services, cuts to social spending and deregulation ... It was the most extreme capitalist makeover ever attempted anywhere, and it became known as the 'Chicago School' revolution, since so many of Pinochet's economists had studied under Friedman at the University of Chicago. (8)

Friedman coined the term 'shock treatment' to describe the rapid, sometimes painful, transition to a free market economy.

In *The Shock Doctrine*, Klein continues her critique of corporate ethics begun in *No Logo* (2000) by describing neoliberal interventions following economic, political or natural disasters. Taking her examples from Chile, Argentina and Bolivia, to Hurricane Katrina and the war on terror in the US, Klein argues that crisis provides opportunities to implement Washington Consensus policies. Referring to the aftermath of Hurricane Katrina in 2005, Klein writes that 'orchestrated raids on the public sphere in the wake of catastrophic events, combined with the treatment of disasters as exciting market opportunities' define what she calls 'disaster capitalism' (6). She cites Friedman's related ideas that 'only a crisis – actual or perceived – produces real change', and free market ideas must be implemented quickly (7). This 'shock doctrine' contributed to 'some of the most infamous human rights violations of this era ... either committed with the deliberate intent of terrorising the public or actively harnessed to prepare the ground for the introduction of radical free market "reforms"' (11). For Klein, the attacks of 9/11 brought the shock doctrine home to America, now waging a war against terror using an increasingly privatised military and security apparatus funded with public taxes. She concludes: 'The history of the contemporary free market – better understood as the rise of corporatism – was written in shocks' (22).

Klein compares this 'shock treatment' to CIA-funded experiments secretly conducted between 1957 and 1961 and only revealed in the late 1970s (Klein 2007; Marks 1979). Working through the CIA's Project MKUltra programme, Scottish psychiatrist Ewen Cameron at McGill University used electroshock, drugs and sensory deprivation ostensibly to treat psychiatric ailments. In reality, he was researching mind control and psychic 'de-patterning' to create a blank slate of the subject's mind (Klein 2007: 34; Marks 1979: 133). In comparing the two 'Doctor Shocks' – Friedman and Cameron – Klein hopes to reveal the 'underlying logic of disaster capitalism':

> Like the free-market economists who are convinced that only a large-scale disaster . . . can prepare the ground for their 'reforms', Cameron believed that by inflicting an array of shocks to the human brain, he could unmake and erase faulty minds, then rebuild new personalities on that ever-elusive clean slate. (2007: 31–2)

And, 'where Cameron dreamed of returning the human mind to that pristine state, Friedman dreamed of de-patterning societies, of returning them to a state of pure capitalism, cleansed of all interruptions – government regulations, trade barriers and entrenched interests' (57).

The Project MKUltra experiments were not simply concerned with brainwashing, where they were considered a failure. Instead, they were seeking 'special interrogation techniques . . . to break prisoners suspected of being Communists and double agents' (36). Cameron's shock therapy experiments were actually studies in torture and eventually contributed to the CIA's torture handbook, *Kubark Counterintelligence Interrogation* (1963), declassified in 1997. Klein risks making a false analogy between economic shock treatment and CIA torture, but the analogy allows her to link military interventions and torture – at Abu Ghraib, Guantánamo and other rendition sites – with neoliberal economic reform disguised as democracy. For example, in 2005, President Bush described the challenges facing the US in Iraq:

> [W]e are working with Iraqi forces and Iraqi leaders to help Iraqis improve security and restore order, to rebuild cities taken from the enemy, and to help the national government revitalize Iraq's infrastructure and economy. Today I'm going to speak in depth about another vital element of our strategy: our efforts to help the Iraqi people build a lasting democracy in the heart of the Middle East. (Bush 2005: n.p.)

Despite multiple ironies, Bush's statement expresses the interdependence of war, economic opportunity and democracy. The 'Shock and Awe' military campaign by the US-UK coalition destroyed sizable portions of Iraq's infrastructure and included the torture of enemy combatants. Presidential envoy Paul Bremer directed Iraq's reconstruction using private US contractors, such as Halliburton and Blackwater (now Academi). Disaster, torture and economic reconstruction followed in quick succession, thus giving some credence to Klein's analogy.

Further evidence comes from a capitalist operative. John Perkins (2004) reveals that 'economic hit men' channel funds from the World Bank, the US Agency for International Development (USAID) and other aid organisations to corporations and influential individuals who control resources in developing countries. Funds are used to finance major infrastructure projects, such as dams and power grids; develop oil and gas resources; and construct telecommunications systems, highways, airports and other projects requiring the technologies and expertise of nations contributing funds. These 'economic advisors' attempt to persuade decision-makers in the receiving nation to make investments and accept loan conditions following Washington Consensus guidelines.

Economic hit men like Perkins also rig elections, submit false studies and financial reports, offer bribes and encourage corruption. Frequently, corruption and fraud prevent the appropriate use of funds, and the debt is passed on to the public, with little to show for it. Countries that subsequently defaulted on their debts are now in crisis and vulnerable to economic shock therapy. If the efforts of hit men are unsuccessful – as they were with Jaime Roldos, Ecuador's former president, or Omar Torrijos of Panama – 'jackals' are sent in to apply other forms of coercion. During an interview in 2007, Perkins stated that both Roldos and Torrijos died when their private jets crashed in 1981, implying they were assassinated.

Stiglitz, Klein and Perkins report remarkably congruent narratives of corporate influence operating through international financial institutions, security organisations and occasionally with military assistance. Although Perkins denies these activities are conspiratorial – 'They don't need to conspire. They all know what serves their best interest' (2007: n.p.) – he describes them as the stratagems of a 'corporatocracy' operating through the World Bank, IMF and other aid organisations. In this analysis, government, military and corporate propaganda work in tandem to insist that the world is safer for democracy, more materially prosperous than ever before, but increasingly under threat from terrorists.

Capitalism's magic: the invisible hand and animal spirits

> . . . he intends only his own gain, and he is in this . . . led by an invisible hand to promote an end which was no part of his intention . . .

By pursuing his own interest he frequently promotes that of the society more effectually than when he really intends to promote it. (Smith [1776] 1976: 456)

Economists often use Adam Smith's analogy of the 'invisible hand' to justify the argument that capitalist markets function best when left to regulate themselves without interference (though Smith seems to say that acting in self-interest merely has unintended consequences). When corrections and adjustments are required in the economy, the invisible hand will make those adjustments and restore equilibrium. The invisible hand analogy resembles the biological concept of homeostasis, in which self-regulating systems automatically seek equilibrium, so the image adopts the status of natural law. It has come to symbolise *laissez-faire* capitalism, its capacity for self-regulation and its inherent rationality.

Critics of this interpretation concede that those acting in self-interest benefit society, but unregulated markets can also lead to disaster:

Capitalist societies, as correctly seen by the old economics, can be tremendously creative. Government should interfere as little as possible with that creativity. On the other hand, *left to their own devices*, capitalist economies will pursue excess, as current times bear witness. There will be *manias*. The manias will be followed by *panics*. (Akerlof and Shiller [2009] 2010: xxiii)

Without some kind of planning to 'set the stage' (xxiv), capitalist markets can become volatile and unpredictable. Marx and Engels note that capitalism has the force of practical magic:

Modern bourgeois society . . . a society that has conjured up such gigantic means of production and of exchange, is like the sorcerer, who is no longer able to control the powers of the nether world whom he has called up by his spells. ([1848] 2011: 70)

In the Faust legend they refer to, a man of learning makes a pact with the devil Mephistopheles to exchange his soul for worldly power – an allusion that captures communism's criticism of capitalist excess.

Many economists now consider the invisible hand analogy to be more myth than science. While it correctly predicts some market behaviours, it is inadequate for predicting anomalies driven by non-rational forces. Akerlof and Shiller resurrect John Maynard Keynes' idea that 'animal spirits' can play a determining role in market behaviour and influence investment decisions. Making economic predictions and taking risks involves uncertainty and conjures up animal spirits – 'a restless and inconsistent element in the economy' ([2009] 2010: 4). Animal spirits are the tricksters of the economy, revealing its myths and blind spots and replacing market rationality with subjectivity. Akerlof and Shiller identify five different animal spirits affecting economic decisions (5):

1. *Confidence* in the market is the foremost animal spirit and plays a role in the other factors. Without confidence, investors will hesitate and hedge their bets; people will not invest in homes, consumer goods or the market. Confidence involves trust.

2. *Fairness* is important in wage and price negotiations. Economics is a theory of exchange: who will trade what, with whom, for how much. Often, the exchange involves other things of value besides money, services and labour. Time, energy, relations, status, face-saving, gratitude and social norms are all subject to negotiation and contribute to perceptions of fairness. Akerlof and Shiller cite research finding that subjects were willing to punish people who acted selfishly, even when it cost them to do so (23).

3. *Corruption* by politicians, investors, brokers, banks, lending institutions and accountants undermines confidence in the whole system. In 2001, Enron was discovered using deceptive accounting practices to claim enormous – and unrealised – profits. Lack of regulatory oversight contributed to the sub-prime mortgage scandal.

4. *Money illusion* results from public confusion about inflation and deflation. What is the true value of money today, in the future or enhanced by compound interest? Without a cost of living allowance in contracts, workers' real wages will decline during inflationary times, while company profits can increase if inflationary costs are passed on to consumers.

5. *Stories* communicate the economy's status. Capitalist propaganda attempts to obscure the excess, manias and panics of unregulated markets. Economists, politicians, corporate representatives and lobbyists try to influence public perceptions with their narratives, usually with underlying morals. When the internet became a popular public utility in the mid-90s, the exuberant narrative of a new era in global communications stimulated wild speculation in internet enterprises. The resulting dot-com boom and bust joined Tulip Mania (1630s) and the South Sea Bubble (1720s), as historical examples of economic narratives fuelling irrational speculation (Mackay [1841] 1995).

Animal spirits create uncertainty and unsettle capitalism's logics, and this uncertainty creates openings for persuasion and propaganda to play on biases and stereotypes. Increasingly, behavioural economics and discoveries in neuroscience are 'humanising' economic assumptions and shifting neoliberalism's rhetoric.

Libertarian paternalism

Classical economics makes a basic assumption about rational decision-making: 'that each of us thinks and chooses unfailingly well' (Thaler and Sunstein [2008] 2009: 7). The economic human – *homo economicus* or Econ for short – is a person who pays 'full attention', possesses 'complete information', has 'unlimited cognitive abilities' and exercises 'complete self-control' (5). As the authors note, however, Humans – including some economists they know – do not behave this predictably (7). It is false to assume that 'almost all people, almost all of the time, make choices that are in their best interest' (10).

Unlike Econs, Humans have predictable biases and frequently fall prey to such pitfalls as the availability bias or loss aversion. Following the work of Kahneman and Tversky (1979) on biases and heuristics, Thaler and Sunstein identify predictable errors Humans are prone to make. These are the new logical fallacies:

- *Anchor*: influences expectations, estimates and price negotiations.
- *Availability*: shapes assessments of risk likelihood, based on how quickly examples come to mind: a recent hurricane, epidemic or terrorist incident will affect predictions of similar events occurring.
- *Salience*: the perceived importance of the risk increases the impact of the availability heuristic.
- *Loss aversion*: humans dislike losing more than they value winning.
- *Status quo bias*: humans prefer to continue with existing conditions, a bias often caused by lack of attention. Inertia is a powerful force and can be 'harnessed' (9) through appropriate default options (for example, enforced saving or investing plans, setting software preferences).
- *Representativeness*: humans make judgements based on similarity and stereotypes. They look for patterns of meaning, even in random configurations.
- *Framing*: establishes the context of decision-making and is easily manipulated. ([2008] 2009: 24–39)

Cognitive miscalculations result when people are insufficiently reflective and rely instead on automatic (fast, System 1) thinking. Thaler and Sunstein comment that 'busy people trying to cope in a complex world . . . cannot afford to think deeply about every choice they have to make' ([2008] 2009: 40). They conclude that 'choice architects' can 'nudge' people toward making better decisions for themselves.

Their approach modifies the one proposed by Lippmann and Bernays, in which intellectual elites operate as invisible agents to manufacture consent. Thaler and Sunstein's paternalism includes the libertarian principle of the 'freedom to choose' (see Friedman 1962), resulting in a hybrid form of influence – libertarian paternalism. A nudge 'is any aspect of the choice architecture that alters people's behaviour in a predictable way without forbidding any options or significantly changing their economic incentives' (Thaler and Sunstein [2008] 2009: 6). Nudges must be 'easy and cheap to avoid' and 'are not mandates' (6). Freedom of choice safeguards against faulty or manipulative choice architecture. Good choice architecture:

- uses carefully chosen defaults or mandated choice to combat inertia;
- accommodates human error with forgiving system design;
- gives feedback when errors are made;
- provides 'mapping' to help users understand the issues when selecting options; and
- structures complex choices to foster optimal decision-making.

Humans should be free, for example, to choose from a range of health-care options, both public and private, but they should also be guided by choice architects to select pharmaceutical plans most suitable for their needs. More controversially, the authors recommend that marriage should be privatised as a 'civil union' – defined as a 'domestic partnership between any two people' ([2008] 2009: 211) – where the union is registered and legal obligations are established. Religious and other organisations could still perform marriages as a private option and 'would be free to choose whatever rules they like' (212). In other examples, they propose the use of carefully chosen incentives to encourage environmental sustainability and organ donations.

As libertarians, Thaler and Sunstein insist that transparency plays an important role in their version of paternalism to avoid abuse. Examples abound of private enterprises selling insurance, credit, securities, cellular plans, mortgages and other products where choice architecture is misleading, overly complex or obscured in fine print. Similarly, governments routinely negotiate diplomatic arrangements, trade agreements and even legislation out of public view. The authors cite with approval Rawls' publicity principle prohibiting governments from adopting any policy or practice they are unwilling to defend in public.

'The government should respect the people whom it governs, and if it adopts policies that it cannot defend in public, it fails to manifest that respect' (Rawls 1971: 244). By invoking the publicity principle, Thaler and Sunstein imply that libertarian paternalism will only be successful if it is built on transparency, trust and mutual respect; otherwise, it is a form of planning on its way to authoritarianism. Freedom to choose is corrupted by lack of information, and benevolent paternalism reverts to manufacturing consent.

Through guided choice, libertarian paternalism seeks a middle path between socialist planning and capitalist *laissez-faire*. In Thaler and Sunstein's scheme, citizens would be free to choose between civic unions and marriage; between public and private healthcare; between donating organs automatically or not; between saving enough or too little. The mantram that people should be free to choose obscures their assumption that free market capitalism is the only viable option and market incentives are necessary for social change. Their proposals prompted Prime Minister Cameron to assemble a Behavioural Insights Team (www.inudgeyou.com) – dubbed the 'Nudge Unit' – to advise government on using behavioural economics and market signals 'to persuade citizens to behave in a more socially integrated way' (Wintour 2010: n.p.). Choice architects are suspiciously similar to engineers of consent, and distinctions between the two rest on transparency, generous intentions and good faith. As with a surveillance apparatus designed to protect national security, behavioural economics in the service of 'social integration' could overstep its mandate and continue engineering consent in another guise.

Corporations under fire

Since the 1970s, think tanks, political lobbying and corporate media have advanced capitalism's cause against socialism, workers' rights and environmental protection. In response, independent documentary films have advocated alternate perspectives to challenge corporate narratives.

- *Roger and Me*, directed by Michael Moore (1989): In his first documentary, populist filmmaker Moore attempts to question General Motors CEO Roger Smith on the decision to close the automaker's plant in Flint, Michigan – Moore's hometown and the birthplace of the United Auto Workers.
- *Who's Counting? Marilyn Waring on Sex, Lies and Global Economics*, directed by Terre Nash (1995): Waring, a former New Zealand

legislator, explains that accounting practices and emphasis on gross national product (GNP) enshrine ideas about economic value. Some humans, often women, just do not count.

- *A Place Called Chiapas*, directed by Nettie Wild (1998): Wild journeys to Mexico's southernmost province searching for the Zapatista Army of National Liberation (EZLN). Following ratification of the North America Free Trade Agreement (NAFTA) in 1993, the Zapatistas took control of large areas of Chiapas to defend their traditional territory and way of life from corporate exploitation.

- *This is What Democracy Looks Like*, directed by Jill Friedberg and Rick Rowley (2000): In 1999, protests against the World Trade Organisation (WTO) in Seattle turned violent when police used excessive force responding to isolated incidents of property damage.

- *The Corporation*, directed by J. Abbott and M. Achbar (2003): This influential documentary traces the consequences of defining the corporation as a 'person', and then analyses the corporate personality using standard psychological diagnostic tools. The corporation – the instrument of free market capitalism – is diagnosed as psychopathic.

- *Enron: The Smartest Guys in the Room*, directed by A. Gibney (2005): The energy trading company Enron was caught in a notorious corporate scandal in 2001–2. Chief executives relied on creative accounting to manipulate California's deregulated energy market, deceive banks and brokerages and defraud billions of dollars from investors.

- *L'encerclement – La démocratie dans les rets du néolibéralisme*, directed by R. Brouillette (2008): This French-language documentary unpacks neoliberal ideology and tactics through interviews with international scholars and commentators.

- *Food, Inc.*, directed by R. Kenner (2008): Kenner exposes the disturbing underbelly of corporate food production and its industrialised practices, largely hidden from consumers through the complicity of regulatory agencies, industry and lobby groups.

- *Capitalism: A Love Story*, directed by Michael Moore (2009): Moore's film is a populist and satirical critique of capitalism, the housing crisis of 2008 and the Wall Street bail out. Moore's America has become a 'plutonomy' – a society 'where economic growth is powered by and largely consumed by the wealthy few'.

- *Inside Job*, directed by Charles Ferguson (2010): Ferguson won an Academy Award in 2010 for his thorough condemnation of the US financial industry and its betrayal of investors and the public trust. The film recounts a complex story of deregulation, economic crises, speculative booms and financial crashes leading to 'the systemic corruption of the United States by the financial services industry'.

- *Not Business As Usual*, directed by L. Le Lam and R. Kingle-Watt (2014): This documentary challenges Milton Friedman's doctrine that 'the social responsibility of business is to increase its profits' by profiling entrepreneurs motivated by more than profit. There are examples of conscious capitalism pursuing shared values through social venture networks.

Exercise questions

1. If you were in a position to advise your government on its economic policies, what would you recommend? Be prepared to defend your recommendations.
2. Divide your learning group into capitalists and socialists to debate the benefits of your economic ideology. As much as possible, try to focus on the means of achieving your preferred model, as opposed to the ideal ends you have in mind.
3. Update Klein's ideas about disaster capitalism with contemporary examples.
4. Identify examples of Akerlof and Shiller's 'animal spirits' in financial news reporting.
5. What are your thoughts on implementing policies based on libertarian paternalism?
6. Interview someone with strong opinions on economic ideology, challenging your subject, where necessary, by presenting your own counter-arguments. Your interview can be recorded and edited for broadcast or written for print publication.
7. Write a short policy paper (1,000 words) for a think tank of your choice on the theme of corporate responsibility.
8. Research media coverage of the Occupy movement and evaluate its successes and failures. Comment on the relative objectivity and/or bias you found in the media reports.

Figure 13 'Religion and politics: layers of influence'. Photo: M. Soules, Kerala, 2012.

9 Making News

Trust and journalism

In 2013, an Ipsos MORI poll found that trust in journalists had fallen to 21 per cent in the UK, equal to bankers, but not yet at the bottom of the list. That position, at 18 per cent, was occupied by politicians in general, who could not compete against business leaders (34 per cent), the ordinary person in the street (64 per cent) or against doctors, teachers, scientists and judges, all registering over 80 per cent in the trust survey (Ipsos MORI 2013). The poll notes the 'disconnect' between voters and 'political elites' to explain politicians' poor showing, but does not otherwise speculate on public trust levels. A wary public may be suspicious that politicians and journalists are too influential and unaccountable; perhaps they work in tandem to manufacture consent and deceive the public to hold their positions. Both professions must perform in complex information environments. They work for influential masters and are forced into compromising positions. Ultimately, bad publicity for journalists and politicians has undermined their credibility, keeping them at the bottom of the trust index poll since it began in 1983.

In many accounts, politicians and the mainstream media join forces against an identified enemy. According to Rutherford, politicians, generals and corporate media worked together to bring coalition forces into war with Iraq using 'weapons of mass persuasion'. The war was 'narrative and spectacle . . . a branded war, a co-production of the Pentagon and of newsrooms' (2004: 4). In an earlier example, Seumas Milne's reporting on the 'smear campaign' against Arthur Scargill and the National Union of Mineworkers reveals a unified effort by Thatcher's Conservative government, the corporate media lead by newspaper baron Robert Maxwell, the judiciary and the British security apparatus to discredit the coal miners' union as the 'enemy within' throughout the 1980s and early 1990s:

The campaign was a bizarre, almost surreal, episode which revealed much about the way British public life works: its double standards and workaday corruption; the myriad ties and connections which allow different parts of the establishment to move in tandem as soon as the need arises; the comfortable relationship between sections of the Labour hierarchy and the government and security apparatus; the way politicians, government and its various agencies, newspapers, broadcasters and professionals feed off the same political menu as if to order. It also served to highlight, in exemplary fashion, the political venality and pliability of the bulk of the British media. (Milne [1994] 2005: 310–11)

No accusations against Scargill and his closest colleagues in the union were substantiated. Milne's trenchant commentary provides insight into the perennial lack of public trust in politicians and journalists identified by the Ipsos MORI polls over the past thirty years.

Web of influence

Curtis (2003) argues that the British news media contribute to a 'web of deceit' woven by the government of the day to hide activities from a public who would never agree to these policies carried out in its name. Political realists claim that deception and propaganda are necessary in democracies to support a state apparatus capable of decisive action, while protecting national interests in a competitive, international arena. Without secrecy, deception and propaganda, competitive advantage and information dominance are lost. To counter this defence, Curtis documents patterns of deception exercised by the British Government since WWII. While government rhetoric proclaims its 'basic benevolence' (380), Curtis demonstrates that Britain 'is a systematic violator of international law and ethical standards in its foreign policy' (1). A 'tirade of propaganda' disguises 'actual policies that are directly opposite to [elite] rhetoric' (2–3). Curtis cites convincing examples from Indonesia, Malaya, Kenya, South Africa, Rwanda, Kosovo, Palestine, Chechnya, Afghanistan, Iraq and Iran to illustrate his thesis that the British Government pursues polices that the majority of citizens would find morally repugnant. 'It is not a conspiracy', he writes, 'rather, the system works by journalists and academics *internalising* sets of values, generally accepted wisdom and styles of reporting' (4).

News reporting distorts reality when it fails to report on important stories and policies; frames stories to exclude relevant history, context or information; and repeats stories without challenging official explanations (376–7). The pretext of bringing balance to stories often means that official statements and opinions overpower independent commentary. Curtis cites James Curran's idea that 'the modern mass media in Britain now perform many of the integrative functions of the church in the middle ages' (377) by identifying deviant and anti-social behaviour, marginalising radical opinions and demonising infidels and outsiders, from trade union activists to immigrants. News media explain and legitimise the social order and thereby reinforce existing power structures.

Television news is particularly susceptible to distortion, since it is structured around striking visuals and sound bite commentary. Any extended analysis involves experts, officials and pundits express-ing opinions, telling audiences what to think and repeating official talking points. Deviations from this pattern risk a deluge of criticism (flak) from interest groups, publicists and authorities. The Glasgow University Media Group concludes that 'the news is not a neutral and natural phenomenon; it is rather the manufactured production of ideol-ogy' (Curtis 2003: 379). While news reporting at its worst can involve a web of deceit, it is more frequently caught up in a web of influence.

Political idealists maintain that government and corporate trans-parency are required for meaningful democratic decision-making, and media concentration limits diversity of opinion (Schiller 1991; Bagdikian 2004; McChesney 2008). When public relations masquer-ades as objective journalism, public cynicism increases and contributes to an 'increase of depoliticisation' (McChesney 2013: 59). Diminished trust, credibility and transparency contribute to apathy in the politi-cal process and are even encouraged by those who understand that increased political engagement means greater opposition to policies benefiting elites (Carey 1997; Lessig 2011; Stiglitz 2013). 'I don't want everybody to vote', claimed Heritage Foundation founder Paul Weyrich in 1980, 'our leverage in the elections quite candidly goes up as the voting populace goes down' (McChesney 2013: 59). In *Republic, Lost* (2011), Lessig argues that political campaign financing and special interest lobbying in the US Congress have created 'dependence cor-ruption' in an 'economy of influence' (17), where politicians and advisors depend on financial incentives (bribes) and positive publicity to stay in power. For economist Stiglitz ([2012] 2013), the 'price of inequality' includes widespread perceptions of unfairness and decep-tion. Zak (2012) confirms the importance of trust in sustaining 'moral markets', social fairness and national prosperity. As perceptions of inequality increase, trust in the messengers declines.

Greater access to information and increasing diversity of viewpoints promised by digital media are clearly having an impact on news reporting (Rowland 1997; Benkler 2006; Castells 2012). At the same time, the desire for information dominance encourages surveillance, massive data collection and 'trading' and leads to asymmetries of information as much as disparities of wealth (Stiglitz [2012] 2013: 347). The digital revolution is closely monitored by power elites, with legions of publicists, advertisers, organisations and individuals contributing opinion as news in a torrent of influence. In a media environment saturated with blogs, Tweets, spectacle and churnalism, finding the scarce attention of audiences is the contemporary equivalent of a gold rush. Still, as with the muckrakers in the early twentieth century, investigative journalists play an influential role speaking truth to power.

Investigative journalism: exceptions prove the rule

Responsible investigative journalism shines a spotlight on underreported news stories and even agitates for political and social reform. In his collection of articles written since 1945, Australian journalist and filmmaker John Pilger ([2004] 2005) celebrates journalists who 'bear witness and investigate ideas' neglected or distorted in the mainstream media and mount, in the words of activist Vandana Shiva, an 'insurrection of subjugated knowledge' in the face of 'dominant knowledge' (xvi). Pilger's heroes range from Martha Gellhorn (reporting on Dachau in 1945), Wilfred Burchett (atomic radiation at Hiroshima in 1945), Edward R. Murrow (McCarthyism from 1947 to 1954), Seymour Hersh (Vietnam in 1970), Seumas Milne (UK coal miners in the 1980s and 1990s), Amira Hass (Gaza in 1996), Anna Politkovskaya (Chechnya from 1999 to 2002), Greg Palast (the US election fraud in 2000) and Robert Fisk (reporting on Iraq in 2003). Today, we might extend Pilger's list to include Glenn Greenwald and Laura Poitras, Naomi Klein, Charles Ferguson, Nick Davies, Mark Dowie, Robert Greenwald, Greg Philo and Mike Berry, and Jeremy Scahill among many others who dig beneath conventional wisdom, official statements and outright spin to restore trust and credibility in journalism.

Pilger's story begins in 1820s Australia, when Edward Smith Hall stood up to the virtual dictatorship of General Ralph Darling: '[Hall's] campaigns for the rights of convicts and freed prisoners and his exposure of the corruption of officials, magistrates and the Governor's hangers-on made him a target of the draconian laws of criminal libel' (xviii). Almost 200 years later, whistle-blowers are facing draconian laws for revealing secret government activity, but they are no longer charged with criminal libel. Instead, they are cast as traitors betraying national interests and are charged with espionage. In 2014, a Pulitzer Prize for journalism was awarded jointly to reporters from *The Guardian* and the *Washington Post* who worked on Edward Snowden's revelations of mass surveillance.

Pilger does not believe a conspiracy theory is necessary to explain a news apparatus in the service of power: 'Journalists and broadcasters are no different from historians and teachers in internalising the priorities and fashions and propriety of established power' (xvii). They, too, are subject to received wisdom, patriotic pride and cultural values. To advance in their professions, journalists are 'trained', 'groomed' and encouraged to 'set aside serious doubts'. Stories are framed to be about 'us' and thus tend toward narcissism and self-interest. Conflict in news reporting is expressed in dichotomies: their actions are threatening; our intentions are noble; they are terrorists; we are protecting our interests. This psychological approach leverages fear of a hostile Other (Keen 1986), with the effect that it forges community, promotes national self-interest, reinforces allegiances, defines a way of life and appeals to the status quo. Power needs good publicity at home and bad news elsewhere to justify its status. While cooperation between governments, corporations, security establishments and powerful media actors is defensible during a national crisis, manipulative cooperation done secretively betrays principles of trust and transparency necessary to democracy. A noble lie is required, to use Edward Herman's phrase, to 'normalise the unthinkable for the general public' (Herman, in Pilger [2004] 2005: xxvi). As Pilger concludes: 'Instead, noble words and concepts like "democracy" and "freedom" and "liberation" are emptied of their true meaning and pressed into the service of conquest' (xxvi). Good investigative journalism challenges this trend to prove an exception to the rule.

News propaganda model

Perhaps foremost among critics of media complicity in the service of power is the linguist and cultural critic Noam Chomsky. A prolific researcher, author and commentator, Chomsky openly condemns US policy in the Middle East and considers the US a 'failed state' for its unilateral approach to foreign affairs. Chomsky's overall project responds to Lippmann's ([1922] 1997: 158) notion of the 'manufacture of consent', where state-corporate hegemony is amplified to the condition of propaganda. With Edward Herman, Chomsky developed a propaganda model in the 1980s to account for biased corporate news reporting, both in the US and elsewhere (Herman and Chomsky 1988).

The propaganda model describes a communications environment for 'thought control in democratic societies'. It identifies five filters that frame news reporting and set the agenda for public discourse. To defend the model, power elites assert that media do not have to be controlled, because they are legitimate actors in the influence business. The principle of press freedom makes reform difficult and provides an illusion of the separation of powers. The newspaper scandals involving Rupert Murdoch and his News Corporation discussed later in this chapter are a case study in the application and defence of the propaganda model. The five filters include:

1. *Ownership and editorial policy*: Major media operations are corporations and share interests with the corporate community. Their owners are frequently wealthy entrepreneurs, who cultivate political alliances and who can exert influence over politicians. News organisations are subject to direction by owners and editors, who ultimately shape and enforce editorial policy.

2. *Funding sources and advertising*: News organisations depend on government subsidies (in the form of tax incentives) and advertising dollars to make a profit, and these funding sources exert pressure on news reporting.

3. *News sources*: Government and corporate public relations, sources of opinion (advisors, pundits, think tanks) and news services dominate news supply, especially when news organisations fire reporters and close foreign bureaus to economise.

4. *Flak*: Negative responses to news articles or programmes are submitted from interest groups, lobbyists, publicists, politicians and lawyers, who dispute the facts or tone of news reports. They may threaten to sue, ask for retractions or request equal time for rebuttal. Fear of flak has a dampening effect on reporting and contributes to the common practice of quoting official representatives without challenge.

5. *Ideology/fear*: The propaganda model was developed during the Cold War, and Chomsky and Herman specified anti-communist bias as the final filter. In subsequent writing, they revised their model to specify that any ideology threatening elite interests – unionism, socialism or terrorism – will shape news coverage and its interpretation. (Herman and Chomsky 1988)

The model predicts that corporate news has built-in conflicts of interest, making it less able to balance power between elites and citizens.

By implication, ideal news reporting in democratic societies should be free of these biases or at least more transparent about them. Chomsky advises that 'citizens of the democratic societies should undertake a course of intellectual self-defence to protect themselves from manipulation and control', because corporate media no longer perform this function (1989: viii). Intellectual self-defence involves seeking out alternate news sources and opinions, questioning source credibility and researching the context for important stories.

Illustrations of the propaganda model at work:

- *Containing the enemy (appeal to fear)*: During the Cold War, government intervention was justified as a defence against creeping socialism, even when that defence was pre-emptive or aggressive. Chomsky discusses the CIA-backed interventions in Guatemala (1954) and Nicaragua (1980s) and the war in Southeast Asia as examples. After the fall of the Iron Curtain and demise of the former USSR, a new enemy for containment was needed. On 11 September 2001, the perennial threat of terrorism became the necessary illusion. In a literal sense, the Israeli security wall was built to contain Palestinian 'terrorists' and is justified on that basis.
- *Setting the agenda (framing)*: Top-tier newspapers such as the *The New York Times, Washington Post, Boston Globe* and *Los Angeles Times* in the US set the news agenda by deciding what is newsworthy and, in turn, set the agenda for second-tier news coverage. (The same principles apply in other news markets.) Chomsky's chief example in 1989 was media coverage of the Sandinista government in Nicaragua, where debate was limited to the methods most suitable to remove the Sandinistas from power, not whether it was legitimate to do so. Similar restraints are placed on the question of nuclear capability in Iran and North Korea, without mentioning Israel, India and Pakistan.
- *Failing to report on stories (selection/censorship)*: The media's failure to report adequately on mass killings in Cambodia, Rwanda and East Timor or to probe the role of private contractors in Iraq and Afghanistan excludes newsworthy stories from public view. Commercial interests in war zones are seldom acknowledged to explain causes of conflict. While the US, UK, Canada, New Zealand and Australia collaborated on a global surveillance network called Project Echelon for years (Schmid 2001; Asser 2000), secret agreements to cooperate between intelligence agencies were virtually ignored in the media long before Edward Snowden revealed more advanced surveillance operations in 2013.

- *Interpreting world events along ideological or self-congratulatory lines*: In Iraq, the US and UK Governments explained pre-emptive aggression and regime change as a defence of democracy and human rights. 'Democracy' is achieved when the former failed state is safely in the hands of those who wield economic and political power (Chomsky [1989] 1991: 106). British foreign policy exhibits a 'basic benevolence' (Curtis 2003: 380). Canadian tar sands oil is 'ethical' because it is produced in a democracy, not a totalitarian state.

The boundaries of legitimate debate are drawn by official sources who define issues of concern and marginalise opinions by non-officials. For the necessary illusion to persist, debate must be tolerated within certain bounds to confirm that democracy thrives on controversy and differences of opinion, as long as elite views remain paramount.

Case study in flak: the Israel lobby

In March 2009, British MP George Galloway was denied entry into Canada because he supported Hamas, an elected political party in Gaza identified as a terrorist organisation by the Canadian Government. Galloway was trying to enter Canada from New York, where he had advocated a one-state solution to the Israeli-Palestinian conflict to Columbia University students. Galloway, who helped organise and fund an aid convoy to Hamas, suggested that the presiding judge's decision was influenced by 'external lobbying' and 'political influence' (Wallace and MacCharles 2009). He experienced first-hand the pro-Israel lobby's power and its influence on the governments, judiciary and media of the day.

The pro-Israel lobby is a significant source of flak challenging media reports on Israeli-Palestinian relations. Journalists reporting both sides of the conflict face 'an uphill task', since 'to criticise Israel can create major problems' (Philo and Berry [2004] 2011: 2). For their research on *More Bad News from Israel*, Philo and Berry heard from journalists about 'the extraordinary number of complaints which they receive' (2) if their reporting implies criticism of Israel. Davies notes that contemporary public relations has rules, one of which is to 'avoid the electric fence' by paying 'deference to any organisation or individual with the power to hurt news organisations' ([2008] 2009: 122). In Davies' opinion, the 'most potent electric fence in the world is the one erected on behalf of the Israeli government' (123).

> Journalists who write stories which offend the politics of the Israeli lobby are subjected to a campaign of formal complaints and pressure on their editors; most of all, they are inundated with letters and emails which can be extravagant in their hostility. (123)

Davies refers here to an international network of organisations that specialise in condemning critics of Israel. Their orchestration of complaints approaches the status of propaganda, argues Davies, and supplements Israeli *hasbara* (public diplomacy) to explain its policies to international audiences (Shabi 2009). Organisations such as HonestReporting, Give Israel Your United Support (GIYUS), the Middle East Media Research Institute (MEMRI), Palestine Media Watch and the Britain Israel Communications and Research Centre (BICOM) collectively exert pressure on news media and public figures to condemn Palestinian 'terrorism' and endorse Israeli 'peacekeeping' initiatives.

The Israel lobby in the US is a 'loose coalition of individuals and organisations' pursuing two broad strategies: (1) to pressure Congress and the executive to support Israeli policies (often in consultation with Israeli politicians); and (2) to 'ensure that public discourse portrays Israel in a positive light' (Mearsheimer and Walt 2011: n.p.). As with other US interest groups, the Israel lobby makes campaign contributions, influences elected representatives and bureaucrats and shapes public opinion. Key lobby organisations include the American-Israel Public Affairs Committee (AIPAC) and the Conference of Presidents of Major Jewish Organisations. Many Christian evangelicals support the lobby, seeing the triumph of Israel as a matter of biblical prophecy.

Lobbying power is based on the ability to reward or punish politicians during elections, especially with campaign contributions and threats of negative publicity. AIPAC organises letter-writing campaigns to pressure newspaper editors to include pro-Israel opinion pieces. The Committee for Accurate Middle East Reporting in America (CAMERA) organised demonstrations against National Public Radio (NPR) and persuaded network contributors to withdraw their funding, because NPR's coverage was not sympathetic enough to Israel (Levin 2002). On university campuses, support groups such as the Caravan for Democracy, Jewish Council for Public Affairs, Hillel and the Israel on Campus Coalition actively promote Israel. In 2002, Daniel Pipes established the controversial Campus Watch to monitor Middle East studies courses and report any anti-Israel activity by professors (McNeil 2002).

The Israel lobby intimidates critics with ad hominem attacks, calling them 'anti-Semitic' or 'self-hating Jews' or even making physical threats (Davies [2008] 2009: 123). 'Indeed, anyone who merely claims that there is an Israel lobby runs the risk of being charged with anti-Semitism, even though the Israeli media refer to America's "Jewish Lobby"' (Mearsheimer and Walt 2011: n.p.). In July 2011, an aid flotilla to Gaza was blocked by the Greek Government under pressure from Israel and the United States (McGovern 2011). Alan Dershowitz, a prominent pro-Israel supporter and Harvard law professor, described the flotilla as 'ships of fools, knaves hypocrites [sic], bigots, and supporters of terrorism that tried to break Israel's naval blockade of Gaza' (Dershowitz 2011: n.p.). His attack continues:

> A common virus among many on these ships is a hatred for Jews, the Jewish state, America, and the West. Some are self-haters, because they themselves are Jews, Israelis or Westerners. Others are Arabs who cannot abide the notion of the Jewish state, regardless of its size or borders, anywhere in the Middle East. (Dershowitz 2011: n.p.)

McGovern observes that one of the 'self-hating Jews' on the US ship was Hedy Epstein, an 86-year-old Holocaust survivor (2011).

In their investigation of the Israel lobby, Mearsheimer and Walt (2011) question why the US Government would jeopardise its own security to provide financial, political and moral support to a country identified by the United Nations as engaging in human rights abuses and illegal annexation of territory. 'The combination of unwavering support for Israel and the related effort to spread "democracy" throughout the region has inflamed Arab and Islamic opinion and jeopardized not only US security but that of much of the rest of the world' (2011: n.p.). Their argument was confirmed in Osama bin Laden's letter 'To the Americans' (October 2002), where he asserted that the US had become a target for terrorist attacks because it continued to support Israeli aggression in the Middle East and was itself engaged in imperialist adventures in the region (bin Laden 2005: 162). While US solidarity with Israel is presented as a common fight against terrorism,

> saying that Israel and the US are united by a shared terrorist threat has the causal relationship backwards: the US has a terrorism problem in good part because it is so closely allied with Israel, not the other way around. (Mearsheimer and Walt 2011: n.p.)

For its part, the Israeli Government's National Information Directorate continues its *hasbara* efforts with its own talking points: 'that Hamas broke the ceasefire agreements with Israel; that Israel's objective is the defence of its population; and that Hamas is a terror organisation targeting Israeli civilians' (Shabi 2009: n.p.). Israel's need for security is a legitimate matter of global concern, but building separation barriers with both concrete and words may be counterproductive. When US Secretary of State John Kerry warned in 2014 that Israel was in danger of becoming 'an apartheid state' like South Africa, he was immediately criticised by the pro-Israel lobby and even President Obama, who countered: 'Injecting a term like apartheid into the discussion doesn't advance that goal [of peace] . . . It's emotionally loaded, historically inaccurate, and it's not what I believe' (Rogin 2014: n.p.).

Anti-Semitism is real and has a long and terrible history. Following Russian and Soviet pogroms and the Nazi Holocaust, understanding the intense desire for a Jewish homeland and sanctuary in Israel is a matter of empathy and compassion. Peace has been difficult and painful to negotiate and crimes have been committed on all sides. Discourse that further inflames polarisation and enmity is not helpful and endangers lives, both in the region and elsewhere. As Brendan Nyhan comments, there is a 'downside' to 'registering outrage', because 'drawing attention to group differences can amplify divisions' (2014: n.p.).

Another way forward is suggested by the collaboration between Edward Said and Argentine-Israeli conductor Daniel Barenboim on the West-Eastern Divan Orchestra. A film about their collaboration called *Knowledge is the Beginning* (2005) tells the story of young musicians coming together from Egypt, Iran, Israel, Jordan, Lebanon, Palestine, Syria and Spain to perform selections from classical repertoires. Barenboim describes the project as intended to promote understanding and peace in the Arab-Israeli conflict:

> The Divan was conceived as a project against ignorance. A project against the fact that it is absolutely essential for people to get to know the other, to understand what the other thinks and feels, without necessarily agreeing with it . . . I want to . . . create a platform where the two sides can disagree and not resort to knives. (Vulliamy 2008: n.p.)

Fox News and post-truth politics

We live in a cynical time, when words like 'fair' and 'balanced' are used as slogans to sell content that is anything but. When the words of lobbyists and the politicians they support are given equal weight with the consensus of scientific experts, by journalists who think a news story is a competition between opposing narratives rather than a judicious search for truth. (Brock and Rabin-Havt 2012: 11)

In 2004, filmmaker Robert Greenwald used leaked emails from a senior editor at Fox News as the centrepiece of his film *Outfoxed: Rupert Murdoch's War on Journalism*. Among other accusations, the film criticises management interference in news reporting, particularly coverage of the Iraq War. Hosts such as O'Reilly and Hannity routinely intimidate guests they disagree with. Citing unidentified sources ('some people say . . .'), hosts are able to make accusations with impunity, using constant repetition and talking points to set the agenda for discussion. Greenwald's film is not balanced in its critique, but it raises serious issues about journalistic ethics and management interference, especially when that interference is sustained, partisan and inflammatory.

In *The Fox Effect* (2012), Brock, Rabin-Havt and the research team at Media Matters for America use content analysis to document the evolution of Fox News from a partisan news organisation to an active political player and 'propaganda machine'. They reveal an extreme version of management interference – the first propaganda news filter – as well as a trend toward advocacy journalism unconstrained by balance and objectivity. The authors spotlight the influence of Fox News President Roger Ailes and his senior managers on editorial opinion, story coverage and ideological slanting. They conclude that far from being 'fair and balanced', the network broadcasts 'demonstrable lies and distortions with a consistent conservative spin' (12). They cite studies revealing that viewers who regularly watch Fox News are among the most misinformed on a variety of issues (13) and are subjected to rhetoric filled with 'violent imagery and demonisation' (12).

Fox News acted as a Republican cheerleader during the Bush presidency, but it quickly took the offensive against Obama and Congressional Democrats after the 2008 election. 'Now the network would wag the elephant, transforming itself from a news and opinion outlet into the leading communications, fund-raising, and mobilising arm of the Republican Party' (Brock and Rabin-Havt 2012: 17–18). Just days into his presidency, Obama's 'socialist' policies were deemed a failure. He was compared to genocidal leaders, accused of racism, of not being American (the birtherism controversy), of being soft on terrorism. Personal attacks and name-calling soon extended to his healthcare reforms ('death panels' would decide who lived or died), economic reforms and environmental policies. When host Glenn Beck went too far and accused Obama of racism, over seventy advertisers noted the public outrage and cancelled their contracts (148).

As the 2010 elections approached, Fox News crossed another ethical line for news organisations when it allowed Republican candidates to promote their campaigns on the air. 'Over the course of the 2010 election cycle, more than thirty Fox News employees endorsed, raised funds, or campaigned for over three hundred Republican candidates and organisations' (213). Fox was no longer a news broadcaster; it had become a political player making a difference in the polls, especially for conservative Tea Party candidates.

Brock and Rabin-Havt conclude that Roger Ailes, increasingly out of favour with Murdoch for his single-minded leadership, became a 'king maker' for Republican candidates, who depended on Fox for favourable coverage. Ailes, they suggest, 'has ushered in the era of post-truth politics', where 'the facts no longer matter, only what is politically expedient, sensationalistic, and designed to confirm the pre-existing opinions of a large audience' (283). Significantly, the Fox audience is large enough to influence the politics of the world's most heavily militarised state.

Journalism's dark arts

One of the prerogatives of a free press is the power to influence, and Rupert Murdoch became a master of the game, first in Australia, then Britain and most recently in the US, with his various acquisitions including *The Wall Street Journal* and the Fox Network. As a self-confessed libertarian, Murdoch built a media empire to influence his diverse publics on an industrial scale toward his politically conservative views.

Murdoch was an innovator in electronic newspaper publication in the 1980s when he built state-of-the-art facilities at Wapping in the London dockyards. The new production methods anticipated the challenges of distributing news on the internet, through social media and mobile computing, but led to lay-offs and labour unrest. He courted those in positions of power, was courted in return and successfully positioned his news properties to comment on and influence politics: in the 1980s and early 90s, he supported Margaret Thatcher and the Conservatives, he switched allegiance to Tony Blair and Labour in the late 1990s and then he swung back to the Cameron Conservatives after 2005 (Pilger [2004] 2005: xx–xxi; Watson and Hickman 2012: 6–7). Murdoch cultivated a reputation as a 'hands-on' proprietor, shaped editorial policy and fostered a competitive, profit-driven newsroom atmosphere.

In July 2011, stories began to emerge that *News of the World* and other Murdoch newspapers had been paying private investigators to hack the telephones of politicians, celebrities, members of the royal family and crime victims, often with the help of corrupt police officers. Known as 'blagging' – obtaining something by persuasion or guile – this breach of journalistic ethics was condemned in the corporate media, even though the practice was widely suspected for years (Davies [2008] 2009; Watson and Hickman 2012).

While the complex story of the 'phone hacking scandal' is still being written, reporters and a parliamentary investigation have pieced together facts, allegations and denials into a tale of journalism sacrificing ethics and truth for sensationalism and profit. The 'dark arts' of the new journalism (Davies [2008] 2009: 259) used various blagging techniques to gather information for stories, including: phone hacking; accessing databases, criminal records, telephone numbers, billing records, credit card and bank statements; searching through trash; corrupting public officials; and influencing members of government. Investigations and courtroom testimony revealed an extensive network of bribery and collusion extending into the London Metropolitan Police and Scotland Yard, following years of denial and inaction on their part.

Watson and Hickman (2012) explain

> how a particular global media company . . . came to exert a poisonous, secretive influence on public life in Britain, how it used its huge power to bully, intimidate and to cover up, and how its exposure has changed the way we look at our politicians, our police service and our press. (xvi)

Their indignant tone telegraphs the authors' bias, but captures the sense of outrage at revelations that *News of the World* and other publications routinely violated the privacy of British subjects, published their findings to increase circulation and then denied the practice. Senior editors at *News of the World*, along with Rupert Murdoch and his son James, were called to testify before the parliamentary committee, but essentially denied all foreknowledge of private investigators, eavesdropping and blagging until convictions had been secured and evidence accumulated to the point where further denials were impossible.

When the phone hacking scandal reached a crescendo, *News of the World* closed its doors after 160 years of reporting. Murdoch's bid for control of the BSkyB satellite network was withdrawn in July 2011. Rupert Murdoch was deemed 'not a fit person to exercise stewardship of a major international company' and was proven to have demonstrated 'wilful blindness' toward illegal activities in News

Corporation properties ('Rupert Murdoch' BBC 2012: n.p.). By 2012, it was public knowledge that the dark arts were not isolated to News Corporation, but endemic across the British press. At the height of the controversy, Carl Bernstein – of Watergate reporting fame – commented:

> As anyone in the business will tell you, the standards and culture of a journalistic institution are set from the top down, by its owner, publisher, and top editors. Reporters and editors do not routinely break the law, bribe policemen, wiretap, and generally conduct themselves like thugs unless it is a matter of recognized and understood policy. Private detectives and phone hackers do not become the primary sources of a newspaper's information without the tacit knowledge and approval of the people at the top, all the more so in the case of newspapers owned by Rupert Murdoch, according to those who know him best. (Bernstein 2011: n.p.)

Bernstein goes on to quote a former executive and close Murdoch aide as saying the scandal could have happened

> [o]nly in Murdoch's orbit . . . More than anyone, Murdoch invented and established this culture in the newsroom, where you do whatever it takes to get the story, take no prisoners, destroy the competition, and the end will justify the means. (2011: n.p.)

Press reform: holding power to account

Freedom of the press has been enshrined in British common law for 300 years. In his inquiry into the phone hacking scandal, Justice Leveson commented: 'The press, operating properly and in the public interest is one of the true safeguards of our democracy' (Leveson 2012: 3). In that role,

> the press is given significant and special rights . . . With these rights, however, come responsibilities to the public interest: to respect the truth, to obey the law and to uphold the rights and liberties of individuals. In short, to honour the very principles proclaimed and articulated by the industry itself. (3)

The *News of the World* scandal raises widespread concern, because it sits at the nexus of technological change, journalistic ethics and influence and the highest aspirations of democratic societies. In Australia, the Finkelstein media inquiry report (2012) expressed similar concerns about a market with a higher concentration of newspaper ownership than the other twenty-six countries studied. News Corporation controls 65 per cent of metropolitan and daily news circulation in Australia (Bacon 2012). If the function of the press is 'to hold those with power to account' (5), its failure during the UK phone hacking scandal to investigate its own crimes is a breach of public trust.

Leveson is cautious not to make any recommendations undermining press freedom and independence, especially by the government, but insists there must be a mechanism for protecting the public interest. He condemns inaction by the Press Complaints Commission and calls for its reformation to become independent of the industry and capable of robust and timely complaint arbitration. He concludes that the relationship between the Metropolitan Police Service and *News of the World* was 'too close' (20) and contributed to a failure to investigate crimes coming to light beginning in 2007 (Underhill 2011). Leveson also accuses the press of 'recklessness in prioritising sensational stories, almost irrespective of the harm that the stories may cause . . . all the while heedless of the public interest' (2012: 10). *News of the World* 'lost its way', he concludes, with a 'significant and reckless disregard for accuracy' (11).

Politician Tom Watson reached his own conclusions: 'Ultimately this scandal is about the failure of politicians to act in the interests of the powerless rather than themselves' (Watson and Hickman 2012: xvi). Without the press or politicians to protect the 'powerless', who will hold those with power to account? Al Jazeera is one news organisation attempting to do just that.

Al Jazeera under fire

Egyptian-American filmmaker Jehane Noujaim made *Control Room*, her 2004 documentary on Al Jazeera, on a shoestring budget. She was eventually granted extraordinary access to reporters and producers working for the Qatar-based broadcaster. Prominent figures in the film include Hassan Ibrahim, a Sudanese journalist formerly at the BBC; Samir Khader and Deema Khatib, senior producers at Al Jazeera; and Lt Josh Rushing, a press officer at US Central Command in Doha. With an audience of 40 million viewers in the Arab world during the Iraq War, Al Jazeera's satellite broadcasts made it an influential player on the brink of notoriety.

In the film, Secretary of Defense Donald Rumsfeld accuses Al Jazeera of propaganda for showing the dead bodies of US soldiers and Iraqi civilians. The network tells lies and encourages resistance, he asserts. It is 'not being helpful'. George W. Bush calls Al Jazeera the 'mouthpiece of Osama bin Laden'. From the other side of the conflict, Muhammad Saeed al-Sahhaf, the Iraqi Minister of Information, says Al Jazeera transmits American propaganda. Since its founding in 1996, Al Jazeera's support of democracy and modernisation in the Arab world has made it vulnerable to criticism and censorship from repressive Arab regimes. Its motto is 'the opinion and the other opinion'.

Early in the film, Josh Rushing performs his duty of presenting the coalition talking points that they are liberating Iraq from a tyrant willing to use weapons of mass destruction on his own people, and Iraqis will welcome their liberators with open arms. Rushing accuses Al Jazeera of bias in its focus on civilian casualties, but he also acknowledges the biased coverage of Fox News. Khader explains that Al Jazeera's coverage reveals the real costs of war on both sides. Images transcend language barriers, he argues, and communicate information to both sides of the conflict when they are not contrived. Later in the film, while watching television images of wounded civilians, Khader comments: 'Rumsfeld calls this incitement. I call this true journalism'.

Rumsfeld's accusations that Al Jazeera's coverage is not helpful takes on ominous overtones when the film shows a US fighter attack on Al Jazeera's Baghdad headquarters on 8 April 2003. (Previously, Al Jazeera had reported its location coordinates to the US military to prevent any mistaken attacks.) Journalist Tareq Ayyoub is killed in the attack, and his widow is later shown on television pleading with journalists to 'tell the truth' about his death. On the same day as the Al Jazeera bombing, US forces open fire on the Palestine Hotel in Baghdad, killing two cameramen, and attack the Abu Dhabi television network. These three attacks on non-embedded journalists were considered deliberate by eyewitnesses.

In his writing on the Iraq conflict, Paul William Roberts explains that journalism is considered 'an aspect or wing of psychological warfare operations', whose purpose is to gain 'information dominance'. The attacks on non-embedded news organisations by US forces were another facet of 'full-spectrum dominance' (2004: 89–90). Commenting on the question of balance when reporting war casualties, Roberts concludes: 'With the ubiquity of personal computers and internet access, not to mention Al Jazeera, our bias is increasingly available for all to see, and we are rightly despised for it, regarded as hypocrites and liars' (210).

Control Room documents how difficult it is for journalists and news organisations to report accurately in the 'fog of war', especially when modern warfare relies so heavily on psychological operations to dominate the 'human terrain'. A 2009 Associated Press investigation identified the US$4.7 billion annual budget for Pentagon public relations, with the fastest-growing area going to psychological operations directed at foreign audiences ('Pentagon Spending Billions on PR' 2009). Thus, a significant emotional fulcrum of the film balances on the character of Josh Rushing. Through his interactions with the spirited and cynical Hassan Ibrahim, Rushing begins to express doubts about his role as a military apologist. The film captures his growing indecision about the US mission, and his character evolution is frequently noted in film reviews. Rushing's horror at seeing images of dead Iraqis finally prompts him to express his hatred for war. During discussions with Ibrahim, who explains the importance of optics for television audiences, Rushing begins to exhibit genuine curiosity about world events, such as the Israeli-Palestinian conflict. His character arc provides a powerful emblem of the film's message: reporting truth about war can be transformative.

Postscript: when his military superiors refused to allow Rushing to discuss his involvement in the film or give interviews, he resigned his commission and within a year helped launch Al Jazeera English.

> As soon as I hired on with Al Jazeera, I was blistered by hate mail and death threats from people who had never seen a minute of the Arabic news channel. Once, to promote my appearance on Hannity & Colmes, Fox News ran a picture of me in uniform. Beneath it the word traitor was punctuated with a question mark. Five years later, that image is still one of the first pictures that pop up in a Google image search of my name – despite the fact that my reporting has taken me to Iraq and Afghanistan ten times, often embedded with soldiers and Marines at the invitation of their commanders. (Rushing 2011: n.p.)

In August 2013, Al Jazeera America (america.aljazeera.com/) launched a new twenty-four hour news channel to compete with MSNBC, Fox News and CNN, with over 400 investigative journalists on staff. Ehab Al Shihabi, acting chief executive, promised: 'There will be less opinion, less yelling and fewer celebrity sightings' (Stelter 2013: n.p.).

Samizdat journalism: information wants to be free

Dissident Cuban blogger Yoani Sanchez, on a 2013 Mexican lecture tour, told newspaper publishers that press freedom in her country 'is calamitous', but Cubans had discovered a new form of *samizdat* using memory sticks. 'Information circulates hand to hand through this wonderful gadget known as the memory stick . . . and it is difficult for the government to intercept them' (Johnson 2013: n.p.). Sanchez reports that 'underground blogs, digital portals and illicit e-magazines proliferate' in a new incarnation of samizdat (self-publishing) that originated in 1950s USSR to circumvent state censorship. Risking harsh punishment, individuals reproduced censored documents and passed them hand-to-hand. Samizdat was distinguished by retrograde reproduction techniques and nondescript covers designed to avoid detection. In time, the ad hoc production techniques came to symbolise the resourcefulness and the rebellious spirit of dissident Soviet citizens.

Generally, samizdat was directed at intellectual elites, many of whom held positions of power and practiced 'dual consciousness': reading censored material to know how to censor it (Komaromi 2004; Alfaro and Komaromi 2012). Samizdat literary works included Bulgakov's *The Master and Margarita*, Pasternak's *Doctor Zhivago* and Solzhenitsyn's *Gulag Archipelago*, but samizdat documents were predominantly political or social in nature and included Medvedev's series *The Political Journal*, circulated from 1964 to 1970, and *Chronicle of Current Events*, which focused on human rights issues using readers' contributions. In Czechoslovakia, Václav Havel's essay 'The Power of the Powerless' (1978) was distributed in this manner and is credited with inspiring hope throughout a dispirited populace. In Northern Ireland, the IRA's secretive *Green Book* functioned as both induction manual and propaganda source. Samizdat – both its material form and system of distribution – has come to refer to dissident publications circulating through grassroots, rhisomatic networks to avoid state censorship (Komaromi 2004). Samizdat can be a valuable source of news in repressive regimes and, when mimicked, can function as propaganda.

While parallels are not precise, the activities of WikiLeaks have samizdat qualities: self-publication of censored documents by Julian Assange and the WikiLeaks network requires circuitous (decentralised) routes to reach a wider audience and exposes main players to considerable risk. WikiLeaks uses the tools and techniques of computer hacking and encryption to circulate files and avoid denial of service attacks trying to shut down its website (Kaplan 2012). Despite the risks, Sifry (2011) says that WikiLeaks heralds an 'age of transparency' and will inspire other attempts at citizen-powered advocacy, crowdsourcing and 'copyleft' creativity. 'If anything, Assange's greatest contribution to global enlightenment is the idea of a viable "stateless news organisation" . . . beholden to no country's laws and dedicated to bringing government information into public view' (173).

WikiLeaks is on the front lines of a global cyberwar to influence what becomes news and reveal what remains hidden from public view. In *Top Secret America* (2011), Priest and Arkin document the extraordinary growth of the US security infrastructure after 9/11, its labyrinthine and unaccountable activities hidden behind firewalls of secrecy.

> Regardless of Assange's publicly stated bias against U.S. policies and the allegations against his personal behaviour, this unprecedented trove of material has allowed reporters around the world to write some of the most insightful and revealing stories of our time. ([2011] 2012: xxiv)

Priest and Arkin offer a counterproposal to the burgeoning security state they document: '[O]nly more transparency and debate will make us safe from terrorism . . . Terrorism is not just about indiscriminate violence. As the name suggests, it is about instilling paranoia and profound anxiety' (xxv).

To ensure credibility and accountability, WikiLeaks worked with five well-regarded news organisations to publish documents 'responsibly'. This collaboration proved difficult, but raised important legal and ethical questions about reporting on secretive government activities. Alan Rusbridger, editor at *The Guardian*, commented: 'It was surprising to see the widespread reluctance among American journalists to support the general ideal and work of WikiLeaks. For some it simply boiled down to a reluctance to admit Assange was a journalist' (Leigh and Harding 2011: 10–11). If Assange is guilty of a crime for publishing classified documents, so, too, are investigative journalists and reputable news organisations. Rusbridger notes that 'it would be virtually impossible to prosecute Assange for the act of publication of the war logs or state department cables without also putting five editors in the dock. That would be the media case of the century' (11).

More than a publisher and journalist, Assange is a whistle-blower, someone who discovers corporate or government wrongdoing and brings it to public attention. The US Office of Special Counsel defines whistle-blowers as those who disclose the violation of laws, rules or regulations; significant mismanagement or waste of funds; abuse of authority; or specific danger to public health and safety (www.osc. gov). The whistle-blower policy rests on the principle that laws have been broken and is intended to protect those made vulnerable by their revelations. Whistle-blower protection remains in doubt, however, when secret legislation changes laws to give governments additional powers. For example, the US Congress passed secret legislation to authorise citizen surveillance, and Edward Snowden was not protected by whistle-blower safeguards (Greenwald 2014).

The revelations of WikiLeaks, Manning, Snowden and others reached a tipping point in 2012–13, as numerous accounts of state secrecy and surveillance were covered in mainstream news and full-length studies (Priest and Arkin 2011; Morozov 2012; Bennett et al. 2014). It became increasingly difficult for governments to deny they were secretly watching their own citizens or spying on foreign governments and businesses (Hopkins and Borger 2013; Freeze 2013). These governments did not need to deny any wrongdoing. They now possessed technologies to watch everyone, and information dominance was theirs. Security had trumped transparency.

Citizen journalists and networks of power

In her study of US diplomacy and propaganda, Snow recommends a combination of citizen diplomacy and media reform to repair damage to the US image at home and abroad ([1998] 2010). Citizen-based diplomacy 'places civic-mindedness and civic activism at the centre of the body politic by emphasising human rights, human security, and environmental and cultural preservation' (38). Snow despairs of reforming the mainstream media (49) and instead recommends expanding citizen journalism and independent media outlets through the internet: 'The public is migrating to the internet and mainstream media are going to have to meet the public there' (50). Public, commercial-free media require subsidies, but are necessary in her view: 'Democracy cannot function and will not survive without a sufficient medium by which citizens can inform each other and engage in public policy debates' (50).

Similarly, McChesney and Nichols call for publicly funded media (along the lines of the BBC in the UK, CBC in Canada and ABC and SBS in Australia), as long as they are adequately funded and independent of government interference (McChesney 2013). Public broadcasting, however, has not always reached its potential, because politicians and corporate leaders fear its independence of opinion or object to it on ideological grounds. Given the challenges facing a robust public broadcasting system, media critics have turned their attention to the internet as an information and news source – and promising stimulus to media reform – because it provides greater diversity of opinion if one looks for it. Independent news agencies, NGO websites, blogs and social media operate in tandem with established news channels to circulate stories. Audiences can independently triangulate information by comparing different sources. Underlying this participatory approach to news making is the hacker's ethic, and the idea that information wants to be free (Levy 1984).

Spanish sociologist Manuel Castells established his reputation as a theorist of the networked society with his ambitious trilogy *The Information Age* (1996–2004). Widely cited for his description of the 'space of flows' – where data and ideas traverse global information networks to coordinate economies and circulate culture – Castells maintains that networks and social movements in combination can revolutionise power distribution. 'Mass self-communication' is the ability of the internet to communicate one-to-many and many-to-many through extensive networks. It is difficult, but not impossible to control and provides a stage for the autonomous social actor, whether an individual or a group. This ability to communicate autonomously outside the usual networks of power, with their monopolies and gate-keepers, explains 'why governments are afraid of the Internet' and 'corporations have a love-hate relationship with it and are trying to extract profits while limiting its potential for freedom' ([2012] 2013: 7). Snowden's revelations of digital surveillance complicate Castells' analysis, since mass self-communication leaves tracks across the networks.

Networks of power intersect at 'switching points' to give global financial networks and media networks immense influence when they join forces. But this power still has to compete with political networks, production networks, military and security networks, criminal networks and networks dedicated to sharing knowledge. For Castells, power in the network society depends on 'programmers' in charge of individual networks and 'switchers' who control the intersections between networks. Switchers include 'media moguls introduced in the political class, financial elites bankrolling political elites, political elites bailing out financial institutions, media corporations intertwined with financial corporations, academic institutions financed by big business' ([2012] 2013: 8–9). Those wishing to challenge the status quo of power need to programme their own networks to express their interests and values and build switches to connect with other networks. They join the conversation, despite the existing noise, by 'occupying the medium and creating the message' (9). They hack the news by hacking the networks. For progressive media critics, Castells' description acts as a roadmap for thinking about social change in networked societies.

Castells' model of networked power has obvious application to the news organisation – a production network intersecting with political and social networks to form a matrix of information, entertainment, advertising and persuasion. With Amelia Arsenault, Castells researched the 'switching power' of Rupert Murdoch's 'global business of media politics' as a case study for testing his model of networked power. They examine News Corporation operations to learn how media actors such as Murdoch navigate networks and manage switches to serve their business interests. Strategies to increase market share and influence audiences include 'political brokering, leveraging public opinion, instituting sensationalist news formulas, customising media content, and diversifying and adapting media holdings in the face of technological and regulatory changes' (2008: n.p.). Arsenault and Castells describe the contemporary news organisation as an influencing machine adapted for the networked political economy.

'Any theory of cultural transmission must now account for a new mode of production', writes Strangelove, 'one that enables massive volumes and varieties of non-corporate cultural products to circulate through the social system' (2005: 11). He rejects the 'normalisation thesis' advanced by McChesney and others that government and market forces will eventually assert control over the internet, as they did with radio and television. He argues instead that capitalism's empire can be challenged by internet audiences producing their own counter-narratives and systems of meanings. In this chapter, we have seen that public trust in politicians and journalists is perennially low, with their lack of credibility being a constant complaint. In the final chapter, we consider the ethics of deception, activism as counter-propaganda and the possibility of a democratic media. Digital media and their networks will require discerning and savvy switchers, programmers and watchers to keep them accessible, credible and trustworthy.

Exercise questions

1. Illustrate Chomsky and Herman's (1988) five filters of news propaganda with short case studies.
2. Either online or in the classroom, discuss the opposing positions in the Israeli-Palestinian conflict. Whenever possible, use reliable statements from the media to support your position.
3. After discussing journalism practices and ethics online or in class (see Alia 2004), upload a three minute video report on an event you attend as a 'journalist'.
4. Review a piece of investigative journalism that you find informative, credible and fair. What techniques has the writer used to give the piece these qualities?
5. In a letter to the editor or op-ed piece, respond to a news report where you think the weight of opinion is not supported by evidence.

6. Define what 'in the public interest' means and explain why this notion is important to news reporting.
7. Identify significant problems with the media in your country and suggest realistic proposals for reform.
8. Review an example of journalism where framing excludes issues important for understanding the story's meaning.

Figure 14 'Vinyl wars'. Photo: M. Soules, Vancouver, 2011.
Popular culture is a messy collective performance with gifts to offer.
Disguises are common.

10 Performing Propaganda

A paradox: reframing deception

> A prince ... must imitate the fox and the lion, for the lion cannot
> protect himself from traps, and the fox cannot defend himself from
> wolves. One must therefore be a fox to recognise traps, and a lion
> to frighten wolves ... But it is necessary to be able to disguise
> this character well, and to be a great feigner and dissembler ...
> (Machiavelli [1532] 1997: Chapter 18; Bok [1978] 1979: 143)

In this final chapter, we explore the double standards of deception
and lying – deception used for self-defence, subterfuge and art – and
the performance of propaganda as a form of dissent. Deception for
self-defence and subterfuge is motivated by lack of trust and fuelled
by indignation over betrayed values and beliefs. But we encounter
a paradox at this ethical crossroads, because we meet our own self-
interest face-to-face and must wrestle with self-deception and idealism. Behavioural sciences are teaching us that we deceive ourselves as
much as we are deceived by others. Here, we come full circle back to
the trickster who shakes up the status quo, crosses boundaries, makes a
mess and teaches us how to know others by knowing ourselves. Eshu's
trick with his cap shows us that our black is another's white. We are
both wrong and both right – this is the paradox we consider here. To
solve this riddle, we need ethics, discernment and compassion. We
need autonomous zones to express ourselves. We need communities
and networks for strength, protection and creative play.

Machiavelli advises his prince that he must act with the fox's cunning
and the lion's force to protect his power, but he must also disguise his
actions to preserve trust and protect his reputation. Machiavelli understands that deception is a performance and often perceived as a matter
of survival to the deceiver: if the prince is not deceptive, his enemies
will take his power. Sissela Bok ([1978] 1979) says that deception
involves a double standard: one standard for the deceiver and another

for the deceived. Liars want a 'free-ride', she argues; 'their choice to lie is one which they would like to reserve for themselves while insisting that others be honest' (24). When governments take this free-ride approach, they give themselves a monopoly on both violence and deception – 'deliberate' assaults to coerce people against their will. 'Most harm that can befall victims through violence can come to them also through deceit. But deceit controls more subtly, for it works on belief as well as action' (19). Machiavelli advises the prince to act with cunning and force and to disguise his actions by dissembling.

Deceit corrodes communities and whole nations, because it undermines both the victim's trust and the liar's integrity (Chambers 2013; Bok 1978). Significantly, 'lies affect the distribution of power; they add to that of the liar, and diminish that of the deceived' (Bok [1978] 1979: 20). As we saw in the case of climate change denial, lies create uncertainty, affect risk assessment and encourage inaction. Power remains with the big energy companies and is removed from scientists, environmentalists and anyone advocating action on climate change. The energy lobby tries to normalise extraordinary conditions by asserting that there is no real threat – events are being managed appropriately – and embeds these messages in the codes of popular culture through advertising and public relations. 'This is the essence of camouflage and of the cover-up – the creation of apparent normality to avert suspicion' (21).

Bok condemns lying as a covert form of violence, but she also notes that lying to create uncertainty or when used as camouflage for survival in the non-human world is not considered unethical. The chameleon or leopard blending into its surroundings is being deceptive, but is more properly adapting by fitting into its immediate environment. 'For both violence and deception are means not only to unjust coercion, but also to self-defence and survival' (31). Here, in a nutshell, is the most common defence for waging wars, even pre-emptive attacks to avoid further conflict. Whether morally justified or not, people and nations lie to defend themselves. Some tricks can save us.

In St. Augustine's extreme ethical position, lies are immoral, even to protect the innocent from murderers. Bok does not agree that all lies are immoral, but she argues that the 'principle of veracity' should be a first test for lying. This principle gives an 'initial negative weight to lies', because 'lying requires explanation, whereas truth ordinarily does not', and it 'places the burden of proof squarely on those who assume the liar's perspective' (32). Truth is preferable to falsehood, because it builds trust. '*Whatever* matters to human beings, trust is the atmosphere in which it thrives' (33).

In the following discussion, I want to keep Bok's principle of veracity in mind when exploring the idea that persuasion and propaganda are performances expressed through acting and storytelling and proliferating in the persuasive arts of publicity, advertising and advocacy of all forms. As Daniel Pink argues: 'We're all in sales now' (2012: 9). This approach requires us to hold ethical objections in temporary suspension to see more clearly the ways deception can be an adaptive strategy for survival. It allows us to consider the role of counter-propaganda and activism for social change. Many propagandists think of themselves as teachers, not deceivers. Followers of a spiritual path want to share that path with others. Parents, caregivers and healers want to help those in their care and sometimes use deception to achieve their ends. Patriots love their countries and will make sacrifices for their beliefs, even if that means using subterfuge. Still, we need ethical principles to guide us beyond Machiavelli's amoral pragmatism, since deception can irreparably damage trust and social coherence. We can predict with certainty that others will deceive for personal power and gain, and we need discernment to recognise their deceptions for what they are.

Lying and dissembling

> Tell all the truth but tell it slant,/ Success in circuit lies/ . . .
> The truth must dazzle gradually/ Or every man be blind.
>
> (Emily Dickinson, 'Tell all the truth')

Paul Ekman's early research discovered a universal repertoire of facial expressions to communicate human emotions, while physical gestures are culturally specific. Building on this early work, and inspired by Goffman's (1959) *The Presentation of Self in Everyday Life*, Ekman studied the detection of lying and deception by observing body language, gestures and split-second 'micro-expressions' signalling an intention to deceive. He tells an anecdote about a meeting between British Prime Minister Neville Chamberlain and Adolf Hitler on 15 September 1938. Chamberlain hoped to avoid war with Germany, despite its aggression against Austria, while Hitler wanted to buy time to mobilise his armies secretly and attack Czechoslovakia before it could prepare a defence. Chamberlain was fooled by Hitler's reassurance that 'peace can be preserved if the Czechs will meet his demands' and wrote that: 'in spite of the hardness and ruthlessness I thought I saw in his face, I got the impression that here was a man who could be relied upon when he had given his word' (1985: 15–16). Ekman concludes that Hitler was a 'natural performer . . . practiced in deceit', who had the 'advantage of deceiving someone who wanted to be misled' (19). Chamberlain's political reputation depended on a successful appeasement policy; he gambled his interests against Hitler's, and lost.

This anecdote raises an important, often neglected feature of deception: the deceived person's willingness to maintain the fiction. History confirms that Hitler was certainly being deceptive, but history cannot be certain if Chamberlain was deceived by Hitler or whether he was deceiving himself with wishful thinking. Frequently, both parties have something at stake in the deception. Partners ignore obvious signs of contempt, infidelity or addiction to preserve their relationship. 'Some lies, many fewer than liars will claim, are altruistic. Some social relationships are enjoyed because of the myths they preserve' (Ekman 1985: 23). Buyers overlook obvious sales tricks and fine print to pursue their desires. And, more costly, citizens wishing only for security and prosperity suspend disbelief in political propaganda about motives for war, new legislation or government policies.

Deception does not always require telling lies, but instead conceals by omission, equivocation or ambiguity. Ekman distinguishes between lying by omission and telling falsehoods. Liars choose to mislead; they know the difference between lying and telling the truth; they do so deliberately; do not announce their purpose; and have not been asked to lie by the intended target (26–7). Falsehoods require an additional step: liars both 'withhold true information' and present 'false information as if it were true' (28). Ekman recalls that Nixon 'denied *lying* but acknowledged that he, like other politicians, had *dissembled*' (25). Bok cites an example of dissembling when Lyndon Johnson campaigned as the peace candidate against the hawkish Barry Goldwater in the 1964 presidential election, even though he knew the US was planning a major military offensive in Vietnam after the election ([1978] 1979: 180–1). George W. Bush, Colin Powell and Tony Blair told falsehoods when they claimed there were weapons of mass destruction in Iraq if they knew the evidence was false. The US, UK and Canadian Governments continued to deny unwarranted mass citizen surveillance, even when faced with overwhelming contradictory evidence – a falsehood. Government leaders justify their falsehoods by citing national security concerns and the need for camouflage. They are considered patriotic, while whistle-blowers, who reveal the deception, are cast as threats to national security and traitors. Propaganda is a battle for mindshare using opposing narratives, sometimes fictional, sometimes not.

Penelope's ruse

For the Romantic poet Coleridge, participation in literature's fictional worlds requires a 'willing suspension of disbelief' (*Biographia Literaria* [1817] 2013: n.p.). To immerse ourselves in stories and experience their pleasures, we suspend disbelief while reading novels, watching movies or playing computer games. Watching a production of *Othello*, we can be deeply troubled by Iago's deception of Othello, but equally appreciate the actor's performance. We praise the actor and condemn the character. 'It would be bizarre to call actors liars', Ekman suggests. 'Their audience agrees to be misled, for a time . . . Actors do not impersonate, as does the con man, without giving notice that it is a pose put on for a time' (1985: 27). Boyd (2009) places fiction and storytelling in the context of evolutionary theory to suggest that these art forms are adaptive, necessary for reproduction and survival. Determining whether another human will cooperate or compete with us is a complex and important calculation, and fiction prepares humans for social interactions with hypothetical scenarios: 'What if you were in this situation?' Stories from *The Odyssey* to the *Harry Potter* series place protagonists in situations demanding both subterfuge and ethical choices. Experiencing *Othello* allows us to rehearse the consequences of deception motivated by envy and desire for revenge. Storytelling is practice for 'complex situational thought' (Boyd 2009: 49), nowhere more useful than when someone is attempting to deceive us.

According to the theory of mind, humans infer the beliefs, desires and intentions of others through empathy and observation. We use these inferences to run through possible scenarios and test courses of action. Homer's epic poem *The Odyssey* provides an early example of rehearsing fictional scenarios, or scripts, to explore deception's intricate manoeuvres. The hero, Odysseus, inhabits a world where trust is scarce and the threat of deception is constant. Odysseus himself is wily, an expert at deception, who uses cunning to survive constant dangers. Typically, he deceives by withholding information, evading questions about his identity and disguising his motivations, even when he returns to his wife Penelope after years of absence following the Trojan War. Penelope is equally accomplished at deception, successfully keeping many suitors at bay while waiting for Odysseus to return to their marriage bed. When Odysseus continues his deception to test Penelope's faithfulness, she unmasks him by pretending the bed he built for them from a tree still rooted in the ground can now be moved, as if she herself could be moved in her affections for him. His anger at her ruse reveals his identity as her long-awaited husband. When trust is low,

'Machiavellian intelligence' may be necessary to combat those trying to deceive us (Boyd 2009: 276). But as this ancient story suggests, social harmony thrives when trust is restored.

On the wing: tactics and strategies for everyday life

In his influential analysis of cultural participation, Michel de Certeau (1984) distinguishes between the 'strategies' of the powerful – those who claim to know what is 'proper' – and the 'tactics' of less powerful players trying to think and act for themselves. What is proper must be rhetorically defined and aggressively pursued, because it is constantly being contested, both inside and outside places of power. For example, copyright requires that the ownership of cultural properties be defined and limited to certain uses, then defended by litigation if necessary. In journalism, only authorities, officials and experts are granted credibility to speak on certain issues, even if they are involved in a conflict of interest. (Curiously, politicians and journalists rank far below the average person in the street when it comes to credibility.) During mass demonstrations against official state policies, authorities communicate their tolerance of public expression by allowing the event to occur, but also make it clear who is ultimately in control by strictly defining the demonstration space (Harvey 2012). In contrast, tactics are used by those who cannot make a convincing claim to what is proper, whether through lack of authority, credibility or resources. They might not have the resources, but they do have time to 'watch for opportunities that must be seized "on the wing"' (de Certeau [1984] 1988: xix). Both tactics and strategies communicate power relations and have a performative dimension. Against the tactic of mass demonstration is opposed the strategy of state security measures combined with mainstream media commentary.

People resist dominant narratives, says de Certeau, by 'poaching' what they want from media messages and making them useful for themselves. Public protestors carry signs to express their dissent, hoping their message will be seen by a larger audience through various media. Participants in the Ukrainian protest movement Femen write slogans on their bodies, turning the objectification of women's bodies into a weapon of dissent. Are their theatrics deceptive? What these poachers make of popular culture is not always visible, because powerful networks of production dominate the stage and leave little room for unruly actors to play their parts. Noise in the public sphere threatens to drown out all but the loudest and most insistent voices. Ultimately, individual attempts to reclaim social space with tactics merge into a 'network of antidiscipline' with political force: 'The tactics of consumption, the ingenious ways in which the weak make use of the strong, thus lend a political dimension to everyday practices', concludes de Certeau ([1984] 1988: xvii). Similarly, Ellul observes that tactics become another source of propaganda when organised and networked: 'If the action obtained by propaganda is to be appropriate, it cannot be individual; it must be collective. Propaganda has meaning only when it obtains convergence . . . through the intermediary of an organisation' (Ellul [1965] 1973: 28). In this sense, organisation results from convergence, not bureaucratic planning, and networked tactics become counter-propaganda.

Tactics are enacted in 'temporary autonomous zones' (Bey [1985] 1991: n.p.), where opportunities can be seized as they arise. Flash mobs give the impression of spontaneity because they occur in unexpected locations, even though they depend on organisation and planning. They are surprising because they redefine the public sphere and give it new uses. If strategies are calculated, tactics are more spontaneous, improvised, rhisomatic and nomadic – what Deleuze and Guattari (1986) ironically compare to the 'war machine' operating outside system control. War must be waged just beyond the control of politicians to take advantage of opportunities as they arise. Similarly, tactics for social change require the flexibility and stealth of the war machine working rhisomatically – horizontally, with multiple nodes of entry and exit – through communication networks. Demonstrators in Tahrir Square, Wall Street and Westminster used social media and mobile phones to organise and temporarily occupy powerful places and provide visual evidence of dissent. In 2012, Pussy Riot – the Russian protest collective – staged a guerrilla performance in Moscow's Cathedral of Christ the Saviour before being removed by security guards. They quickly turned their performance into a music video distributed on the internet ('Punk Prayer'). Unfortunately, their profane criticism of Putin and the Orthodox Christian church resulted in prison sentences.

Tactics like this are ruled by the trickster; they repeat, revise, translate, strain against all effort to contain popular culture, keep it in its place, make it proper. In cities around the world, graffiti 'writers' improvise on the dominant culture's script, deface its walls and messages, redefine literacy, transform the aesthetics of the city proper, 'distorting it, fragmenting it, and diverting it from its immobile order' (de Certeau [1984] 1988: 102). Or, in Banksy's version: 'Some people become cops because they want to make the world a better place. Some people become vandals because they want to make the world a better *looking* place' (2006: 8).

Convergence culture and collective intelligence

Henry Jenkins argues that media convergence, participatory culture and collective intelligence are redefining discourse in the public sphere and shifting power imbalances. He extends de Certeau's concept of poaching by defining convergence as 'the flow of content across multiple media platforms . . . and the migratory behaviour of media audiences who will go almost anywhere in search of the kinds of entertainment experiences they want' (2006: 4). He is particularly interested in fan and gamer culture and resists defining convergence as a purely technological process. Instead, the 'circulation of media content . . . depends heavily on consumers' active participation' (3). Media consumers work, play and perform in convergence culture. While there are still obvious imbalances between corporate and individual creators, convergence culture provides evidence of collective intelligence – a concept Jenkins borrows from cyberspace theorist Pierre Lévy.

Collective intelligence starts with global conversations enabled by the internet and mobile communication devices, further focused by social networking and aggregated as social capital: the potential of human relationships interacting through social networks to take action and create things. Collective intelligence is nothing new, but networked communications have accelerated the speed of interaction and extended the reach of communities, making their dialogue just as possible globally as locally, at least for mediated conversations. Face-to-face interaction – an effective theatre of persuasion – is still a local affair.

Virtual geography, media vectors, communicative capitalism

Megan Boler (2008) takes de Certeau's concept of poaching and his distinction between strategies and tactics as frameworks to explore dissent in the networked world. Boler is also influenced by McKenzie Wark's ideas of 'virtual geography': a global media space crossed by proliferating communication channels called the 'media vector' (1994: n.p.). 'The paradox of the media vector [is that] the technical properties are hard and fast and fixed . . . but it is an oxymoronic relay system: a rigorous indeterminacy; a determinate imprecision; a precise ambiguity; and ambiguous determinism' (Wark 1994: 12; Boler 2008: 7). Wark's 'oxymoronic' language expresses the idea that the technical infrastructure of a global communications network is consistent and predictable (hardwired and with protocols; see Galloway 2004), while the content flowing through this infrastructure can be unruly and chaotic. The convergence of print, electronic and digital technologies in the virtual geography opens up opportunities for intervention within a zone of ambiguity and paradox. Content leaking from secretive diplomatic networks through disclosures from whistle-blowers like Chelsey Manning and Julian Assange demonstrates loss of system control and poses a threat to powerful interests when their digital data is translated into print and broadcast media. Increasingly, however, the celebrated libertarian autonomy of the internet (Barlow 1996) – associated with the principle of 'net neutrality', where every user has equal access – is threatened by traffic shaping, content filtering, censorship and government surveillance.

Jodi Dean's concept of 'communicative capitalism' suggests it will not be easy to hold power brokers accountable to dissenting publics. Dean sees a significant difference between what is discussed as politics in the media and what actually occurs as politics: 'Today, the circulation of content in the dense, intensive networks of global communications relieves top-level actors (corporate, institutional, and governmental) from the obligation to respond' (2008: 102). While these top-level actors do not have to respond directly to challenges, they can add their own messages to the media vector. There is intense competition in the free market of messages, with media monopolies holding an advantage. '[F]ar from enhancing governance or resistance', Dean argues, communicative capitalism 'results in precisely the opposite' (102). The global communications environment is filled with noise, and it takes compelling performance skills to gain attention for dissenting messages.

In her search to find opportunities for social activism in this virtual geography, Boler asked Amy Goodman of *Democracy Now!* if media are more powerful than bombs. Goodman responded: 'But the people who are being impacted, the people who are having the bombs dropped on them – something happens to pave the way for the bombs. That's what the media does. It manufactures consent for war' (Boler 2008: 12). Turning this idea around, Boler suggests that digital media can equally pave the way for dissent as for violence, though it is not yet clear if new communication networks can effectively advance and sustain social change.

Agitprop theatre

Contemporary performances of dissent are influenced by a long tradition of mass demonstrations and street theatre. In the Introduction, we encountered Ellul's distinction between agitation and integration propaganda and noted connections with Lenin's plans for revolution in Russia. In *What Is to Be Done?* (1902), Lenin advocated agitation propaganda (agitprop) for the working classes to provoke them to 'definite, concrete actions', while propaganda proper was simply education in communist principles for the more advanced vanguard (Lenin [1902] 1999: n.p.). In the 1920s, European and Soviet agit-prop theatre groups took their ideological messages to the working classes. In the USSR, for example, the Blue Blouse collective (*Sinyaya Bluza*) was established in 1923 by the Moscow Institute of Journalism and grew to 5,000 troupes with over 100,000 members. In 1927, the original Blue Blouse troupe performed in Erwin Piscator's theatre in Berlin, where it inspired the Epic theatre style adopted by Bertolt Brecht and influenced such German agitprop companies as the Red Rockets (*Rote Raketen*). A communist newspaper of the time described the Red Rockets as

> shopfloor workers and apprentices using the little time and energy left over from wage-slaving to make theatre after work . . . What do they play? Everything that concerns the worker: scenes from his life, his daily needs, the factory, and the revolutionary struggle. (Clark 1997: 26)

The agitprop style blended vaudeville, cabaret, acrobatics, singing and jazz music to keep its proletarian audiences engaged. Typically, the troupe traveled in trucks, quickly setting up their few props in small towns and factories, performing under threat of arrest and just as quickly packing up and leaving. The Red Rockets were banned in 1929 and driven underground in 1933 when the Nazis came to power. As one performer explained:

> Our first and foremost task is to explain with our images and scenes, satire and vivid presentation to young people what words alone leave unexplained. We must make them warm to our slogans, awaken and develop their class consciousness, their sense of belonging to the oppressed and exploited and their understanding that it is their duty to join our ranks and take part in the struggle. (Clark 1997: 26)

In our own time, public demonstrations, advocacy protests, media hacks and documentary films perform a similar agitprop function, often with the same social justice themes.

Brecht's 'Alienation-effect' (*Verfremdungs-Effekt*) is an important concept emerging from agitprop theatre. The A-effect undermines conventions of dramatic realism by using simple props, ignoring the fourth-wall convention and directing actors to demonstrate their characters through actions and gestures (*Gestus*). Characters are shaped by history, politics and power; they are not merely individuals preoccupied by psychological motivations as they are, for example, in the dramatic realism of Ibsen, Chekhov or Tennessee Williams. In the Epic performance style, audiences are 'alienated' or 'estranged': discouraged from focusing on character psychology and individual tragedy, deflected away from empathy and catharsis toward contemplation of history's epic narratives of power and subjugation. Audiences are provoked to remain observant and critically engaged in the complex social issues confronting the characters. Brecht wants audiences to take their new awareness of exploitation outside the theatre and into the streets.

Mother Courage and Her Children (1941) is a parable set during the Thirty Years' War of 1618 to 1648 and warned Brecht's audiences not to cooperate with the Nazis. Mother Courage loses her three children in succession as she follows one army or another, Catholic or Protestant, trading goods from her cart. Having made her decision to trade with both sides for her own profit, Courage remains alone in the final scene to pull her trademark cart on the revolving stage. Written in less than a month following the German invasion of Poland, *Mother Courage* is one of the great anti-war plays of the twentieth century and illustrates Brecht's use of historicisation to suggest that injustice repeats itself if people are not vigilant and prepared to act ethically.

Case study: *Ai Wei Wei: Never Sorry*

In his notorious 1995 performance piece, dissident Chinese artist Ai Wei Wei photographs himself dropping an ancient Han Dynasty urn, which smashes at his feet. His iconoclastic performance at first appears to comment on contemporary artists abandoning traditional Chinese art, until one understands that Ai Wei Wei is angry about crass efforts to modernise society and suppress freedom of expression in China. Alison Klayman's documentary *Ai Wei Wei: Never Sorry* (2012) is a compelling portrait of her subject, an internationally recognised artist intimidated and imprisoned by the Chinese Government. He has become an icon of the dissident artist speaking truth to power, praised equally for his courage and creativity of epic proportions.

After helping design the Beijing National Stadium ('Olympic Bird's Nest'), Ai Wei Wei dissociated himself from the project and the Olympics, criticising state security and the hypocrisy of its 'pretend smile'. His attention shifted instead to the disastrous 2008 earthquake in Sichuan Province, where thousands of children died when poorly constructed schools crumbled like tofu. His efforts to account for the missing children and film the aftermath of the tragedy were posted on his blog and circulated through a Twitter account, embarrassing authorities who tried to suppress details of the deaths. 'What counts', instead of Olympic gold medals, he wrote, are

> the tens of thousands of lives ruined because of poor construction of schools in Sichuan, because of blood sellers in Henan, because of industrial accidents in Guangdong and because of the death penalty. These are the figures that really tell the tale of our era. (Dargis 2012: n.p.)

Known for his collaborative approach to art – epitomised by his monumental 2010 installation *Sunflower Seeds* at the Tate Modern – Ai Wei Wei is a complex, confrontational, media-savvy artist capable of surprising provocations. In 2013, his agitprop music video 'Dumbass' used explicit lyrics and imagery to dramatise his three-month imprisonment for crimes against the state (aiweiwei.com/music/dumbass). Threatened by a repressive government, Ai Wei Wei has become a hero of dissent for critics of China's human rights policies, while his Chinese opponents accuse him of propagandising against the state and subverting government power.

Street art class war

USE WHAT IS DOMINANT IN A CULTURE TO CHANGE IT QUICKLY.

(Jenny Holzer 1990)

Given the high barriers to meaningful public participation in corporate media, the subversive art of graffiti, posters and stencils is an important form of expression at the local level, especially in large urban centres. Widely seen as the scourge of vandals, contemporary graffiti and other forms of street art compete with consumer culture for mindshare. The early form of graffiti known as 'tagging' emerged from poor urban neighbourhoods of Philadelphia and New York City in the 1960s and 1970s (Jenkins 2007: 11) and allowed marginalised youth to be noticed and recognised. Tags are personal brands 'thrown up' on every available surface, with the more elaborate 'piece' (for masterpiece) circulating through the urban landscape on trains, buses and delivery trucks. The large and colourful pieces painted on concrete walls are anti-billboards promoting public space and class wars against private property and privilege.

Norman Mailer's 1974 introduction to *The Faith of Graffiti* is an early defence of graffiti as art and expression of the *Zeitgeist*. For

Mailer, the tag is a logo layered over the competing logos of corporations and businesses already covering urban walls: 'For now your name is over their name, over the subway manufacturer, the Transit Authority, the city administration . . . your alias hangs over their scene' (Mailer 1974: 6). UK street artist Banksy elaborates:

> The people who truly deface our neighbourhoods are the companies that scrawl giant slogans across buildings and buses trying to make us feel inadequate unless we buy their stuff. They expect to be able to shout their message in your face from every available surface but you're never allowed to answer back. Well, they started the fight and the wall is the weapon of choice to hit them back. (Banksy 2006: 8)

By the 1980s, this class war of signs had spread virally to cities around the globe and become a significant, if controversial, artistic movement. It was 'a wake-up call to the Establishment from the underprivileged, a plaintive *cri de coeur* from people wanting to be heard, putting up their tags and watching their names go by' (Naar 2007: 19).

Now, graffiti, stencils, posters and social murals compete with billboards, logos and commercial signage for visual dominance. The resulting palimpsest – writing surfaces erased and written over again – signifies an urban aesthetic deeply encoded with messages of dissent carried forward from the revolutionary art of the twentieth century: Cubism, Dada, Surrealism, Pop Art, cartoons. 'While commercialisation and market incentives unquestionably dominate in these times, there are plenty of dissident sub-currents . . . for the production of a new kind of commons' (Harvey 2012: 89).

Political performance art

Even major television networks can be hacked with media pranks, though rarely. On 15 October 2004, comedian Jon Stewart appeared on *CNN*'s *Crossfire* – a television programme specialising in political debate hosted by Paul Begala and Tucker Carlson. Stewart took this opportunity to confront his hosts and hold them to account. After some opening banter, Stewart begged his hosts to 'stop, stop, stop, stop hurting America'.

> See, the thing is, we need your help. Right now, you're helping the politicians and the corporations . . . You're part of their strategies. You are partisan, what do you call it, hacks . . . I'm here to confront you, because we need help from the media and they're hurting us . . .

you have a responsibility to the public discourse, and you fail miserably. (*Jon Stewart on Crossfire* 2004)

His hosts struggled to keep their composure, but frequent laughter and applause from the audience signalled its delight with Stewart's trickster performance. Like the Fool in *King Lear*, Stewart delivered the hard truth to cynical masters and used humour to instruct *and* entertain.

Even more remarkable is the number of times this episode has been replayed since it was first broadcast in 2004. At the time of broadcast, *Crossfire* had 867,000 viewers. Shortly afterwards, the fourteen minute clip was uploaded to YouTube, where it has been viewed over 6.5 million times as of April 2014. Performances by other culture jamming activists reach wider exposure when the meme they construct goes 'viral' in the mainstream media, as happened with Stewart's *Crossfire* interview or Colbert's speech at the White House correspondents' dinner in 2006. As Stewart observed to his *CNN* hosts, it is sadly ironic when television audiences rely on comedians for news analysis.

The Yes Men (Jacques Servin and Igor Vamos) engage in pranks under a variety of disguises, including their characters Andy Bichlbaum and Mike Bonanno. Their films document media pranks where they impersonate officials and issue fake news releases. Beginning with their satire of presidential candidate G. W. Bush in 1999, their main targets have been corporations, such as Dow Chemical, Royal Dutch Shell and ExxonMobil; the World Trade Organisation; and governments contributing to climate change (Canada) or global conflict. At their most successful, these hoaxes are reported in the media and elicit denials from the prank's victim. In 2004, twenty years after the Bhopal disaster, Andy Bichlbaum appeared on *BBC World* as 'Jude Finisterra', a Dow Chemical official, to announce that Dow was accepting full responsibility for the disaster and would compensate the victims (*Bhopal Disaster* 2004). The story was quickly revealed as a hoax and denied by Dow Chemical, but only after causing significant controversy. In 2008, the Yes Men and their supporters distributed over one million copies of a fake issue of *The New York Times*, with a headline announcing the end of the Iraq War ('Pranksters' 2008). During the 2009 United Nations Climate Change Conference in Copenhagen, they distributed an email appearing to be from Environment Canada Minister Jim Prentice, pledging to cut carbon emissions by 40 per cent and committing up to 5 per cent of Canada's GDP to help developing countries adapt to climate change. A subsequent series of fake communications extended the hoax. 'And who better?' commented journalist

Suzanne Goldenberg. 'The Canadians have emerged as the villain of the climate change negotiations for pumping out greenhouse gas emissions with the full-on exploitation of the Alberta tar sands' (2009: n.p.).

The Yes Men join a diverse collection of culture jammers and media pranksters that Dery (1993) traces back to medieval carnival, the anti-fascist collages of John Heartfield and his Dada colleagues in Nazi Germany, the Situationist International *détournement* and pirate radio, among other precursors. As practised by the Yes Men, Joey Skaggs, Reverend Billy, Micah Wright, Shepard Fairey, the Billboard Liberation Front, BUGA-UP and Adbusters, culture jamming draws attention to misleading corporate and commercial messaging by unmasking their veiled fictions.

> Brandalism: Any advertisement in public space that gives you no choice whether you see it or not is yours. It belongs to you. It's yours to take, re-arrange and re-use. Asking for permission is like asking to keep a rock someone just threw at your head. (Banksy 2006: 196)

These interventions and stunts circulate as memes and gain currency through the internet and social media. Kalle Lasn, founder of *Adbusters* magazine in Vancouver and one of the foremost proponents of culture jamming, argues that the most effective interventions use meta-memes – a two-tier viral message deflating a commercial message on one level, while challenging some wider political or social issue on another level (Pickerel et al. 2002). The counter-branding of 'conflict' or 'blood' diamonds draws attention to diamonds as an extravagant luxury commodity also used to fund conflicts and purchase weapons. Brand recognition is turned back against the brand to expose – often with humour – its darker side. An internet search for 'BP satire' reveals scores of images showing that the former British Petroleum, now called BP and branded with the slogan 'Beyond Petroleum', is not Beyond Parody. In 2001, Jonah Paretti's request to have his custom-made Nikes labelled with 'sweatshop' was rejected, so he published his email exchange with a Nike representative on the internet, where it became news. Paretti went on to help found *BuzzFeed* and *The Huffington Post*, while gaining a reputation as a viral marketing expert (Carr 2006).

Culture jamming tactics interrupt commercial rhetoric and challenge consumers to think beyond their personal interests to consider issues of wider significance. As Klein argues in *No Logo*, becoming aware of corporate branding's domination of public space is a step toward 'a citizen-centered alternative to the international rule of brands'. The goal of culture jamming is to 'build a resistance – both high-tech and grassroots, both focused and fragmented – that is as global, and as capable of coordinated action, as the multinational corporations it seeks to subvert' (2000: 446).

Lasn gained international attention when he and his colleagues at Adbusters registered the hash tag #occupywallstreet and posted the following on their blog in July 2011: 'Are you ready for a Tahrir moment? On September 17th, flood into Lower Manhattan, set up tents, kitchens, peaceful barricades and occupy Wall Street' (Castells [2012] 2013: 159). Adbusters effectively branded an emerging movement with their meta-meme, linking widespread frustration with economic inequality in the US to Egyptian demands for democratic reform (Yardley 2011). Adbusters was making news with alternate memes, challenging the Wall Street brand with its own Occupy brand.

Networks of protest

Without trust, the social contract corrodes and citizens seek new opportunities for meaningful communication. Castells ([2012] 2013) argues that public protests beginning in Tunisia in 2011 signalled a new hybrid 'space of autonomy' based on the convergence of physical spaces and digital networks (24). The 'space of places' brings people together to experience community and solidarity, often in locations of symbolic importance, such as Tahrir Square in Cairo and Zucotti Park in NYC. Digital networking ('space of flows') builds on social networks, both on- and offline, and provides a suite of tools for networking independent of corporate media. In Egypt, for example, soccer clubs became important sites for physical networking. Research by the Dubai School of Government in 2011 confirmed the significant role played by Facebook and Twitter in 'civil movements' throughout the Arab region. The space of flows is more agile and far-reaching than word-of-mouth, samizdat publications, posters and graffiti. In the space of autonomy, civil movements establish themselves through 'autonomous communication, free from the control of those holding institutional power' (9) and extend the dialogue occurring in the space of places.

Castells' formula for protest combines public space, social networks, digital media, outrage and hope into a potent demand for change. Civil movements ignite when emotion and reason transform into action. They must struggle within themselves to balance anxiety and outrage with hope and enthusiasm to produce 'affective intelligence' (Neuman et al. 2007). One of the slogans circulating during the *Indignada* protests in Spain was 'Real Democracy Now!' to communicate the sense that protestors felt betrayed by undemocratic politicians not listening to them, but they were equally enthusiastic about immediate political reform.

Civil movements propagate when social media express emotions and tell stories that fuel affective intelligence. 'The faster and more interactive the process of communication is, the more likely the formation of a process of collective action becomes' (Castells [2012] 2013: 15). Howard and Hussain (2010, 2013) demonstrate that information technology and digital networks increased participation by a well-educated, unemployed, younger generation in Arab country movements and fuelled demands for democratic reform against the ruling dictatorships. Unlike the repressive public sphere in Egypt, the internet became a 'sphere of dissidence' (Castells [2012] 2013: 58), where people could share their narratives. The video blogs of Egyptian student Asmaa Mafhouz documented revolution as it progressed (asmamahfouz.com). Videos of police brutality during the Egyptian protests – including the beating of a woman identified as 'blue bra girl' – were uploaded to YouTube. Al Jazeera covered the protests consistently and in depth, frequently using citizen journalists for their reporting. The internet did more than foster the Arab Spring and Occupy movements; it continues to host a deep repository of written and visual archival materials. Until this repository is censored or erased, it will support future research into news coverage of these historic civil protests.

Problem of the media

Biased media coverage of these protest movements spotlight what McChesney calls the 'problem of the media'. His political economy approach begins from the assumption that media analysis must always account for the political and economic forces operating on media systems. 'Media are the centre of struggles for power and control in any society, and they are arguably even more vital players in democratic nations' (McChesney 2004: 17). The problem of the media at first appears to concern content, but is more importantly about the 'structure that generates that content' (16). While his focus is primarily US media, his assessment applies to the UK, Canada and Australia, all of which are operating under the same general conditions of state regulation, corporate ownership, media monopolies and copyright laws. Propaganda filters slant the news toward elite views; public relations competes with unbiased journalism; and advertising infuses all commercial media with the free-market 'catechism' (McChesney 2013: 23). These influences create a democratic deficit that progressively erodes citizens' ability to engage in meaningful debate. 'On balance', McChesney concludes, 'the media system has become . . . a significantly anti-democratic force' (18).

His analysis predicts that mainstream media coverage of the Arab Spring and Occupy movements would favour the status quo over populist dissent – a prediction confirmed by content analysis of Occupy Wall Street coverage in *The New York Times* and *USA Today* (Xu 2013). Systemic bias in the mainstream media is a problem for those advocating progressive change.

McChesney challenges the 'celebrants' of internet culture – and he includes Castells in this category – for failing to account adequately for capitalism's resistance to reform. While he acknowledges the potential importance of digital networks in social transformation ([2012] 2013: 8), he argues that the celebrants and sceptics talk past one another. Sceptics believe the internet does not add to collective intelligence (Carr 2008; Lanier 2010) and increasingly contributes to isolation (Pariser 2011; Turkle 2011; Rosen 2005). Those who manage the internet have the ability to regulate, control, censor and disable the internet – as was imposed temporarily in Egypt in 2011 and routinely in China – thus rendering the internet 'mostly impotent as a democratic organising force' (McChesney 2013: 10). At the same time, power elites use these technologies to conduct political campaigns, engage in public relations and sell products and ideas in an environment of communicative capitalism (Dean 2008). Giant internet corporations and internet service providers turn over data to authorities, all under the pretext of fighting crime and protecting national security. The 'relationship between the Internet giants and the military and national security agencies of the US government' is a 'marriage made in heaven, with dire implications for liberty and democracy' (McChesney 2013: 21). Anyone using Google Mail or Facebook soon learns that algorithms are monitoring content and displaying ads based on keywords.

Since elites will resist demands to democratise the media, McChesney argues that reform should occur within the existing system by curtailing media monopolies, diversifying ownership and investing in public media. Journalism is 'a public good and if it is to thrive, it will require . . . large public investments' (2013: 21). McChesney's vision of a more democratic media includes greater community control, decentralised planning, commitment to cooperatives and non-profits, democratic governance of media institutions,

public discussion of long-term goals and environmentally responsible production and distribution practices (230). To achieve these
goals, he recommends a two-pronged approach: protect the internet
as a forum for democratic dialogue; and reform the existing political economy of communications through state oversight and public
funding, especially for journalism.

Castells notes that progressive intellectuals are frequently 'looking
for the politics of their dreams' ([2012] 2013: 187) – an observation he might apply to McChesney's democratic media system.
McChesney does not specify what would motivate those in power to
curtail monopolies, diversify ownership and invest in public media,
unless through political leadership. What would induce the military-
corporate-government complex to relinquish its dominance of the
capitalist media system? Who will provide leadership for the transition
and where will funding come from? This is the problem of the media:
not whether it needs reform, but how to do it. Will change come from
inside the system, through democratic reform, or from the outside,
through subversive guerrilla tactics or even revolution? Is there a
future for independent media capable of competing for influence with
the majors?

Secular ethics and common humanity

This chapter begins with an exploration of lying and deception and
entertains the idea that deception can be adaptive. The trickster
archetype embodies the idea that some deceptions keep cultures
fresh and vital by shaking up conventions. Plato suggests that a
noble lie can be useful to statecraft – a theme Machiavelli elaborates for his prince. All the great religions use myths and stories to
communicate their teachings. Are they deceptions or beliefs to live
by? Penelope's ruse was a self-protective trick to unmask Odysseus.
Similarly, the hackers collectively known as Anonymous hide their
identities to dispense their version of online justice. Corporations
act anonymously through interest groups, think tanks and political
action committees. Trade negotiations are conducted behind closed
doors. Governments deceive to protect their national interests and
security. Protestors, dissenters, culture jammers and street artists
all use theatrics and art to hack the media spectacle. Are their
deceptions advocacy or propaganda? Symbolic communications are
seldom black or white.

Bok and Ekman remind us that lying is ethically complex and often
rationalised as self-protection, similar to the camouflage and eva-

sions found in nature. Bok prefers truth to lies because truth needs no defence, while Ekman makes a useful distinction between dissembling and telling falsehoods. In an earlier chapter, we saw that our own stereotypes and biases often prevent us from distinguishing between threats and opportunities, deception and truth. Lippmann, Cialdini, Kahneman, Mlodinow, Ariely, Tavris and Aronson, Lehrer and many others encountered in this text confirm that we deceive ourselves as much as we are deceived by others.

Deception can be ethically confusing, and we need common ground to discuss what we believe is right and wrong if we hope to build trust in human society. In *Beyond Religion* (2011), the Dalai Lama proposes that humanity needs a system of secular ethics not specific to any religion and acceptable to atheists. Secular ethics recognises our 'common humanity' and is founded on compassion and the golden rule that we should treat others as we want to be treated. Compassion flourishes in an environment of cooperation, transparency and trust and languishes in times of fear, competition, secrecy and deception. Research has discovered that thinking about money reduces compassion, empathy and sociability (DeSteno 2014: 140; Vohs et al. 2006). Cultures 'primed' by money consciousness may be disadvantaged in the long term:

> [L]iving in a culture that surrounds us with reminders of money may shape our behaviour and our attitudes in ways that we do not know about and of which we may not be proud. Some cultures provide frequent reminders of respect, others constantly remind their members of God, and some societies prime obedience by large images of the Dear Leader. (Kahneman 2011: 56)

As various indices illustrate, prosperous countries measured by gross national product are not equally rich in measures of well-being and happiness (see World Values Survey; Happy Planet Index; OECD Better Life Index).

Recognising our common humanity is an antidote to despair. Velcrow Ripper's remarkable trilogy of films – *Scared Sacred* (2004), *Fierce Light* (2008) and *Occupy Love* (2012) – document the spiritual dimensions of activism emerging out of crisis, from the killing fields of Cambodia and the aftermath of 9/11 in the US to the Occupy movements. The Dalai Lama, in exile from his home in Tibet, travels the world to promote the virtues of compassion and discernment. Ai Wei Wei unmasks his nation's fictions with terrifying wit and creativity. Snowden, Assange, Greenwald, Poitras, Politkovskaya and a diverse army of journalists risk their freedom, and lives, to report information in the public interest. Legions of artists, writers, performers and protesting citizens resist complacency, cynicism and self-absorption to speak truth to power. They are the counterforce to deception and secrecy. They are all making news in their own ways, though we have to seek them out.

Media scholar and journalist Valerie Alia makes a convincing argument that media 'malpractice' is as consequential as medical malpractice and recommends the professional 'obligation to clarify and codify standards and make media practitioners accountable to the public' (Alia 2004: 174). Amy Goodman's observation that stories in the media 'pave the way for bombs' underscores the importance of media accountability and the consequences of deception. Citizen journalists and bloggers and dissident reporters of all political stripes need to be especially scrupulous in their claims, because they are holding powerful adversaries to account.

Any meaningful reform of the media – or of society – will have to be built on a foundation of secular ethics that does not discriminate between people with different spiritual beliefs. The creative stories of our clever and adaptive species will always play an important role in shaping the direction of our interdependent journey. Tell your stories with compassion, discernment and as much truth as you can muster.

Exercise questions

1. Describe your participation in popular culture.
2. In what situations, if any, is your government justified in deceiving its citizens?
3. Define social justice using examples to distinguish between justice and injustice in your society.
4. Profile an artist notable for protesting against social norms or perceived injustice. How effective do you think protest art can be?
5. Create a slideshow of images documenting memorable graffiti, street art and social murals in your community. What messages do they communicate?
6. Write a report for your supervisor evaluating the role of digital networks for a marketing or advocacy campaign.
7. Research the Arab Spring, Occupy or one of the other protest movements from recent years, and write an article summarising the protest, its objectives and key features. Be conscious of how you frame the narrative to convey your support, neutrality or disapproval of the events.

8. Make a three- to five-minute advocacy video and upload it to the internet.
9. What are the most effective strategies to reform your country's media?

Figure 15 'Playing for stakes'. Photo: M. Soules, Toronto, 2007.

Bibliography

Unless otherwise noted, all URLs were last accessed on 8 September 2014.

Aaronovitch, D. [2009] (2010), *Voodoo Histories: The Role of Conspiracy Theory in Shaping Modern History*, New York: Riverhead.

'Abu Ghraib files' (2006), *Salon.com*, 14 March, www.salon.com/2006/03/14/introduction_2/

Adamic, L. and N. Glance (2005), 'The political blogosphere and the 2004 U.S. election: divided they blog', www2.scedu.unibo.it/roversi/SocioNet/AdamicGlanceBlogWWW.pdf

Adbusters, www.adbusters.org/

Akerlof, G. and R. Shiller [2009] (2010), *Animal Spirits: How Human Psychology Drives the Economy*, Princeton: Princeton University Press.

Alfaro, K. and A. Komaromi (2012), 'Uncertified copies: on samizdat', *Triple Canopy*, 8 May, canopycanopycanopy.com/updates/189

Alia, V. (1999), *Un/Covering the North: News, Media, and Aboriginal People*, Vancouver: UBC Press.

Alia, V. (2004), *Media Ethics and Social Change*, Edinburgh: Edinburgh University Press.

Alia, V. [2010] (2012), *The New Media Nation: Indigenous Peoples and Global Communication*, New York: Berghahn Books.

Alia, V. (2014), Personal correspondence on ethnographic filmmaking.

Alia, V. and S. Bull (2005), *Media and Ethnic Minorities*, Edinburgh: Edinburgh University Press.

'The Alibaba phenomenon' (2013), *The Economist*, 23 March, www.economist.com/news/leaders/21573981-chinas-e-commerce-giant-could-generate-enormous-wealthprovided-countrys-rulers-leave-it

Althusser, L. [1971] (2006), 'Ideology and ideological state apparatuses (notes towards an investigation)', in M. Durham and D. Kellner (eds), *Media and Cultural Studies KeyWorks*, Malden: Blackwell Publishing, pp. 79–87.

Anders, G. (2012), 'Inside Amazon's idea machine: how Bezos decodes customers', *Forbes*, 23 April, www.forbes.com/sites/georgeanders/2012/04/04/inside-amazon/

Anderson, B. [1983] (2006), *Imagined Communities: Reflections on the Origins and Spread of Nationalism*, London: Verso.

Anderson, C. (2006), *The Long Tail: Why the Future of Business is Selling Less of More*, New York: Hyperion.

Anderson, J. L. (1997), *Che Guevara: A Revolutionary Life*, New York: Grove Press.

Andrews, W. and T. Lindeman (2013), 'The black budget: top secret U.S. intelligence funding', *The Washington Post*, 29 August, www.washington-post.com/wp-srv/special/national/black-budget/

Angilirq, Paul Apak, Z. Kunuk, H. Paniaq, P. Qualitalik, N. Cohen and B. Saladin d'Anglure (2002), *Atanarjuat: The Fast Runner*, Toronto: Coach House Books and Isuma Publishing.

Arab American National Museum (2011), 'What is Orientalism', *Reclaiming Identity: Dismantling Arab Stereotypes*, www.arabstereotypes.org/why-stereotypes/what-orientalism

Arendt, H. (1968), 'Walter Benjamin: 1892–1940', in W. Benjamin [1936] (1968), *Illuminations*, trans. H. Zohn, New York: Schocken Books, pp. 217–51.

Ariely, D. [2008] (2010), *Predictably Irrational: The Hidden Forces That Shape Our Decisions*, New York: HarperCollins.

Aristotle [350 BCE] (1994–2009), *Politics*, Internet Classics Archive (MIT), trans. B. Jowett, classics.mit.edu/Aristotle/politics.html

Aristotle [350 BCE] (1994–2014), *Poetics*, Internet Classics Archive (MIT), trans. S. Butcher, classics.mit.edu/Aristotle/poetics.html

Aristotle [350 BCE] (2011), *Rhetoric*, Rhetoric and Composition Eserver, trans. W. Rhys Roberts, rhetoric.eserver.org/aristotle/index.html

Arsenault, A. and M. Castells (2008), 'Switching power: Rupert Murdoch and the global business of media politics: a sociological analysis', *International Sociology* 23.4: 488ff, iss.sagepub.com/content/23/4/488.abstract

Asser, M. (2000), 'Echelon: big brother without a cause?' *BBC News*, 6 July, news.bbc.co.uk/2/hi/europe/820758.stm

Auerbach, D. (2013), 'You are what you click: on microtargeting', *The Nation*, 13 February, www.thenation.com/article/172887/you-are-what-you-click-microtargeting

Auerbach, E. [1946] (2003), *Mimesis: The Representation of Reality in Western Literature*, trans. W. Trask, Princeton: Princeton University Press.

Aufderheide, P. (2007), *Documentary Film: A Very Short Introduction*, Oxford: Oxford University Press.

Avaaz, www.avaaz.org

'Ayman al-Zawahiri appointed as al-Qaeda leader' (2011), *BBC News*, 16 June, www.bbc.co.uk/news/world-middle-east-13788594

Babcock-Abrahams, B. (1975), '"A tolerated margin of mess": the trickster and his tales reconsidered', *Journal of the Folklore Institute* 11.3 (March): 147–86.

Bacon, W. (2012), 'Why the market can't ensure a free press', *New Matilda*, 6 March, newmatilda.com/2012/03/06/why-market-cant-ensure-free-press

Bagdikian, B. (2004), *The New Media Monopoly*, Boston: Beacon Press.

Bakhtin, M. (1981), *The Dialogic Imagination: Four Essays*, trans. C. Emerson and M. Holquist, Austin: University of Texas Press.

Ball, K., K. Haggerty and D. Lyon (eds) (2012), *Routledge Handbook of Surveillance Studies*, New York: Routledge.

Bandura, A., D. Ross and S. Ross (1961), 'Transmission of aggression through the imitation of aggressive models', *Journal of Abnormal and Social Psychology* 63: 575–82.

Bandura, A., D. Ross and S. Ross (1963), 'Imitation of film-mediated aggressive models', *Journal of Abnormal and Social Psychology* 66.1: 3–11.

Banksy (2006), *Wall and Piece*, London: Century.

Baram, M. (2010), 'WikiLeaks' Iraq War logs: U.S. troops abused prisoners for years after Abu Ghraib', *Huffington Post*, 22 October, www.huffingtonpost.com/2010/10/22/WikiLeaks-iraq-war-logs-i_n_772658.html (accessed 21 January 2014)

Barlow, J. P. (1996), 'A declaration of the independence of cyberspace', *Electronic Frontier Foundation*, w2.eff.org/Censorship/Internet_censorship_bills/barlow_0296.declaration

Barnard, T. (2009), 'Translator's notes', in A. Bazin (2009), *What is Cinema?* Montreal: Caboose, pp. 251–312.

Barnouw, E. [1974] (1993), *Documentary: A History of the Non-Fiction Film*, New York: Oxford University Press.

Barstow, D. (2008), 'Behind TV analysts, Pentagon's hidden hand', *The New York Times*, 20 April, www.nytimes.com/2008/04/20/us/20generals.html

Barthes, R. [1977] (1978), *Image/Music/Text*, trans. S. Heath, New York: Hill and Wang.

Barthes, R. [1980] (2000), *Camera Lucida: Reflections on Photography*, trans. R. Howard, London: Vintage.

Basen, I. (2007), *Spin Cycles*, CBC Radio, www.cbc.ca/andthewinneris/2012/06/26/spin-cycles-episode-one/

Bataille, G. [1961] (1989), *The Tears of Eros*, trans. P. Connor, San Francisco: City Lights.

Baudrillard, J. (1988), *Selected Writings*, ed. M. Poster, Stanford: Stanford University Press.

Baudrillard, J. (2005), *The Intelligence of Evil or the Lucidity Pact*, trans. C. Turner, Oxford: Berg.

Bazin, A. (2009), *What is Cinema?* trans. T. Barnard, Montreal: Caboose.

Benjamin, W. [1936] (1968), 'The work of art in the age of mechanical reproduction', in *Illuminations*, trans. H. Zohn, New York: Schocken Books, pp. 217–51.

Benkler, Y. (2006), *The Wealth of Networks: How Social Production Transforms Markets and Freedom*, New Haven: Yale University Press.

Bennett, C., K. Haggerty, D. Lyon, and V. Steeves (eds) (2014), *Transparent Lives: Surveillance in Canada*, Edmonton: Athabasca University Press.

Bentham, J. [1787] (1995), *The Panopticon Writings*, ed. M. Bozovic, London: Verso.

Berger, J. (1972), *Ways of Seeing*, London: BBC/Penguin.

Berman, M. (2011), 'Introduction: tearing away the veils: *The Communist Manifesto*', in K. Marx and F. Engels [1848] (2011), *The Communist Manifesto*, New York: Penguin, pp. 1–17.

Bernard, S. (2005), 'Eyes on the rights: the rising cost of putting history on screen', *International Documentary*, June: 26–32.

Bernardi, D. (2005), '*The Birth of a Nation*: integrating race into the narrator system', in J. Geiger and R. Rutsky (eds) (2005), *Film Analysis*, New York: W. W. Norton, pp. 83–96.

Bernays, E. [1928] (2005), *Propaganda*, New York: Ig Publishing.

Bernays, E. (1947), 'The engineering of consent', *Annals of the American Academy of Political and Social Science* 250: 113ff.

Bernstein, C. (2011), 'Is phone-hacking scandal Murdoch's Watergate?' *Newsweek*, 11 July, www.newsweek.com/carl-bernstein-phone-hacking-scandal-murdochs-watergate-68411

Berry, J. (2000), *The New Liberalism: The Rising Power of Citizen Groups*, Washington, DC: Brookings Institution Press.

Bey, H. [1985] (1991), *T. A. Z.: The Temporary Autonomous Zone, Ontological Anarchy, Poetic Terrorism*, New York: Automedia.

Bhabha, H. (1994), *The Location of Culture*, New York: Routledge.

bin Laden, Osama (2005), *Messages to the World: The Statements of Osama bin Laden*, ed. B. Lawrence, London: Verso.

Blackmore, S. [1999] (2000), *The Meme Machine*, Oxford: Oxford University Press.

Blair, T. (2003), 'Speech to the US Congress', *The Guardian*, 18 July, www.theguardian.com/politics/2003/jul/18/iraq.speeches

Bok, S. [1978] (1979), *Lying: Moral Choice in Public and Private Life*, New York: Vintage.

Boler, M. (2008), *Digital Media and Democracy: Tactics in Hard Times*, Cambridge, MA: MIT Press.

Boorstin, D. [1961] (1992), *The Image: A Guide to Pseudo-Events in America*, New York: Vintage Books.

Boyd, B. (2009), *On the Origin of Stories: Evolution, Cognition, and Fiction*, Cambridge, MA: Harvard University Press.

Boyden, J. (2013), *The Orenda*, Toronto: Hamish Hamilton/Penguin.

Boykoff, M. and J. Boykoff (2004), 'Balance as bias: global warming and the US prestige press', *Global Environmental Change* 14: 125–36.

Brasch, W. (1990), *Forerunners of Revolution: Muckrakers and the American Social Conscience*, Lanham: University Press of America.

Breazeal, C. (2011), 'The rise of personal robots', *TED Talks*, www.youtube.com/watch?v=eAnHjuTQF3M

Brecht, B. [1941] (1991), *Mother Courage and her Children*, trans. E. Bentley, New York: Grove Weidenfeld.

Brecht, B. [1947] (1994), *The Caucasian Chalk Circle*, in *Two Plays by Bertolt Brecht*, trans. E. Bentley, New York: Penguin.

Bredekamp, H. (2006), *Hyperrealism: One Step Beyond*, London: Tate Museum.

Brehm, J. (1966), *A Theory of Psychological Reactance*, Waltham: Academic Press.

Brehm, S. and J. Brehm (1981), *Psychological Reactance: A Theory of Freedom and Control*, Waltham: Academic Press.

Bringhurst, R. (1999), *A Story as Sharp as a Knife: The Classical Haida Mythtellers and their World*, Vancouver: Douglas and McIntyre.

British Army website, www.army.mod.uk/

Brock, D. and A. Rabin-Havt, with Media Matters for America (2012), *The Fox Effect: How Roger Ailes Turned a Network Into a Propaganda Machine*, New York: Anchor.

Brooks, X. (2013), 'The Birth of a Nation: a gripping masterpiece . . . and a stain on history', *The Guardian*, 29 July, www.guardian.co.uk/film/film-blog/2013/jul/29/birth-of-a-nation-dw-griffith-masterpiece

Brown, E. (2014), 'In Gallup Poll, the biggest threat to world peace is . . . America?' *International Business Times*, 2 January, www.ibtimes.com/gallup-poll-biggest-threat-world-peace-america-1525008

Burke, K. [1941a] (1973), *The Philosophy of Literary Form*, Berkeley: University of California Press.

Burke, K. [1941b] (2006), 'The rhetoric of Hitler's "battle"', in G. Jowett and V. O'Donnell (eds) (2006), *Readings in Propaganda and Persuasion: New and Classic Essays*, Thousand Oaks: Sage, pp. 149–68.

Burke, K. [1950] (1969), *A Rhetoric of Motives*, Berkeley: University of California Press.

Burnett, R. (2008), 'Reflections on the documentary cinema', *Critical Approaches to Culture + Media* (weblog), rburnett.ecuad.ca/archive/2008/8/29/reflections-on-the-documentary-cinema.html

Bush, G. W. (2001), 'Remarks by the President upon arrival', *White House Press Release*, 16 September, georgewbush-whitehouse.archives.gov/news/releases/2001/09/20010916-2.html

Bush, G. W. (2005), 'The struggle for democracy in Iraq: speech to the World Affairs Council of Philadelphia', *Presidential Rhetoric*, 12 December, www.presidentialrhetoric.com/speeches/12.12.05.html

'Canadian Forces ads zoom in on combat mission' (2006), *CTV News*, 13 September.

Canetti, E. [1960] (1973), *Crowds and Power*, trans. C. Stewart, Harmondsworth: Penguin.

Caplan, G. (2012), 'Harper is right: foreign radicals are after the oil sands', *The Globe and Mail*, 26 May, www.theglobeandmail.com/news/politics/second-reading/harper-is-right-foreign-radicals-are-after-the-oil-sands/article4209920/

Capra, F. (1971), *The Name Above the Title: An Autobiography*, New York: Macmillan Company.

Carey, A. [1995] (1997), *Taking the Risk Out of Democracy*, Urbana: University of Illinois Press.

Carlson, M. (1996), *Performance: A Critical Introduction*, London: Routledge.

Carpenter, E. (1972), *Oh, What a Blow That Phantom Gave Me!* New York: Holt, Rinehart and Winston.

Carr, D. (2006), 'Building a brand with a blog', *The New York Times*, 15 May, www.nytimes.com/2006/05/15/technology/15carr.html

Carr, N. (2008), 'Is Google making us stupid?' *Atlantic Magazine*, July/August, www.theatlantic.com/magazine/archive/2008/07/is-google-making-us-stupid/306868/

Carr, N. [2008] (2009), *The Big Switch: Rewiring the World, From Edison to Google*, New York: W. W. Norton.

Cassel, M. (2013), 'Identity and exile: an American's struggle with Zionism', *Al Jazeera*, 29 November, www.aljazeera.com/programmes/aljazeeracorrespondent/2013/11/identity-exile-20131124121757352111.html

Castells, M. [2012] (2013), *Networks of Outrage and Hope: Social Movements in the Internet Age*, Cambridge: Polity.

Central Intelligence Agency (CIA) (1963), *Kubark Counterintelligence Interrogation*, US Government manual, www.gwu.edu/~nsarchiv/NSAEBB/NSAEBB122/CIA%20Kubark%201-60.pdf

Chambers, C. (2013), 'NSA and GCHQ: the flawed psychology of government mass surveillance', *The Guardian*, 26 August, www.theguardian.com/science/head-quarters/2013/aug/26/nsa-gchq-psychology-government-mass-surveillance

Chanan, M. (2000), 'The documentary chronotope', *Jump Cut* 43 (July): 56–61, www.ejumpcut.org/archive/onlinessays/JC43folder/DocyChronotope.html

Chen, C., K. Wu, V. Srinivasan and X. Zhang (2011), 'Battling the internet water army: detection of hidden paid posters', *Social and Information Networks*, 18 November, arxiv.org/abs/1111.4297

Chomsky, N. [1989] (1991), *Necessary Illusions: Thought Control in Democratic Societies*, Toronto: House of Anansi.

Chomsky, N. (2006), *Failed States: The Abuse of Power and the Assault on Democracy*, New York: Henry Holt.

Chomsky, N. (2012), *Occupy*, New York: Occupied Media Pamphlet Series.

Christopher, R. (2005), *Robert and Frances Flaherty: A Documentary Life, 1883–1922*, Montreal and Kingston: McGill-Queen's University Press.

Cialdini, R. [1984] (2007), *Influence: The Psychology of Persuasion*, New York: Collins.

Clark, T. (1997), *Art and Propaganda in the Twentieth Century: The Political Image in the Age of Mass Culture*, New York: Harry N. Abrams.

Clinton, H. (2001), 'Interview with Dan Rather', *CBS Evening News*, 13 September.

Cockburn, A. (2002), 'The tenth crusade', *CounterPunch*, 7 September, www.counterpunch.org/2002/09/07/the-tenth-crusade/

Cockcroft, E. (1974), 'Abstract Expressionism, weapon of the Cold War', *Artforum* xii.10 (June): 39–41.

Cohen, P. (2009), 'Yale Press bans images of Muhammad in new book', *The New York Times*, 12 August, www.nytimes.com/2009/08/13/books/13book.html

Cohen, S. [1972] (2002), *Folk Devils and Moral Panics: The Creation of the Mods and Rockers*, London: Routledge.

Cohen, S. (2001), *States of Denial: Knowing About Atrocities and Suffering*, Oxford: Polity Press.

Coleridge, S. [1817] (2013), 'Chapter XIV', *Biographia Literaria*, Project Gutenberg, www.gutenberg.org/files/6081/6081-h/6081-h.htm

Collins, R. (1998), 'Introduction', in M. Weber [1904] (1998), *The Protestant Ethic and the Spirit of Capitalism*, Los Angeles: Roxbury Publishing, pp. vii–lxxiv.

Corporate Watch UK (2003), 'Public relations and lobbying industry: an overview', www.corporatewatch.org.uk/?lid=1570

Creamer, M. (2008), 'Obama wins! . . . Ad Age's marketer of the year', *Ad Age*, 17 October, adage.com/article/moy-2008/obama-wins-ad-age-s-marketer-year/131810/

Creel, G. (1920), *How We Advertised America: The First Telling of the Amazing Story of the Committee on Public Information, 1917–1919*, New York: Harper and Row.

Crozier, M., S. Huntington and J. Watanuki (1975), *The Crisis of Democracy: Report on the Governability of Democracies to the Trilateral Commission*, New York: New York University Press, www.trilateral.org/download/doc/crisis_of_democracy.pdf

Curtis, M. (2003), *Web of Deceit: Britain's Real Role in the World*, London: Vintage Books.

Dalai Lama [2011] (2012), *Beyond Religion: Ethics for a Whole World*, London: Rider.

Damasio, A. (1994), *Descartes' Error: Emotion, Reason, and the Human Brain*, New York: Penguin.

Dargis, M. (2012), 'Giving voice to a big picture thinker', *The New York Times*, 26 July.

Davies, J. (1962), 'Toward a theory of revolution', *American Sociological Review* 27: 5–19.

Davies, N. [2008] (2009), *Flat Earth News*, London: Vintage Books.

Davis, E. (1991), 'Trickster at the crossroads: West Africa's god of messages, sex and deceit', *Gnosis* 19 (Spring): 37–45.

Davis, W. (2011), *Into the Silence: The Great War, Mallory, and the Conquest of Everest*, New York: Alfred A. Knopf.

Dean, J. (2008), 'Communicative capitalism: circulation and the foreclosure of politics', in M. Boler (ed.) (2008), *Digital Media and Democracy: Tactics in Hard Times*, Cambridge, MA: MIT Press, pp. 101–21.

Debord, G. [1967] (1983), *Society of the Spectacle*, Detroit: Black and Red.

de Certeau, M. [1984] (1988), *The Practice of Everyday Life*, trans. S. Rendall, Berkeley: University of California Press.

Deci, E. and R. Ryan (1985), *Intrinsic Motivation and Self-Determination in Human Behaviour*, New York: Plenum.

Deibert, R. (2013), *Black Code: Inside the Battle for Cyberspace*, Toronto: McClelland and Stewart.

Deleuze, G. and F. Guattari (1986), *Nomadology: The War Machine*, trans. B. Massumi, New York: Semiotext(e).

DeLisi, M., M. Vaughn, D. Gentile, C. Anderson and J. Shook (2013), 'Violent video games, delinquency, and youth violence: new evidence', *Youth Violence and Juvenile Justice* 11.2: 132–42.

Dershowitz, A. (2011), '"Human rights activists" ignore Israel under siege', *Newsmax*, 10 July, www.newsmax.com/AlanDershowitz/israel-gaza-arabs-iran/2011/07/10/id/403072

Dery, M. (1993), *Culture Jamming: Hacking, Slashing, and Sniping in the Empire of the Signs*, New York: Open Magazine Pamphlet, project.cyberpunk.ru/idb/culture_jamming.html

Descartes, R. [1637] (1960), *Discourse on the Method*, trans. L. Lafleur, New York: Liberal Arts Press.

de Souza, M. (2011), 'Tories left oil sands data out of UN report: numbers indicate rise in annual pollution', *Ottawa Citizen*, 29 May, ecosocialism-canada.blogspot.ca/2011/05/tories-left-oilsands-data-out-of-un.html

DeSteno, D. (2014), *The Truth About Trust: How It Determines Success in Life, Love, Learning, and More*, New York: Hudson Street Press.

Dhardhowa, Y. (2011), 'UN commemorates 10th anniversary of Afghan giant Buddha statues', *The Tibet Post International*, 1 March, www.thetibetpost.com/en/news/international/1497-un-commemorates-10th-anniversary-of-afghan-giant-buddha-statues

DiNucci, D. (1999), 'Fragmented future', *Print* 53.4: 32ff.

Donnelly, T., with D. Kagan and G. Schmitt (project co-chairmen) (2000), 'Rebuilding America's defences: strategy, forces and resources for a new century', report for The Project for the New American Century, www.informationclearinghouse.info/pdf/RebuildingAmericasDefenses.pdf

Douglas, M. and A. Wildavsky (1982), *Risk and Culture: An Essay on the Selection of Technological and Environmental Dangers*, Berkeley: University of California Press.

Drury, S. (2007), 'Gurus of endless war', *New Humanist* 122.3 (May/June), rationalist.org.uk/1463

Dubai School of Government (2011), 'Civil movements: the impact of Facebook and Twitter', *Arab Social Media Report* 1.2 (May), www.dsg.ae/en/ASMR2/ASMRHome2.aspx

Eco, U. [1986] (1987), *Travels in Hyperreality*, trans. W. Weaver, London: Picador.

Eisenhower, D. (1961), 'Farewell address', *American Rhetoric*, www.americanrhetoric.com/speeches/dwightdeisenhowerfarewell.html

Eisenstein, E. (1980), *The Printing Press as an Agent of Change: Communications and Cultural Transformations in Early-Modern Europe*, Cambridge: Cambridge University Press.

Eisenstein, S. [1923] (1957), 'Montage of attractions: an essay', *The Film Sense*:

Two Complete and Unabridged Works, trans. J. Leyda, Cleveland: Meridian, pp. 230–3.

Ekman, P. (1985), *Telling Lies: Clues to Deceit in the Marketplace, Politics, and Marriage*, New York: W. W. Norton.

Ellis, J. and B. McLane [2005] (2008), *A New History of Documentary Film*, New York: Continuum.

Ellul, J. [1965] (1973), *Propaganda: The Formation of Men's Attitudes*, New York: Vintage Books.

Emerson, R. W. [1839] (1957), 'Self-reliance', in *Selections from Ralph Waldo Emerson*, ed. S. Whicher, Boston: Riverside Editions.

Emery, C. (1994), *Public Opinion Polling in Canada*, Government of Canada report, www.parl.gc.ca/Content/LOP/researchpublications/bp371-e.htm

European Parliament (2009), *A Review of the Increased Use of CCTV and Video-Surveillance for Crime Prevention Purposes in Europe*, report by the Directorate General Internal Policies, www.statewatch.org/news/2009/apr/ep-study-norris-cctv-video-surveillance.pdf

Ewen, S. (1996), *PR! A Social History of Spin*, New York: Basic Books.

Ewen, S. and E. Ewen [1982] (1992), *Channels of Desire: Mass Images and the Shaping of American Consciousness*, Minneapolis: University of Minnesota Press.

Farsetta, D. and D. Price (2006), 'Fake TV news: widespread and undisclosed', Center for Media and Democracy, 16 March, www.prwatch.org/fakenews/execsummary

Femen, femen.org/en

Festinger, L. (1957), *A Theory of Cognitive Dissonance*, Redwood City: Stanford University Press.

Fielding, N. and I. Cobain (2011), 'Revealed: US spy operation that manipulates social media', *The Guardian*, 17 March, www.guardian.co.uk/technology/2011/mar/17/us-spy-operation-social-networks

Filler, L. (1939), *Crusaders for American Liberalism*, New York: Harcourt, Brace.

Flood, A. (2012), 'Sock puppetry and fake reviews: publish and be damned', *The Guardian*, 4 September, www.guardian.co.uk/books/2012/sep/04/sock-puppetry-publish-be-damned

Florida, R. (2007), *The Flight of the Creative Class: The New Global Competition for Talent*, New York: Collins.

Food Democracy Now, www.fooddemocracynow.org/

Foucault, M. (1984), *The Foucault Reader*, ed. P. Rabinow, London: Penguin.

Frank, J. D. and J. B. Frank [1961] (1993), *Persuasion and Healing: A Comparative Study of Psychotherapy*, Baltimore: Johns Hopkins Press.

Freeman, C. (2014), 'Ukraine crisis: Crimea joining Russia "like Scotland staying in the Union"', *The Telegraph*, 28 March, www.telegraph.co.uk/news/worldnews/europe/ukraine/10730853/Ukraine-crisis-Crimea-joining-Russia-like-Scotland-staying-in-the-Union.html

Freeze, C. (2013), 'How Canada's shadowy metadata-gathering program went awry', *Globe and Mail*, 15 June, www.theglobeandmail.com/news/national/how-canadas-shadowy-metadata-gathering-program-went-awry/article12580225/

French, J. and B. Raven [1960] (1968), 'The bases of social power', in D. Cartwright and A. Zander (eds), *Group Dynamics*, New York: Harper and Row, pp. 607–23.

Friedman, M. (1962), *Capitalism and Freedom*, Chicago: University of Chicago Press.

Froomkin, D. (2005), 'Cheney's "dark side" is showing', *Washington Post*, 7 November, www.washingtonpost.com/wp-dyn/content/blog/2005/11/07/BL2005110700793.html

Fulford, R. (1999), *The Triumph of Narrative: Storytelling in the Age of Mass Culture*, Toronto: Anansi.

Fussell, P. [1989] (1990), *Wartime: Understanding and Behaviour in the Second World War*, New York: Oxford University Press.

Galloway, A. (2004), *Protocol: How Control Exists After Decentralization*, Cambridge, MA: MIT Press.

Gass, R. and J. Seiter [1999] (2007), *Persuasion, Social Influence, and Compliance Gaining*, Boston: Pearson.

Gates, Henry Louis Jr [1988] (1989), *The Signifying Monkey: A Theory of African-American Literary Criticism*, New York: Oxford.

Geiger, J. (2005), 'Fiction, truth, and the documentary contract', in J. Geiger and R. Rutsky (eds), *Film Analysis*, New York: W. W. Norton, pp. 118–37.

Ghamari-Tabrizi, S. (2005), *The Worlds of Herman Kahn: The Intuitive Science of Thermonuclear War*, Cambridge, MA: Harvard University Press.

Giannetti, L. and J. Leach (1998), *Understanding Movies*, Canadian edn, Englewood Cliffs: Prentice-Hall.

Giddens, A. (1997), *Sociology*, 3rd edn, Cambridge, MA: Polity Press.

Giroux, H. (2006), *Beyond the Spectacle of Terrorism: Global Uncertainty and the Challenge of the New Media*, Boulder: Paradigm.

Gladstone, B. and J. Neufeld (2011), *The Influencing Machine*, New York: W. W. Norton.

Glass, A., B. Evans and A. Sanborn (2008), 'Project statement', in *In the Land of the Head Hunters*, Seattle: Moore Theatre presentation programme, p. 2, www.curtisfilm.rutgers.edu/downloads/moa_ec_program.pdf

Gleick, J. [2011] (2012), *The Information: A History, A Theory, A Flood*, New York: Vintage.

Global Terrorism Database, www.start.umd.edu/gtd/

Goebbels, J. [1943] (1998), 'Nation, rise up, and let the storm break loose' (Total war speech), trans. R. Bytwerk, www.calvin.edu/german-propaganda-archive/goeb36.htm

Goebbels, J. (1978), *The Goebbels Diaries: The Last Days*, ed. H. Trevor-Roper, trans. R. Barry, London: Secker and Warburg.

Goffman, E. (1959), *The Presentation of Self in Everyday Life*, Garden City: Doubleday.

Goffman, E. (1974), *Frame Analysis: An Essay on the Organization of Experience*, New York: Harper and Row.

Goldenberg, S. (2009), 'Copenhagen spoof shames Canada on the truth about its emissions', *The Guardian*, 14 December, www.theguardian.com/environment/blog/2009/dec/14/environment-canada-spoof

Goodman, A. (2006), 'Stephen Colbert's blistering performance mocking Bush and the press goes ignored by the media', *Democracy Now!* 3 May, www.democracynow.org/2006/5/3/stephen_colberts_blistering_performance_mocking_bush

Goodman, L-A. (2014), 'Harper addresses Israel Parliament, rails against "new" anti-Semitism', *Huffington Post*, 20 January, www.huffingtonpost.ca/2014/01/20/stephen-harper-israel-parliament_n_4632269.html

Goody, J. (1977), *The Domestication of the Savage Mind*, Cambridge: Cambridge University Press.

'GOP deeply divided over climate change' (2013), Pew Research, www.people-press.org/2013/11/01/gop-deeply-divided-over-climate-change/

Gottschall, J. (2012), *The Storytelling Animal: How Stories Make Us Human*, Boston: Houghton Mifflin Harcourt.

Gourevitch, P. and E. Morris (2008), *Standard Operating Procedure*, New York: Penguin.

Government Accountability Office (GAO) (2005), 'Office of National Drug Control Policy – video news release', US Government report, www.gao.gov/decisions/appro/303495.htm

Gramsci, A. (1971), *Selections from the Prison Notebooks*, New York: International Publishers.

Grant, G. (1969), *Technology and Empire: Perspectives on North America*, Toronto: Anansi.

Greenberg, C. (1939), 'Avant-garde and kitsch', *Partisan Review*, VI.5 (Fall): 34–49.

Greenwald, G. (2014), *No Place to Hide*, New York: Metropolitan Books.

Greenwald, G., E. MacAskill and L. Poitras (2013), 'Edward Snowden: the whistleblower behind the NSA surveillance revelations', *The Guardian*, 10 June, www.theguardian.com/world/2013/jun/09/edward-snowden-nsa-whistleblower-surveillance

Guerrilla Girls, www.guerrillagirls.com

Guevara, E. [1965] (2003), 'Socialism and man in Cuba', in *Che Guevara Reader*, Melbourne: Ocean Press, pp. 212–28.

Gutstein, D. (2009), *Not a Conspiracy Theory: How Business Propaganda Hijacks Democracy*, Toronto: Key Porter Books.

Habermas, J. [1962] (1991), *The Structural Transformation of the Public Sphere: An Inquiry into a Category of Bourgeois Society*, Cambridge, MA: MIT Press.

Hacker, J. and P. Pierson (2010), *Winner-Take-All Politics: How Washington Made the Rich Richer – and Turned Its Back on the Middle Class*, New York: Simon and Schuster.

Hall, S. [1980] (2006), 'Encoding/decoding', in M. Durham and D. Kellner (eds), *Media and Cultural Studies Keyworks*, Malden: Blackwell, pp. 163–73.

Happy Planet Index, happyplanetindex.org/

Harcourt, B. [2001] (2004), *Illusion of Order: The False Promise of Broken Windows Policing*, Cambridge, MA: Harvard University Press.

Hardin, G. (1968), 'The tragedy of the commons', *Science* 162: 1243–8, www.sciencemag.org/content/162/3859/1243.full

Hardt, M. and A. Negri [2000] (2001), *Empire*, Cambridge, MA: Harvard University Press.

Hardy, F. (ed.) (1966), *Grierson on Documentary*, London: Faber.

Harris, R. A. (2013), *Handbook of Rhetorical Devices*, Virtual Salt website, www.virtualsalt.com/rhetoric.htm

Harrison, J. and H. Stein (eds) (1974), *Muckraking: Past, Present and Future*, University Park, PA: Pennsylvania State University Press.

Harvey, D. (2012), *Rebel Cities: From the Right to the City to the Urban Revolution*, London: Verso.

Hasson, U., O. Landesman, B. Knappmeyer, I. Vallines, N. Rubin and D. Heeger (2008), 'Neurocinematics: the neuroscience of film', *Projections: The Journal for Movies and Mind* 2.1 (Summer): 1–23, www.cns.nyu.edu/~nava/MyPubs/Hasson-etal_NeuroCinematics2008.pdf

Havel, V. [1978] (1985), 'The power of the powerless', in J. Keane (ed.), *The Power of the Powerless: Citizens Against the State in Central-Eastern Europe*, trans. P. Wilson, London: Hutchinson, vaclavhavel.cz/showtrans.php?cat=clanky&val=72_aj_clanky.html&typ=HTML

Havelock, E. (1986), *The Muse Learns to Write: Reflections on Orality and Literacy from Antiquity to the Present*, New Haven: Yale University Press.

Hayek, F. [1944] (2007), *The Road to Serfdom*, ed. B. Caldwell, Chicago: University of Chicago Press.

Hayles, N. K. (1999), *How We Became Posthuman: Virtual Bodies in Cybernetics, Literature, and Informatics*, Chicago: University of Chicago Press.

Hedges, C. [2002] (2003), *War is a Force That Gives Us Meaning*, New York: Anchor Books.

Hedges, C. (2009), *Empire of Illusion: The End of Literacy and the Triumph of Spectacle*, Toronto: Alfred A. Knopf Canada.

Hedges, C. (2010), *Death of the Liberal Class*, New York: Nation Books.

Helfand, J. (2001), *Screen: Essays on Graphic Design, New Media, and Visual Culture*, Princeton: Princeton Architectural Press.

Heller, S. (2008), *Iron Fists: Branding the 20th-Century Totalitarian State*, London: Phaidon.

Herman, E. and N. Chomsky (1988), *Manufacturing Consent: The Political Economy of the Mass Media*, New York: Pantheon.

Hersh, S. (2004), 'Torture at Abu Ghraib', *The New Yorker*, 10 May, www.newyorker.com/archive/2004/05/10/040510fa_fact

Historica Canada, historicacanada.ca

Hitchens, C. (2001), *The Trial of Henry Kissinger*, London: Verso.

Hitchens, P. (2007), 'How to read an opinion poll', Hitchens Blog, *The Mail on Sunday*, 17 December, hitchensblog.mailonsunday.co.uk/2007/12/how-to-read-an.html

Hitchens, P. (2010), *The Cameron Delusion*, London: Continuum.

Hitler, A. [1927] (1971), *Mein Kampf*, trans. R. Manheim, Boston: Houghton Mifflin.

Hobbes, T. [1651] (2010), *Leviathan: Or the Matter, Forme, and Power of a Common-Wealth Ecclesiasticall and Civill*, New Haven: Yale University Press.

Hockney, D. (2006), *Secret Knowledge: Rediscovering the Lost Techniques of the Old Masters*, London: Thames and Hudson.

Hoffmann, H. (1927), 'Hitler rehearsing his oratory', United States Holocaust Memorial Museum website, www.ushmm.org/propaganda/archive/hitler-rehearses-speech-6/

Hoffmann, H. [1955] (2012), *Hitler was My Friend: The Memoirs of Hitler's Photographer*, Bamsley: Frontline Books.

Hoggan, J. (2009), *Climate Cover-Up: The Crusade to Deny Global Warming*, Vancouver: Greystone Books.

Holland, F. (2013), 'Microsoft advertising digital trends and opportunities in 2013', Microsoft report, 9 January, advertising.microsoft.com/en-us/blogpost/121548/microsoft-advertising-blog/microsoft-advertising-digital-trends-and-opportunities-in-2013 (accessed 21 January 2014)

Jenny Holzer website, projects.jennyholzer.com/

Hopkins, N. and J. Borger (2013), 'NSA pays £100m in secret funding for GCHQ', *The Guardian*, 1 August, www.theguardian.com/uk-news/2013/aug/01/nsa-paid-gchq-spying-edward-snowden

Horkheimer, M. and T. Adorno [1944] (2006), 'The culture industry: enlightenment as mass deception', in M. Durham and D. Kellner (eds), *Media and Cultural Studies Keyworks*, Oxford: Blackwell, pp. 41–72.

Howard, P. (2010), *The Digital Origins of Dictatorship and Democracy: Information Technology and Political Islam*, New York: Oxford University Press.

Howard, P. and M. Hussain (2013), *Democracy's Fourth Wave? Digital Media and the Arab Spring*, New York: Oxford University Press.

Hunter, J. (1991), *Culture Wars: The Struggle to Define America*, New York: Basic Books.

Huntington, S. (1993), 'The clash of civilisations?' *Foreign Affairs* 72.3 (Summer): 22–49.

Huxley, A. [1958] (1965), *Brave New World Revisited*, New York: Harper and Row.

Hyde, L. (1998), *Trickster Makes This World: Mischief, Myth, and Art*, New York: Farrar, Straus and Giroux.

Hyde, L. (2011), *Trickster Makes This World*, www.lewishyde.com/publications/trickster

Idle No More, idlenomore.ca/

Implicit Association Test (Project Implicit), implicit.harvard.edu/implicit/

Innis, H. A. [1951] (1984), *The Bias of Communications*, Toronto: University of Toronto Press.

iNudgeYou, www.inudgeyou.com

'Ipsos MORI trust poll' (2013), Ipsos MORI, 11 February, www.ipsos-mori. com/Assets/Docs/Polls/Feb2013_Trust_Topline.PDF

Issenberg, S. (2012), 'How President Obama's campaign used big data to rally individual voters', *Technology Review*, 16 December, www.technologyreview.com/featuredstory/508836/how-obama-used-big-data-to-rally-voters-part-1/

'Ivan Pavlov – biographical' [1904] (1967), Nobel Foundation, Nobelprize. org, www.nobelprize.org/nobel_prizes/medicine/laureates/1904/pavlov-bio.html

Jablonsky, D. (1991), *Churchill, the Great Game and Total War*, London: Frank Cass.

Jenkins, H. (2006), *Convergence Culture: Where Old and New Media Collide*, New York: New York University Press.

Jenkins, S. (2007), 'In a war zone wide-awake: Jon Naar in New York, c. 1973', in J. Naar, *The Birth of Graffiti*, Munich: Prestel, pp. 11–14.

Johnson, T. (2013), 'Cubans evade censorship by exchanging computer memory sticks, blogger says', *McClatchy DC*, 9 March, www.mcclatchydc. com/2013/03/09/185347/cubans-evade-censorship-by-exchanging.html

Jonestown Institute (2014), 'Alternative considerations of Jonestown and the Peoples Temple', jonestown.sdsu.edu/

Jowett, G. and V. O'Donnell (2006), *Propaganda and Persuasion*, 4th edn, Thousand Oaks: Sage.

Judovitz, D. (1987), 'Rendez-vous with Marcel Duchamp: given', *Dada/Surrealism* 16: 184–202.

'Just a few bad apples?' (2005), *The Economist*, 20 January, www.economist. com/node/3577249

Kahn, H. (1960), *On Thermonuclear War*, Princeton: Princeton University Press.

Kahneman, D. (2011), *Thinking, Fast and Slow*, Toronto: Random House (Doubleday).

Kahneman, D. and A. Tversky (1979), 'Prospect theory: an analysis of decision under risk', *Econometrica* XLVII: 263–91.

Kant, E. [1787] (1996), *Critique of Pure Reason*, trans. W. Pluhar, Indianapolis: Hackett.

Kaplan, D. (2012), 'WikiLeaks undergoing massive denial-of-service attack', *SC Magazine*, 10 August, www.scmagazine.com/WikiLeaks-undergoing-massive-denial-of-service-attack/article/254267/

Keeble, A. (ed.) [1961] (2001), *Con El Espíritu de los Maestros Ambulantes: La Campaña de Alfabetización Cubana, 1961* (*In the Spirit of Wandering Teachers: Cuban Literacy Campaign, 1961*), Melbourne: Ocean Press.

Keen, S. [1986] (1991), *Faces of the Enemy: Reflections of the Hostile Imagination*, New York: HarperCollins.

Kellerman, K. (2004), 'A goal-directed approach to gaining compliance: relating differences among goals to differences in behaviours', *Communication Research* 31.4: 347–445.

Kellerman, K. and B. Shea (1996), 'Threats, suggestions, hints, and promises: gaining compliance efficiently and politely', *Communication Quarterly* 44.2: 145–65.

Kelly, K. (2010), *What Technology Wants*, New York: Viking.

Keohane, J. (2010), 'How facts backfire', *Boston Globe*, 11 July, www.boston.com/bostonglobe/ideas/articles/2010/07/11/how_facts_backfire/

Key, W. B. (1973), *Subliminal Seduction*, New York: Prentice Hall.

Keynes, J. M. [1934] (2007), *The General Theory of Employment, Interest and Money*, London: Palgrave Macmillan.

Keysers, C. (2011), *The Empathic Brain: How the Discovery of Mirror Neurons Changes Our Understanding of Human Nature*, Electronic Book: Social Brain Press.

Kirchhoff, S. (2009), 'Advertising industry in the digital age', Congressional Research Service Report R40908, *www.fas.org/sgp/crs/misc/R40908.pdf*

Klausen, J. (2009), *The Cartoons That Shook the World*, New Haven: Yale University Press.

Klein, N. (2000), *No Logo: Taking Aim at the Brand Bullies*, Toronto: Vintage Canada.

Klein, N. (2007), *The Shock Doctrine: The Rise of Disaster Capitalism*, Toronto: Alfred A. Knopf.

Klein, N. (2010), 'Naomi Klein on how corporate branding has taken over America', *The Guardian*, 16 January, www.guardian.co.uk/books/2010/jan/16/naomi-klein-branding-obama-america

Klewes, J. and R. Wreschniok (eds) (2009), *Reputation Capital: Building and Maintaining Trust in the 21st Century*, New York: Springer.

Knightley, P. (1975), *The First Casualty: From the Crimea to Vietnam: The War Correspondent as Hero, Propagandist and Myth-Maker*, New York: Harcourt Brace Jovanovich.

Komaromi, A (2004), 'The material existence of Soviet samizdat', *Slavic Review* 63.3: 597–618.

Kracauer, S. [1926] (1987), 'The cult of distraction: on Berlin's picture palaces', *New German Critique* 40: 91–6.

Kristeva, J. (1980), *Desire in Language: A Semiotic Approach to Literature and Art*, New York: Columbia University Press.

Kristol, I. (1995), *Neo-Conservatism: The Autobiography of an Idea*, Chicago: Ivan R. Dee.

Kristol, W., E. Abrams, G. Bauer, W. J. Bennett, J. Bush, D. Cheney, E. Cohen, M. Decter, P. Dobriansky, S. Forbes, A. Friedberg, F. Fukuyama, F. Gaffney, F. Ikle, D. Kagan, Z. Khalilzad, I. L. Libby, N. Podhoretz, D. Quayle, P. Rodman, S. Rosen, H. Rowen, D. Rumsfeld, V. Weber, G. Weigel and P. Wolfowitz (co-signatories) (1997), 'Statement of principles', Project for a New American Century, www.rightweb.irc-online.org/profile/Project_for_the_New_American_Century

Kunda, Z. (1990), 'The case for motivated reasoning', *Psychological Bulletin* 108.3: 480–98.

Lakoff, G. [2008] (2009), *The Political Mind: A Cognitive Scientist's Guide to Your Brain and its Politics*, New York: Penguin.

Lakoff, G. and M. Johnson [1980] (2003), *Metaphors We Live By*, Chicago: University of Chicago Press.

Landman, A. (2010), 'BP's "Beyond Petroleum" campaign losing its sheen', *PRWatch*, 3 May, www.prwatch.org/node/9038

Lanham, R. (1991), *A Handlist of Rhetorical Terms*, 2nd edn, Berkeley: University of California Press.

Lanier, J. (2010), *You Are Not a Gadget: A Manifesto*, New York: Knopf.

Laningham, S. (2006), 'developerWorks interviews: Tim Berners-Lee', IBM developerWorks, 22 August, www.ibm.com/developerworks/podcast/dwi/cm-int082206txt.html

Lasswell, H., D. Lerner and H. Speier (eds) (1979), *The Symbolic Instrument in Early Times*, Vol. 1 of *Propaganda and Communication in World History*, Honolulu: University Press of Hawaii.

Leahy, S. (2011), 'Cut climate damaging emissions in half and double food production with eco-farming', Stephenleahy.net, 13 March, stephenleahy.net/

Le Bon, G. [1896] (2006), *The Crowd: A Study of the Popular Mind*, West Valley City: Walking Lion Press.

Lehrer, J. [2009] (2010), *How We Decide*, Boston: Mariner Books.

Leigh, D. (2009), 'How UK oil company Trafigura tried to cover up African pollution disaster', *The Guardian*, 16 September, www.guardian.co.uk/world/2009/sep/16/trafigura-african-pollution-disaster

Leigh, D. and L. Harding (2011), *WikiLeaks: Inside Julian Assange's War on Secrecy*, New York: Guardian Books/PublicAffairs.

Leith, S. (2012), *Words Like Loaded Pistols: Rhetoric from Aristotle to Obama*, New York: Basic Books.

Lenin, V. I. [1902] (1999), *What Is To Be Done? Burning Questions of our Movement*, Marxist Internet Archive, www.marxists.org/archive/lenin/works/1901/witbd/

Lessig, L. (2008), *Remix: Making Art and Commerce Thrive in the Hybrid Economy*, New York: Penguin.

Lessig, L. (2011), *Republic, Lost: How Money Corrupts Congress – and a Plan to Stop It*, New York: Twelve.

Levant, E. (2010), *Ethical Oil: The Case for Canada's Oil Sands*, Toronto: McClelland and Stewart.

Leveson, B. (2012), *Leveson Inquiry: Culture, Practices and Ethics of the Press*, report to UK Government, www.levesoninquiry.org.uk/

Levin, A. (2002), 'Eye on the media: just say no to NPR', Committee for Accuracy in Middle East Reporting in America (CAMERA), 9 October, www.camera.org/index.asp?x_context=4&x_outlet=28&x_article=292

Levs, J. and C. Cratty (2013), 'Court considers demand that U.S. release photos of bin Laden's body', *CNN*, 10 January, www.cnn.com/2013/01/10/world/bin-laden-photos/index.html

Lévy, P. (1994), *L'Intelligence Collective: Pour une Anthropologie du Cyberspace*, Paris: La Découverte.

Levy, S. (1984), *Hackers: Heroes of the Computer Revolution*, Garden City: Doubleday.

Lewis, P. (2011), 'You're being watched: there's one CCTV camera for every 32 people in UK', *The Guardian*, 2 March, www.guardian.co.uk/uk/2011/mar/02/cctv-cameras-watching-surveillance

Lichtblau, E. and M. Rich (2012), 'N.R.A. envisions "a good guy with a gun" in every school', *The New York Times*, 21 December, www.nytimes.com/2012/12/22/us/nra-calls-for-armed-guards-at-schools.html

Lifton, R. (1982), 'Beyond psychic numbing: a call to awareness', *American Journal of Orthopsychiatry* 52.4 (October): 619–29.

Linden, M. (2011), 'Rich people's taxes have little to do with job creation', Center for American Progress, 27 June, www.americanprogress.org/issues/tax-reform/news/2011/06/27/9856/rich-peoples-taxes-have-little-to-do-with-job-creation/

Linfield, S. (2010), *The Cruel Radiance: Photography and Political Violence*, Chicago: University of Chicago Press.

Lippmann, W. [1922] (1997), *Public Opinion*, New York: Simon and Schuster.

Littau, K. (2005), 'Arrival of a train at La Ciotat', in J. Geiger and R. Rutsky (eds), *Film Analysis*, New York: W. W. Norton, pp. 43–62.

London School of Economics (2014), 'Ending the drug wars: report of the LSE Expert Group on the economics of drug policy', www.lse.ac.uk/IDEAS/Projects/IDPP/The-Expert-Group-on-the-Economics-of-Drug-Policy.aspx

Lord, A. (1960), *The Singer of Tales*, Cambridge, MA: Harvard University Press.

Lunenfeld, P. (2000), *Snap to Grid: A User's Guide to Digital Arts, Media, and Cultures*, Cambridge, MA: MIT Press.

Lynskey, D. (2013), 'Oblivion with bells', *Q* 318 (January): 82–8.

Lyons, D. (2007), *Surveillance Studies: An Overview*, Cambridge: Polity Press.

McChesney, R. (2004), *The Problem of the Media: U.S. Communication Politics in the 21st Century*, New York: Monthly Review Press.

McChesney, R. (2008), *The Political Economy of Media: Enduring Issues, Emerging Dilemmas*, New York: Monthly Review Press.

McChesney, R. (2013), *Digital Disconnect: How Capitalism is Turning the Internet Against Democracy*, New York: The New Press.

McCracken, G. [1988] (1990), *Culture and Consumption: New Approaches to the Symbolic Character of Consumer Goods and Activities*, Bloomington: Indiana University Press.

McEwan, I. (2012), *Sweet Tooth*, New York: Knopf Doubleday.

McGovern, R. (2011), 'Neocons fume over US boat to Gaza', *Consortium*

News, 16 July, consortiumnews.com/2011/07/16/neocons-fume-over-us-boat-to-gaza/

McKie, R. (2010), '*Merchants of Doubt* by Naomi Oreskes and Erik M Conway', *The Guardian*, 8 August, www.guardian.co.uk/books/2010/aug/08/merchants-of-doubt-oreskes-conway

McLuhan, M. [1951] (1967), *The Mechanical Bride: The Folklore of Industrial Man*, Boston: Beacon Press.

McLuhan, M. [1962] (1965), *The Gutenberg Galaxy: The Making of Typographic Man*, Toronto: University of Toronto Press.

McLuhan, M. [1964] (1994), *Understanding Media: The Extensions of Man*, Cambridge, MA: MIT Press.

McLuhan, M. and E. McLuhan (1988), *Laws of Media: The New Science*, Toronto: University of Toronto Press.

McNeil, K. (2002), 'The war on academic freedom', *The Nation*, 11 November, www.thenation.com/article/war-academic-freedom

Maass, P. (2011), 'The toppling: how the media inflated a minor moment in a long war', *The New Yorker*, 10 January, www.newyorker.com/reporting/2011/01/10/110110fa_fact_maass

Machiavelli, N. [1532] (1997), *The Prince*, trans. C. E. Detmold, London: Wordsworth Editions.

Mackay, C. [1841] (1995), *Extraordinary Popular Delusions and the Madness of Crowds*, Ware: Wordsworth Reference.

Mailer, N. (1974), 'Introduction', in J. Naar, M. Kurlansky and N. Mailer, *The Faith of Graffiti*, New York: Praeger, pp. 4–9.

Malcolm, J. (1990), *The Journalist and the Murderer*, New York: Vintage.

Mander, J. (1978), *Four Arguments for the Elimination of Television*, New York: HarperCollins.

Mann, S. (2013), EyeTap website, www.eyetap.org/research/eyetap.html

Mann, S., J. Nolan and B. Wellmar (2003), 'Sousveillance: inventing and using wearable computing devices for data collection in surveillance environments', *Surveillance and Society* 1.3: 331–55.

Manovich, L. (2001), *The Language of New Media*, Cambridge, MA: MIT Press.

Marcus, G. [1989] (1990), *Lipstick Traces: A Secret History of the Twentieth Century*, Cambridge, MA: Harvard University Press.

Marcuse, H. [1964] (1991), *One-Dimensional Man: Studies in the Ideology of Advanced Industrial Society*, Boston: Beacon Press.

Marinetti, F. T. [1909] (1991), 'Futurist manifesto', in *Let's Murder the Moonshine: The Selected Writings of F. T. Marinetti*, Los Angeles: Sun and Moon Press, pp. 47–52.

Marks, J. (1979), *The Search for the 'Manchurian Candidate': The Story of the CIA's Secret Efforts to Control Human Behaviour*, London: Allen Lane.

Marlin, R. (2002), *Propaganda and the Ethics of Persuasion*, Peterborough, ON: Broadview Press.

Marwell, G. and D. Schmitt (1967), 'Dimensions of compliance gaining behaviour: an empirical analysis', *Sociometry* 30: 350–64.

Marx, K. and F. Engels [1848] (2011), *The Communist Manifesto*, trans. S. Moore, New York: Penguin.

Marx, K. and F. Engels [1872] (2011), 'Preface to the German edition of 1872', *The Communist Manifesto*, trans. S. Moore, New York: Penguin, pp. 21–4.

Mayer, J. (2010), 'Covert operations', *The New Yorker*, 30 August, www.newyorker.com/reporting/2010/08/30/100830fa_fact_mayer

Mayer, J. (2012), 'Bully pulpit', *The New Yorker*, 18 June, www.newyorker.com/reporting/2012/06/18/120618fa_fact_mayer

Mearsheimer, J. and S. Walt (2006), 'The Israel lobby', *The London Review of Books* 28.6 (23 March): 3–12, www.lrb.co.uk/v28/n06/john-mearsheimer/the-israel-lobby

Mechanical Turk, www.mturk.com/mturk/welcome

Media Ecology Association, www.media-ecology.org

Meggs, P. (1998), *The History of Graphic Design*, New York: John Wiley and Sons.

Merlin, D. (1991), *The Origins of the Modern Mind: Three Stages in the Evolution of Culture and Cognition*, Cambridge, MA: Harvard University Press.

Meyrowitz, J. (1985), *No Sense of Place: The Impact of Electronic Media on Social Behaviour*, Oxford: Oxford University Press.

Michie, D. (1998), *The Invisible Persuaders: How Britain's Spin Doctors Manipulate the Media*, London: Bantam.

Milgram, S. [1974] (2009), *Obedience to Authority: An Experimental View*, New York: Harper Perennial.

Miller, M. (2005), 'Introduction', in E. Bernays (1928), *Propaganda*, New York: Ig Publishing, pp. 9–30.

'Millions join global anti-war protests' (2003), *BBC World News*, 17 February, news.bbc.co.uk/2/hi/europe/2765215.stm

Millman, D. (2013), *Brand Thinking and other Noble Pursuits*, New York: Allworth Press.

Milne, S. [1994] (2005), 'The secret war against the miners', in J. Pilger (ed.), *Tell Me No Lies: Investigative Journalism and its Triumphs*, London: Vintage, pp. 284–331.

Mitchell, W. [1986] (1987), *Iconology: Image, Text, Ideology*, Chicago: University of Chicago Press.

Mlodinow, L. (2012), *Subliminal: How Your Unconscious Mind Rules Your Behaviour*, New York: Pantheon Books.

Moeller, S. (1999), *Compassion Fatigue: How the Media Sell Disease, Famine, War and Death*, New York: Routledge.

Moeller, S. (2001), 'Compassion fatigue: graphic, complicated stories numb readers and viewers to atrocities', *Media Studies Journal* (Summer): 108–12.

Monbiot, G. (2002), 'The covert biotech war', *The Guardian*, 19 November, www.guardian.co.uk/science/2002/nov/19/gm.food

Monbiot, G. (2006), 'The denial industry', *The Guardian*, 19 September, www.guardian.co.uk/environment/2006/sep/19/ethicalliving.g2

Monbiot, G. (2011), 'The need to protect the internet from "astroturfing" grows ever more urgent', *The Guardian*, 23 February, www.guardian.co.uk/environment/georgemonbiot/2011/feb/23/need-to-protect-internet-from-astroturfing

Morozov, E. (2012), *The Net Delusion: The Dark Side of Internet Freedom*, New York: PublicAffairs/Perseus Books.

Morris, E. (2004), 'Eye contact', Errol Morris website, www.errolmorris.com/content/eyecontact/interrotron.html

Morris, E. (2011), *Believing is Seeing: Observations on the Mysteries of Photography*, New York: Penguin Press.

Morris, P. (1987), 'Re-thinking Grierson: the ideology of John Grierson', in T. O'Regan and B. Shoesmith (eds), *History on/and/in Film*, Perth: History and Film Association of Australia, pp. 20–30, http://wwwmcc.murdoch.edu.au/ReadingRoom/hfilm/MORRIS.html

Mulvey, L. (1975), 'Visual pleasure and narrative cinema', *Screen* 16.3: 6–18.

Murch, W. [1995] (2001), *In the Blink of an Eye: A Perspective on Film Editing*, 2nd edn, Los Angeles: Silman-James Press.

Murray, J. (1997), *Hamlet on the Holodeck: The Future of Narrative in Cyberspace*, New York: The Free Press.

Naar, J. (2007), *The Birth of Graffiti*, Munich: Prestel.

Naremore, J. (2000), 'The death and rebirth of rhetoric', *Senses of Cinema* 5 (April), sensesofcinema.com/2000/society-for-cinema-studies-conference-2000/rhetoric/

Negroponte, N. [1995] (1996), *Being Digital*, New York: Vintage.

Neuman, W., G. Marcus, A. Crigler and M. MacKuen (eds) (2007), *The Affect Effect: Dynamics of Emotions in Political Thinking and Behaviour*, Chicago: University of Chicago Press.

Nichols, B. (2005), 'Film form and revolution', in J. Geiger and R. Rutsky (eds), *Film Analysis*, New York: W. W. Norton, pp. 158–77.

Nizkor Project, www.nizkor.org/

Noë, A. [2009] (2010), *Out of Our Heads*, New York: Hill and Wang.

Nye, J. (2004), *Soft Power: The Means to Success in World Politics*, New York: Public Affairs.

Nyhan, B. (2014), 'The downside of registering outrage', *The New York Times*, 24 April, www.nytimes.com/2014/04/24/upshot/the-downside-of-registering-outrage.html

Nyhan, B. and J. Reifler (2010), 'When corrections fail: the persistence of political misperceptions', *Political Behavior* 32.2 (June): 303–30.

O'Reilly, Terry and M. Tennant [2009] (2010), *The Age of Persuasion: How Marketing Ate Our Culture*, Toronto: Vintage Canada.

O'Reilly, Tim (2005), 'What is Web 2.0', O'Reilly Network, oreilly.com/web2/archive/what-is-web-20.html

Occupy Wall Street, occupywallst.org/

Okpewho, I. (1979), *The Epic in Africa: Toward a Poetics of the Oral Performance*, New York: Columbia University Press.

Oliver, M. (2005), 'McLibel Two win legal aid case', *The Guardian*, 15 February, www.theguardian.com/uk/2005/feb/15/foodanddrink

Ondaatje, M. (2002), *The Conversations: Walter Murch and the Art of Editing Film*, Toronto: Vintage/Random House Canada.

Ong, W. [1982] (1988), *Orality and Literacy: The Technologising of the Word*, London: Routledge.

Open Secrets (2011), 'Heavy Hitters: Top all-time donors, 1989–2014', www.opensecrets.org/orgs/list.php

Oreskes, N. (2005), 'Beyond the ivory tower, the scientific consensus on climate change (including corrections)', *Science* 306 (21 January): 1686.

Oreskes, N. and E. Conway (2010), *Merchants of Doubt*, New York: Bloomsbury Press.

Organisation for Economic Co-operation and Development (OECD) Better Life Index, oecdbetterlifeindex.org

Ortega, D. (2006), '"En cada barrio": timocracy, Panopticism and the landscape of a normalised community', *Culture Machine* 8, www.culturemachine.net/index.php/cm/article/viewArticle/42/50

Orwell, G. [1949] (1989), *Nineteen Eighty-Four*, London: Penguin.

Packard, V. [1957] (2007), *The Hidden Persuaders*, New York: Ig Publishing.

Pangburn, D. J. (2011), 'Anonymous strikes and "ends" Monsanto PR firm Bivings Group', *Death and Taxes*, 6 December, www.deathandtaxesmag.com/166429/anonymous-strikes-and-ends-monsanto-pr-firm-bivings-group/

'Panopticon' (2014), *Wikipedia*, en.wikipedia.org/wiki/Panopticon

Pariser, E. (2011), *The Filter Bubble: What the Internet is Hiding from You*, New York: Penguin.

Pascal, J. (2005), *Jacob Riis: Reporter and Reformer*, New York: Oxford University Press.

Paxman, J. (2010), 'Jeremy Paxman's photograph of the decade', *The Guardian*, 13 November, www.guardian.co.uk/artanddesign/2010/nov/13/jeremy-paxman-photograph-decade

'Pentagon spending billions on PR to sway world opinion' (2009), *Fox News*, 5 February, www.foxnews.com/politics/2009/02/05/pentagon-spending-billions-pr-sway-world-opinion/

Peretti, J. (2001), 'Nike emails', Timothy Shey weblog, www.shey.net/niked.html

Perez, G. (2000), 'Toward a rhetoric of film: identification and the spectator', *Senses of Cinema* 5 (April), sensesofcinema.com/2000/society-for-cinema-studies-conference-2000/rhetoric2/

Perkins, J. (2004), *Confessions of an Economic Hit Man*, San Francisco: Berrett-Koehler.

Perkins, J. (2007), 'John Perkins on *The Secret History of the American Empire: Economic Hit Men, Jackals, and the Truth about Global Corruption*', interview with A. Goodman, *Democracy Now!*, www.democracynow.org/2007/6/5/john_perkins_on_the_secret_history

Pew Research Center for the People and the Press (2013), 'Public trust in government: 1958–2013', 18 October, www.people-press.org/2013/10/18/trust-in-government-interactive/

Phan, K., I. Liberzon, R. Welsh, J. Britton and S. Taylor (2003), 'Habituation of rostral anterior cingulate cortex to repeated emotionally salient pictures', *Neuropsychopharmacology* 28: 1344–50.

Philo, G. and M. Berry, with Glasgow Media Group [2004] (2011), *More Bad News from Israel*, London: Pluto Press.

Pickerel, W., H. Jorgensen and L. Bennett (2002), 'Culture jams and meme warfare: Kalle Lasn, Adbusters, and media activism', Centre for Communication and Civic Engagement, University of Washington, depts. washington.edu/gcp/pdf/culturejamsandmemewarfare.pdf

Pilger, J. (ed.) [2004] (2005), *Tell Me No Lies: Investigative Journalism and its Triumphs*, London: Verso.

Pilger, J. (2013), 'The new propaganda is liberal. The new slavery is digital', *The New Statesman*, 14 March, www.newstatesman.com/politics/politics/2013/03/new-propaganda-liberal-new-slavery-digital

Pilkington, E. (2014), 'Guardian and Washington Post win Pulitzer Prize for NSA revelations', *The Guardian*, 14 April, www.theguardian.com/media/2014/apr/14/guardian-washington-post-pulitzer-nsa-revelations

Pink, D. [2009] (2011), *Drive: The Surprising Truth about What Motivates Us*, New York: Riverhead Books.

Pink, D. (2012), *To Sell is Human: The Surprising Truth About Moving Others*, New York: Riverhead Books.

Plato [360 BCE] (2009), *The Republic*, Internet Classics Archive (MIT), trans. B. Jowett, classics.mit.edu/Plato/republic.html

Plato [380 BCE] (2009), *Gorgias*, Internet Classics Archive (MIT), trans. B. Jowett, classics.mit.edu/Plato/gorgias.html

Plato [360 BCE] (2009), *Phaedrus*, Internet Classics Archive (MIT), trans. B. Jowett, classics.mit.edu/Plato/phaedrus.html

Polanyi, K. [1944] (2001), *The Great Transformation: The Political and Economic Origins of Our Time*, Boston: Beacon Press.

Polman, L. [2010] (2011), *War Games: The Story of Aid and War in Modern Times*, trans. L. Waters, London: Penguin.

Postman, N. (1985), *Amusing Ourselves to Death: Public Discourse in the Age of Show Business*, New York: Penguin.

Postman, N. (1992), *Technopoly: The Surrender of Culture to Technology*, New York: Vintage.

Powell, C. (2003), 'Full text of Colin Powell's speech', *The Guardian*, 5 February, www.theguardian.com/world/2003/feb/05/iraq.usa

Powell, L. (1971), 'Attack of American free enterprise system' (Powell Manifesto), Confidential Memorandum to E. Sydnor, US Chamber of Commerce, 23 August, reclaimdemocracy.org/powell_memo_lewis/

'Pranksters print spoof NY Times' (2008), *BBC News*, 12 November, news.bbc.co.uk/2/hi/americas/7725973.stm

Pratkanis, A. and E. Aronson [1992] (2001), *Age of Propaganda: The Everyday Use and Abuse of Persuasion*, rev. edn, New York: W. H. Freeman.

Premack, D. and G. Woodruff (1978), 'Does the chimpanzee have a theory of mind?' *Behavioral and Brain Sciences* 1.4: 515–26.

Prevots, N. (1998), *Dance for Export, Cultural Diplomacy and the Cold War*, Middletown: Wesleyan University Press.

Priest, D. and W. Arkin [2011] (2012), *Top Secret America: The Rise of the New American Security State*, New York: Back Bay Books.

Priestland, D. (2009), *The Red Flag: A History of Communism*, New York: Grove Press.

PRWatch, Centre for Media and Democracy, www.prwatch.org/

'Psyops', Information Warfare Site (IWS), www.iwar.org.uk/psyops/index.htm

Pussy Riot, pussy-riot.livejournal.com/

Rabinow, P. (1984), 'Introduction', in M. Foucault, *The Foucault Reader*, London: Penguin, pp. 3–30.

Ramachandran, V. S. [2011] (2012), *The Tell-Tale Brain: A Neuroscientist's Quest for What Makes Us Human*, New York: W. W. Norton.

Rampton, S. and J. Stauber [1995] (2002), *Toxic Sludge is Good for You: Lies, Damn Lies and the Public Relations Industry*, Monroe: Common Courage Press.

Rampton, S. and J. Stauber [2001] (2002), *Trust Us, We're Experts*, New York: Penguin.

'Raw side of Havana life – *Suite Habana* movie' (2003), *Havana Journal*, July, havanajournal.com/culture/entry/raw_side_of_havana_life_suite_habana_movie/

Rawls, J. (1971), *A Theory of Justice*, Cambridge, MA: Harvard University Press.

'Reality TV lures players into sadistic game' (2010), *CBC News*, 17 March, www.cbc.ca/news/arts/tv/story/2010/03/17/game-of-death.html

Rheingold, H. (2003), *Smart Mobs: The Next Social Revolution*, New York: Basic Books.

Richardson, L. (2006), *What Terrorists Want: Understanding the Enemy, Containing the Threat*, New York: Random House.

Richler, N. (2012), *What We Talk About When We Talk About War*, Fredericton: Goose Lane Editions.

Riis, J. [1890] (2010), *How the Other Half Lives: Studies Among the Tenements of New York*, Cambridge, MA: Harvard University Press.

Roberts, P. W. (2004), *A War Against Truth: An Intimate Account of the Invasion of Iraq*, Vancouver: Raincoast Books.

Robin, C. (2012), 'Hayek von Pinochet', Corey Robin Blog, coreyrobin.com/2012/07/08/hayek-von-pinochet/

Rockwell, D., with B. Mau (2006), *Spectacle*, London: Phaidon.

Rogin, J. (2014), 'Kerry warns Israel could become "an apartheid state"', *The Daily Beast*, 27 April, www.thedailybeast.com/articles/2014/04/27/exclusive-kerry-warns-israel-could-become-an-apartheid-state.html

Rokeby, D. (1996), 'Transforming mirrors: subjectivity and control in interactive media', www.davidrokeby.com/mirrors.html

Rony, F. T. (1996), *The Third Eye: Race, Cinema, and Ethnographic Spectacle*, Durham, NC: Duke University Press.

Roosevelt, T. (1906), 'Address of President Roosevelt at the laying of the corner stone of the office building of the House of Representatives', Washington, DC, voicesofdemocracy.umd.edu/theodore-roosevelt-the-man-with-the-muck-rake-speech-text/

Rosen, C. (2005), 'The age of egocasting', *The New Atlantis* (Fall/Winter), www.thenewatlantis.com/publications/the-age-of-egocasting

Rowland, W. [1997] (2006), *The Spirit of the Web: The Age of Information from Telegraph to Internet*, Toronto: Thomas Allen.

Rumsfeld, D. (2002), 'DoD news briefing – Secretary Rumsfeld and Gen. Myers', US Department of Defense, 12 February, www.defense.gov/transcripts/transcript.aspx?transcriptid=2636

Rumsfeld, D. (2004), 'Testimony of Secretary of Defense Donald H. Rumsfeld', The Senate and House Armed Services Committees, www.defense.gov/speeches/speech.aspx?speechid=118

'Rupert Murdoch "not a fit person" to lead News Corp – MPs' (2012), *BBC News*, 1 May, www.bbc.co.uk/news/uk-politics-17898029

Rushe, D. (2010), 'Bernard Madoff trustee sues JP Morgan for $6.4bn', *The Guardian*, 3 December, www.guardian.co.uk/business/2010/dec/03/bernard-madoff-trustee-sues-jp-morgan

Rushing, J. (2011), 'A marine's Arab Spring: Josh Rushing of Al Jazeera', *Reader's Digest* (September), www.rd.com/true-stories/inspiring/a-marines-arab-spring-josh-rushing-of-al-jazeera/

Rutherford, P. (2000), *Endless Propaganda: The Advertising of Public Goods*, Toronto: University of Toronto Press.

Rutherford, P. (2004), *Weapons of Mass Persuasion: Marketing the War Against Iraq*, Toronto: University of Toronto Press.

Ryan, Y. (2011), 'From the Arab Spring to Liverpool?' *Al Jazeera*, 11 August, english.aljazeera.net/indepth/features/2011/08/2011811122931660627.html

Ryan, R. and E. Deci (2000), 'Self-determination theory and the facilitation of intrinsic motivation, social development, and well-being', *American Psychologist* 55: 68–78.

Said, E. [1978] (2000), *Orientalism*, in M. Bayoumi and A. Rubin (eds), *The Edward Said Reader*, New York: Vintage, pp. 63–113.

Said, E. [1981] (1997), *Covering Islam: How the Media and the Experts Determine How We See the Rest of the World*, New York: Vintage.

Said, E. (2001), 'The clash of ignorance', *The Nation*, 4 October, www.thenation.com/article/clash-ignorance

Saladin d'Anglure, B. (2002), 'An ethnographic commentary: the legend of Atanarjuat, Inuit and shamanism', in P. A. Angilirq, Z. Kunuk, H. Paniaq, P. Qualitalik and N. Cohen, *Atanarjuat: The Fast Runner*, Toronto: Coach House Books and Isuma Publishing, pp. 197–229.

Sand, S. [2009] (2010), *The Invention of the Jewish People*, trans. Y. Lotan, London: Verso.

Scahill, J. (2010), 'Blackwater's black ops', *The Nation*, 15 September, www.thenation.com/article/154739/blackwaters-black-ops

Scahill, J. (2013), *Dirty Wars: The World is a Battlefield*, New York: Nation Books.

Schechner, R. (1988), *Performance Theory*, New York: Routledge.

Schiller, H. (1991), *Culture, Inc.: The Corporate Takeover of Public Expression*, New York: Oxford University Press.

Schmid, G. (2001), 'On the existence of a global system for the interception of private and commercial communications (ECHELON interception system)', Temporary Committee on the ECHELON Interception System report, European Parliament.

Schrag, P. (1978), *Mind Control*, New York: Pantheon.

Schudson, M. [1984] (1986), *Advertising, The Uneasy Persuasion: Its Dubious Impact on American Society*, New York: Basic Books.

Schulze, H. and K. Mochalski (2009), 'Internet study 2008/2009', Ipoque report, www.ipoque.com/sites/default/files/mediafiles/documents/internet-study-2008-2009.pdf

Schwartz, T. (1974), *The Responsive Chord*, New York: Anchor Books.

Self-Determination Theory website, www.selfdeterminationtheory.org/

Shabi, R. (2009), 'Special spin body gets media on message, says Israel', *The Guardian*, 2 January, www.guardian.co.uk/world/2009/jan/02/israel-palestine-pr-spin

Shermer, M. [1997] (2002), *Why People Believe Weird Things: Pseudoscience, Superstition, and Other Confusions of Our Time*, New York: St. Martin's Press.

Shirky, C. (2008), *Here Comes Everybody: The Power of Organizing Without Organizations*, New York: Penguin Press.

Shirky, C. (2009), 'How social media can make history', *TED Talks*, www.ted.com/talks/clay_shirky_how_cellphones_twitter_facebook_can_make_history.html

Sifry, M. (2011), *WikiLeaks and the Age of Transparency*, New Haven: Yale University Press.

Silver, N. (2012), *The Signal and the Noise: Why So Many Predictions Fail – But Some Don't*, New York: Penguin.

Singer, N. (2012), 'Mapping, and sharing, the consumer genome', *The New York Times*, 16 June, www.nytimes.com/2012/06/17/technology/acxiom-the-quiet-giant-of-consumer-database-marketing.html

Smith, A. [1776] (1976), *The Wealth of Nations*, in R. Campbell and A. Skinner (eds), *Works and Correspondence of Adam Smith*, Vol. 2A, Oxford: Clarendon Press.

Smith, M. (1994), 'Altered states: character and emotional response in Cinema', *Cinema Journal* 33.4 (Summer): 34–56.

Snell, J. (ed.) (1959), *The Nazi Revolution: Germany's Guilt or Germany's Fate?* Boston: Heath.

Snow, N. [1998] (2010), *Propaganda, Inc.: Selling America's Culture to the World*, New York: Seven Stories Press.

Snyder, J. (2013), 'Keystone foes say 1 million comments show grass-roots power', *Bloomberg*, 23 April, www.bloomberg.com/news/2013-04-23/keystone-xl-foes-say-1-million-comments-show-power-of-grassroots.html

'Sockpuppet (Internet)', *Wikipedia*, en.wikipedia.org/wiki/Sockpuppet_ (Internet)

Solove, D. (2007), *The Future of Reputation: Gossip, Rumour, and Privacy in the Internet*, New Haven: Yale University Press.

Sontag, S. (1977), *On Photography*, New York: Farrar, Straus and Giroux.

Sontag, S. (2003), *Regarding the Pain of Others*, New York: Picador.

Sontag, S. (2004), 'Regarding the torture of others', *The New York Times*, 23 May, www.nytimes.com/2004/05/23/magazine/regarding-the-torture-of-others.html

Southern, T. [1963] (2004), 'Check-up with Dr. Strangelove', *Filmmaker Magazine* (Fall), www.filmmakermagazine.com/archives/issues/fall2004/line_items/strangelove.php

Specter, M. (2003), 'The extremist: the woman behind the most successful radical group in America', *The New Yorker*, 4 April, www.michaelspecter.com/2003/04/the-extremist/

Spin Watch, www.spinwatch.org/

Steffens, L. [1931] (2005), *The Autobiography of Lincoln Steffens*, Berkeley: Heyday Books.

Stelter, B. (2013), 'Al Jazeera America promises a more sober look at the news', *The New York Times*, 18 August, www.nytimes.com/2013/08/19/business/media/al-jazeera-america-promises-a-more-sober-look-at-the-news.html

Stenovec, T. (2012), 'Steve Mann, inventor, allegedly attacked at Paris McDonald's for wearing digital eye glass', *Huffington Post*, 17 July, www.huffingtonpost.com/2012/07/17/steve-mann-attacked-paris-mcdonalds-digital-eye-glass-photos_n_1680263.html

Steven, P. (1993), *Brink of Reality: New Canadian Documentary Film and Video*, Toronto: Between-the-Lines.

Stiglitz, J. [2002] (2003), *Globalisation and Its Discontents*, New York: W. W. Norton.

Stiglitz, J. [2012] (2013), *The Price of Inequality*, London: Penguin.

Stockbauer, B. (2003), '"Rebuilding America's defences" – a summary', *Information Clearing House*, www.informationclearinghouse.info/article3249.htm

Straughan, D. (ed.) (2007), *Women's Use of Public Relations for Progressive-Era Reform*, Lewiston: Edwin Mellen Press.

Strangelove, M. (2005), *The Empire of Mind: Digital Piracy and the Anti-Capitalist Movement*, Toronto: University of Toronto Press.

Sullivan, J. (2011), 'True enough: the second age of PR', *Columbia Journalism Review* (May/June), www.cjr.org/feature/true_enough.php

Sunstein, C. [2007] (2009), *Republic.com 2.0*, Princeton: Princeton University Press.

Sun Tzu [c. 500 BCE] (1962), *The Art of War*, Oxford: Oxford University Press.

Surowiecki, J. [2004] (2005), *The Wisdom of Crowds: Why the Many Are Smarter Than the Few*, London: Abacus.

Swift, J. [1729] (1960), 'A modest proposal', in *Gulliver's Travels and Other Writings*, Boston: Houghton Mifflin, pp. 439–46.

'Syria's media war' (2013), *Al Jazeera*, 25 May, www.aljazeera.com/programmes/listeningpost/2013/05/2013524183512735367.html

Taber, C. and M. Lodge (2006), 'Motivated scepticism in the evaluation of political beliefs', *American Journal of Political Science* 50.3: 755–69.

Taguba, A. (2004), *US Army 15–6 Report of Abuse of Prisoners in Iraq*, Wikisource, en.wikisource.org/wiki/US_Army_15-6_Report_of_Abuse_of_Prisoners_in_Iraq

Taleb, N. (2007), *The Black Swan: The Impact of the Highly Improbable*, New York: Random House.

Tapscott, D. (1996), *The Digital Economy: Promise and Peril in the Age of Networked Intelligence*, New York: McGraw-Hill.

Tarbell, I. (1904), *History of the Standard Oil Company*, Cambridge, MA: Harvard University Press.

Tarde, G. (1969), *On Communication and Social Influence: Selected Papers*, Chicago: University of Chicago Press.

Taussig, M. (1993), *Mimesis and Alterity: A Particular History of the Senses*, New York: Routledge.

Tavris, C. and E. Aronson (2013), *Mistakes Were Made (But Not By Me)*, London: Pinter and Martin.

Taylor, P. (1995), *Munitions of the Mind: A History of Propaganda from the Ancient World to the Present Day*, Manchester: Manchester University Press.

Teitelbaum, M. (1992), 'Preface', in M. Teitelbaum and L. Freiman (eds), *Montage and Modern Life: 1919–1942*, Cambridge, MA: MIT Press, pp. 7–19.

Tetlock, P. (2005), *Expert Political Opinion, How Good Is It? How Can We Know?* Princeton: Princeton University Press.

Thaler, R. and C. Sunstein [2008] (2009), *Nudge: Improving Decisions about Health, Wealth and Happiness*, London: Penguin.

Thompson, R. F. (1983), *Flash of the Spirit: African and Afro-American Art and Philosophy*, New York: Vintage.

'Timeline: Tony Blair's statements on weapons in Iraq' (2009), *BBC News*, 12 December, news.bbc.co.uk/2/hi/uk_news/politics/8409526.stm

Townsend, M. (2006), 'Leak reveals official story of London bombings', *The Observer*, 9 April, www.guardian.co.uk/uk/2006/apr/09/july7.uksecurity

Trevor-Roper, H. (1978), 'Introduction', in J. Goebbels, *The Goebbels Diaries: The Last Days*, trans. R. Barry, London: Secker and Warburg, pp. xv–xxxiii.

Trilateral Commission, www.trilateral.org/

Trotsky, L. [1925] (2005), *Literature and Revolution*, trans. R. Strunsky, Chicago: Haymarket Books.

Truffaut, F. (1983), *Hitchcock Truffaut*, New York: Simon and Schuster.

Tuchman, B. (1984), *The March of Folly: From Troy to Vietnam*, London: Michael Joseph.

Tufte, E. (2006), *Beautiful Evidence*, Cheshire, CT: Graphics Press LLC.

Turkle, S. (1995), *Life on the Screen: Identity in the Age of the Internet*, New York: Simon and Schuster.

Turkle, S. [2011] (2012), *Alone Together: Why We Expect More from Technology and Less from Each Other*, New York: Basic Books.

Turner, V. (1982), *From Ritual to Theatre: The Human Seriousness of Play*, New York: PAJ Publications.

Turner, V. [1987] (1988), *The Anthropology of Performance*, New York: PAJ Publications.

Turse, N. (2014), 'Why are US Special Operations Forces deployed in over 100 countries?' *The Nation*, 7 January, www.thenation.com/article/177797/why-are-us-special-operations-forces-deployed-over-100-countries

Tversky, A. and Kahneman, D. (1981), 'The framing of decisions and the psychology of choice', *Science* 211 (30 January): 453–8.

Twitchell, J. (1996), *ADCULT USA: The Triumph of Advertising in American Culture*, New York: Columbia University Press.

Underhill, W. (2011), 'The man who busted Murdoch', *The Daily Beast*, 17 July, www.thedailybeast.com/articles/2011/07/17/murdoch-hacking-scandal-how-nick-davies-busted-the-news-of-the-world.html

Van Buren, P. (2013), 'Why the invasion of Iraq was the single worst foreign policy decision in American history', *The Nation*, 7 March, www.thenation.com/article/173246/why-invasion-iraq-was-single-worst-foreign-policy-decision-american-history

Vohs, K. and R. Faber (2007), 'Spent resources: self-regulatory resource availability affects impulse buying', *Journal of Consumer Research* 33: 537–47.

Vohs, K., N. Mead and M. Goode (2006), 'The psychological consequences of money', *Science* 314: 1154–6.

Vulliamy, E. (2008), 'Bridging the gap, part two', *The Guardian*, 13 July, www.theguardian.com/music/2008/jul/13/classicalmusicandopera.culture

Wallace, K. and T. MacCharles (2009), 'Judge denies Galloway's bid to enter Canada', *Toronto Star*, 30 March.

Wark, M. (1994), *Virtual Geography: Living with Global Media Events*, Bloomington: Indiana University Press.

Watson, T. and M. Hickman (2012), *Dial M for Murdoch: News Corporation and the Corruption of Britain*, London: Penguin.

Weber, M. [1904] (1998), *The Protestant Ethic and the Spirit of Capitalism*, trans. T. Parsons, Los Angeles: Roxbury Publishing.

Whitaker, B. (2003), 'Flags in the dust', *The Guardian*, 24 March, www.guardian.co.uk/world/2003/mar/24/worlddispatch.iraq

Whitehouse, S. (2014), 'The climate denial beast', US Senate Speech, 4 February, www.whitehouse.senate.gov/news/speeches/the-climate-denial-beast

Who's Lobbying, whoslobbying.com/

Williams, R. (1960), 'The magic system', *The New Left Review* 4 (July–August): 27–32.

World Values Survey, www.worldvaluessurvey.org/

Williamson, J. (1990), 'What Washington means by policy reform', Washington, DC: Peterson Institute for International Economics, www.iie.com/publications/papers/paper.cfm?researchid=486

Wintour, P. (2010), 'David Cameron's "nudge unit" aims to improve economic behaviour', *The Guardian*, 9 September, www.guardian.co.uk/society/2010/sep/09/cameron-nudge-unit-economic-behaviour

Wyler, R. (2004), *Greenpeace: The Inside Story*, Vancouver: Raincoast Books.

Xu, K. (2013), 'Framing Occupy Wall Street: a content analysis of *The New York Times* and *USA Today*', *International Journal of Communication* 7: 2412–32.

Yardley, W. (2011), 'The branding of the Occupy Movement', *The New York Times*, 27 November, www.nytimes.com/2011/11/28/business/media/the-branding-of-the-occupy-movement.html

Yunus, M. (2008), *Creating a World without Poverty: Social Business and the Future of Capitalism*, New York: Public Affairs.

Zak, P. (2008), 'The neurobiology of trust', *Scientific American* 298: 88–95.

Zak, P. (2012), *The Moral Molecule: The Source of Love and Prosperity*, London: Bantam Press.

'"Zarqawi" beheaded US man in Iraq' (2004), *BBC News*, 13 May, news.bbc.co.uk/2/hi/middle_east/3712421.stm

Zinn, H. [1980] (1990), *A People's History of the United States*, New York: Harper and Row.

Zittrain, J. (2008), *The Future of the Internet – and How to Stop It*, New Haven: Yale University Press.

Zittrain, J. (2009), 'Minds for sale', Berkman Center for Internet and Society (Harvard Law School), cyber.law.harvard.edu/interactive/events/2009/11/berkwest

Multimedia

'1984', television ad, directed by Ridley Scott. US: Apple, 1984. www.youtube.com/watch?v=8UZV7PDt8Lw

The Age of Persuasion, radio series, written and hosted by Terry O'Reilly. Canada: CBC Radio 1, 2008–11.

Ai Wei Wei: Never Sorry, film, directed by A. Klayman. US: Expression United Media, 2012.

An American Love Story, television series, directed by J. Fox. US: Independent Television Service/PBS, 1999.

Apocalypse Now, film, directed by F. Coppola. US: Zeotrope Studios, 1979.

Arrival of a Train at La Ciotat, film, directed by A. and L. Lumière. France: Lumière, 1896.

(Astro) Turf Wars: How Corporate America is Faking a Grassroots Revolution, film, directed by T. Oldham. US: Larrikin Films, 2010.

Atanarjuat: The Fast Runner, film, directed by Z. Kunuk, screenplay by Paul Apak Angilirq. Canada: Isuma Productions, 2001.

Avatar, film, directed by J. Cameron. US: 20th Century Fox, 2009.

The Battle of Algiers, film, directed by G. Pontecorvo. Italy/Algeria: Igor Film/Casbah Film, 1966.

The Battle of Russia, film, directed by F. Capra. US: United States Army, 1944.

Battleship Potemkin, film, directed by S. Eisenstein. USSR: Goskino, 1925.

Beirut: The Last Home Movie, film, directed by J. Fox. US: Zohe Film, 1987.

Bhopal Disaster – BBC – The Yes Men, video, produced by BBC/Yes Men. UK/US: BBC/Yes Men, 2004, www.youtube.com/watch?v=LiWlvBro9eI

The Birth of a Nation, film, directed by D. W. Griffith. US: David W. Griffith Corp., 1915.

Black Hawk Down, film, directed by R. Scott. US: Columbia Pictures, 2001.

'Blue Bra' Girl Brutally Beaten by Egyptian Military, video, uploaded by RT to YouTube on 18 December 2011, www.youtube.com/watch?v=mnFVYewkWEY

Burma VJ: Reporting from a Closed Country, film, directed by A. Østergaard. Denmark: Dogwoof Pictures, 2008.

Candid Eye, television series, produced by W. Koenig and R. Kroiter. Canada: NFB, 1958–61.

Capitalism: A Love Story, film, directed by M. Moore. US: Overture Films, 2009.

Century of the Self, film, written and directed by A. Curtis. UK: BBC, 2002.

Charlie Wilson's War, film, directed by M. Nichols. US: Universal Pictures, 2007.

Chronique d'un Été, film, directed by J. Rouch. France: Argos Films, 1961.

Cinéma Vérité: Defining the Moment, film, directed by P. Wintonick. Canada: NFB, 1999.

The Civil War, television series, directed by K. Burns. US: American Documentaries/PBS, 1990.

Colbert Roasts Bush – 2006 White House Correspondents' Dinner, television, produced by C-SPAN, 29 April.

Collateral Murder, video, produced and distributed online by WikiLeaks, 2010, www.collateralmurder.com/

Control Room, film, directed by J. Noujaim. US: Magnolia Pictures, 2004.

Cops, television series, created by M. Barbour and J. Langley. US: 20th Century Fox Television, 1989–2013.

The Corporation, film, directed by J. Abbott and M. Achbar. Canada: Big Picture Media, 2003.

Crisis, film, directed by R. Drew. US: ABC News/Drew Associates, 1963.

Cyberman, film, directed by S. Lynch. Canada: CBC, 2001.

Das Goebbels Experiment, film, directed by L. Hackmeister. Germany: First Run Features, 2005.

Deadly Currents, film, directed by S. Jacobovici. Canada: CITY-TV/Cineplex Odeon, 1991.

The Dirty Wars, directed by R. Rowley. US: Big Noise Films, 2013.

Don't Look Back, film, directed by D. A. Pennebaker. US: Leacock-Pennebaker, 1966.

Downton Abbey, television series, written by J. Fellowes. UK: Carnival Films/Masterpiece Theatre, 2010–.

Django Unchained, film, directed by Q. Tarantino. US: Columbia, 2012.

Dr. Strangelove: Or How I Learned to Stop Worrying and Love the Bomb, film, directed by S. Kubrick. UK: Hawk Films, 1964.

Dumbass, music video, featuring Ai Wei Wei. China: Ai Wei Wei Music, 2013, aiweiwei.com/mixed-media/music-videos/dumbass

L'encerclement – La démocratie dans les rets du néolibéralisme, film, directed by R. Brouillette. Canada: Les films du passeur, 2008.

The English Patient, film, directed by A. Minghella. US/UK: Miramax, 1996.

Enron: The Smartest Guys in the Room, film, directed by A. Gibney. US: Jigsaw Productions, 2005.

Everest, film, directed by M. Freeman. US: MacGillivray Freeman Films, 1998.

Eyes on the Prize, television series, produced by H. Hampton. US: Blackside/PBS, 1987–90.

Fierce Light: When Spirit Meets Action, film, directed by V. Ripper. Canada: Fierce Love Films, 2008.

The Fog of War, film, directed by E. Morris. US: Sony, 2003.

Food, Inc., film, directed by R. Kenner. US: Magnolia Pictures, 2008.

Full Metal Jacket, film, directed by S. Kubrick. US: Warner Bros., 1987.

The Green Zone, film, directed by P. Greengrass. UK/France/US: Universal/ StudioCanal, 2010.

Grierson, film, directed by R. Blais. Canada: NFB, 1973.

Hand-held, interactive installation, created by D. Rokeby. France: Le Fresnoy Studio, 2012, vimeo.com/48946545

Harlan County, USA, film, directed by B. Kopple. US: Cabin Creek Films, 1976.

Hollywood and the War Machine, television documentary, produced by Al Jazeera English. Qatar/US: Al Jazeera, 2012, www.aljazeera.com/programmes/emp ire/2010/12/2010121681345363793.html

Horns and Halos, film, directed by M. Galinsky and S. Hawley. US: MicroFilms, 2002.

The Hour of Furnaces (La hora de los hornos), film, directed by O. Getino and F. Solanas. Argentina: Grupo Cine Liberacion/Solanas Productions, 1968.

The Hurt Locker, film, directed by K. Bigelow. US: Universal, 2008.

I Am Cuba (Soy Cuba), film, directed by M. Kalatozov, cinematography by S. Urusevsky. Cuba/USSR: ICAIC/Mosfilm, 1964.

An Inconvenient Truth, film, directed by D. Guggenheim, written by A. Gore. US: Lawrence Bender Productions, 2006.

Infiltrators, film, directed by K. Jarrar. Palestine: Idiom Films, 2012.

In Search of Palestine: Edward Said Returns Home, film, produced and directed by Charles Bruce. UK: BBC, 1998.

Inside Job, film, directed by C. Ferguson. US: Sony, 2010.

In the Land of the Head Hunters, film, directed by E. Curtis. US: Seattle Film Company, 1914.

Intolerance, film, directed by D. W. Griffith. US: Triangle Film, 1916.

The Invisible Gorilla, video, produced by Daniel Simons. US: Independent, 1999, www.theinvisiblegorilla.com/videos.html

Jon Stewart on Crossfire, television, produced by CNN *Crossfire*, hosted by Tucker Carlson and Paul Begala. US: CNN, 15 October 2004, www. youtube.com/watch?v=aFQFB5YpDZE

JR's TED Prize Wish: Use Art To Turn the World Inside Out, TED Talks, 2011, www.ted.com/talks/jr_s_ted_prize_wish_use_art_to_turn_the_world_ inside_out.html

Kanehsatake: 270 Years of Resistance, film, directed by A. Obomsawin. Canada: NFB, 1993.

Knowledge is the Beginning, film, directed by P. Smaczny. Germany: Arte, 2005.

Kuleshov Effect, film clip, directed by Lev Kuleshov (USSR 1920s). Spain: Amar el Cine, Ministerio de Educación, Cultura y Deporte en colaboración con Televisión española, 2002, www.youtube.com/watch?v=grCPqoFwp5k

Le Jeu de la Mort (The Game of Death), film, written by C. Nick. France: Rezo Films and France 2, 2010.

The Life of Pi, film, directed by Ang Lee. US: 20th Century Fox, 2012.

Listen to Britain, film, directed by H. Jennings and S. McAlister. UK: Crown Film Unit, 1942.

Mad Men, television series, created and produced by M. Weiner. US: Lionsgate, 2007–14.

Man with a Movie Camera, film, directed by D. Vertov. USSR: VUFKU, 1929.

The Matrix, film, directed by A. Wachowski and L. Wachowski. USA: Warner Bros., 1999.

Moana, film, directed by R. Flaherty. US: Paramount, 1926.

Moi, un noir, film, directed by J. Rouch. France: Les Films de la Pléiade, 1958.

Momma Don't Allow, film, directed by K. Reisz and T. Richardson. UK: BFI, 1955.

Mrs. Miniver, film, directed by W. Wyler. US: MGM, 1942.

My Reincarnation, film, directed by J. Fox. US: Jennifer Fox and partners, 2011.

Nanook of the North, film, directed by R. Flaherty. US/France: Les Frères Revillon/Pathé Exchange, 1922.

Nanook Revisited, film, directed by C. Massot. France: IMA Productions, 1988.

Not Business As Usual, directed by L. Le Lam and R. Kingle-Watt. Canada: Institute B, 2014.

Occupy Love, film, directed by V. Ripper. Canada: Fierce Love Films, 2012.

Oh, What a Blow That Phantom Gave Me! film, written and directed by J. Bishop and H. Prins. US: Media Generation, 2003.

Olympia, film, written and directed by L. Riefenstahl. Germany: Olympia Film, 1938.

Outfoxed: Rupert Murdoch's War on Journalism, film, directed by R. Greenwald. US: Brave New Films, 2004.

Pearl Harbor, film, directed by M. Bay. US: Touchstone/Jerry Bruckheimer Films, 2000.

A Place Called Chiapas, directed by N. Wild. Canada: BC Film Commission, 1998.

Platoon, film, directed by O. Stone. US: Orion, 1986.

The Power of Nightmares: The Rise of the Politics of Fear, film, written and directed by A. Curtis. UK: BBC Two Documentary, 2004.

The Price of Peace and Freedom, army information film. US: Office of Information for the Armed Forces Department of Defense/AFL-CIO, 1976.

Primary, film, directed by R. Drew. US: Drew Associates/Time, 1960.

Punk Prayer: Virgin Mary, Put Putin Away, music video, performed by Pussy Riot. Moscow: Pussy Riot, 2012, www.youtube.com/watch?v=lPDkJbTQRCY

Rashomon, film, directed by A. Kurosawa. Japan: Daiei Productions, 1950.

Rendition, film, directed G. Hood. US: New Line Cinema, 2007.

Restrepo, film, directed by T. Hetherington and S. Junger. US: National Geographic, 2010.

Roger and Me, directed by M. Moore. US: Dog Eat Dog Films, 1989.

Salesman, film, directed by A. Maysles and D. Maysles. US: Maysles Films, 1968.

Saturday Night and Sunday Morning, film, directed by K. Reisz. UK: Woodfall Film Productions, 1960.

Scared Sacred, film, directed by V. Ripper. Canada: Scared Sacred Films/NFB, 2004.

Seeing is Believing: Handicams, Human Rights and the News, film, directed by K. Cizek and P. Wintonick. US: Icarus Films, 2003.

Sherry Turkle: Connected, But Alone? TED Talks, February 2012, www.ted.com/talks/sherry_turkle_alone_together.html

The Spanish Earth, film, directed by J. Ivens. US: Contemporary Historians, 1937.

Standard Operating Procedure, film, directed by E. Morris. US: Sony Pictures, 2008.

The Stone Breakers, painting, painted by G. Courbet, Dresden, 1849, en.wikipedia.org/wiki/File:Gustave_Courbet_018.jpg

Stop Making Sense, film, directed by J. Demme. US: Palm Pictures, 1984.

Suite Habana, film, directed by F. Pérez. Cuba: ICAIC, 2003.

Terms and Conditions May Apply, film, directed by C. Hoback. US: Hyrax Films, 2013.

This is Not a Film, film, directed by J. Panahi and M. Mirtahmasb. Iran: Jafar Panahi/Kannibal Films Distribution, 2011.

This is What Democracy Looks Like, film, directed by J. Friedberg and R. Rowley. US: Big Noise Films, 2000.

Titicut Follies, film, directed by F. Wiseman. US: Fred Wiseman/Zipporah Films, 1967.

Top Gun, film, directed by T. Scott. US: Paramount, 1986.

Triumph of the Will (Triumph des Willens), film, directed by L. Riefenstahl. Germany: Reichsparteitag-Film, 1935.

Under the Influence, radio series, hosted by Terry O'Reilly. Canada: CBC Radio 1, 2012–14.

Vertigo, film, directed by A. Hitchcock. US: Paramount, 1958.

Very Nervous System, installation, created by D. Rokeby. Canada: 1986–90, davidrokeby.com/vns.html

Wag the Dog, film, directed by B. Levinson. US: New Line Cinema, 1997.

Waltz with Bashir, film, written and directed by A. Folman. Israel: Bridgit Folman Film Gang, 2008.

The War Tapes, film, directed by D. Scranton. US: Scranton/Lacy Films, 2006.

We Are the Lambeth Boys, film, directed by K. Reisz. UK: Graphic Films/Ford Motor Company, 1958.

Who's Counting? Marilyn Waring on Sex, Lies and Global Economics, directed by T. Nash. Canada: NFB, 1995.

Why We Fight, film series, directed by F. Capra. US: United States Army, 1942–5.

Why We Fight, film, directed by E. Jarecki. US: Sony, 2006.

Women are Heroes, art installation in Brazil and Kenya, created by JR, 2008–9, www.jr-art.net/projects/women-are-heroes-brazil

The Wonderful, Horrible Life of Leni Riefenstahl (*Die Macht der Bilder: Leni Riefenstahl*), film, directed by R. Müller. France/UK/Germany/Belgium: Arte/Channel Four/Nomad, 1993.

The Yes Men, film, directed by C. Smith, D. Ollman and S. Price. US: MGM, 2004.

The Yes Men Fix the World, film, directed by A. Bichlbaum and M. Bonanno. France/UK/US: Renegade Films, 2009.

Zapruder Film, video of JFK assassination, filmed by Abraham Zapruder. US Independent, 1963, www.youtube.com/watch?v=kq1PbgeBoQ4

Zero Dark Thirty, film, directed by K. Bigelow. US: Columbia Pictures, 2012.

Index